THE MAKING OF A RULING CLASS

Two Centuries of Capital Development on Tyneside

Cover Photograph: The battleship HMS Victoria being taken down the Tyne from the Elswick Works of W.G. Armstrong and Co. where it was built in 1887. (Courtesy Newcastle City Libraries).

The Benwell CDP, one of 12 experimental schemes, was set up by the Home Office in conjunction with Newcastle Council and Durham University to examine the nature and causes of urban poverty. This report is one of a final series of 11 which describe the experience and work of the team over the last six years. Further copies of all these reports, as well as many other national and local CDP reports can be obtained from Benwell CDP Publications, 85/87 Adelaide Terrace, Newcastle Upon Tyne, NE4 8BB.

Published in 1978 by Benwell Community Project, 85/87 Adelaide Terrace, Benwell, Newcastle Upon Tyne NE4 8BB.

ISBN 0 906316 04 9

Designed and produced by SIDELINES, 81 Grove Lane, Handsworth, Birmingham B21 9HE.
(021) 551 2351.

Printed and typeset by the Russell Press Ltd., 45 Gamble Street, Forest Road West, Nottingham NG7 4ET.

This report does not necessarily reflect the views of the Home Office, Durham University or Newcastle District Council.

Benwell Community Project would like to thank the staff of the Local History Section of Newcastle Central Library for the help they have given in the preparation of this report.

Contents

INTRODUCTION	5

1
EARLY INDUSTRIALISATION 1770–1844
9

1.1	**INDUSTRIES**	
	1.1A Coal	10
	1.1B Coal Related	13
	1.1C Early engineering	15
1.2	**THE NEW CAPITALISTS**	16
1.3	**CLASS CONFLICT AND THE NEW RULING CLASS**	18

2
1845–1914: GROWTH OF NEW INDUSTRIES
23

2.1	**INDUSTRIES**	
	2.1A Engineering	24
	2.1B Characteristics of Industrial Change in West End	27
	2.1C Coal	30
2.2	**DIVERSIFICATION OF PRIVATE AND PERSONAL CAPITAL**	31
	2.2A Banking	32
	2.2B Finance Capital	33
	2.2C Purchase of Large Estates	35
2.3	**RULING CLASS AS A HEGEMONIC FORCE**	37
	2.3A Growth of a Working Class Movement	39
	2.3B Industrial Organisation	40
	2.3C Involvement in Central and Local State	41
	2.3D Provision of Social Infrastructure	42
	2.3E Cultural and Ideological Role	44

3
THE INTER-WAR YEARS
49

3.1	**WEST NEWCASTLE**	50
	3.1A Housing Development	50
	3.1B Industries	51
	3.1C General Withdrawal	52
3.2	**TYNESIDE AND THE WIDER REGION**	52
	3.2A Heavy engineering and shipbuilding	52
	3.2B Coal, Steel and Public Utilities	55
3.3	**CAPITAL DIVERSIFICATION**	58
	3.3A Banking	58
	3.3B Investment Trusts	59
	3.3C Finance Capital Professions	59
	3.3D Building Societies	60
3.4	**HEGEMONIC ORGANISATION**	60

4
POST-WAR TRANSFORMATION
63

4.1	**FAMILY AND KINSHIP IN THE WIDER ECONOMY**	64
4.2	**STATE INTERVENTION**	65
	4.2A New Towns	67
	4.2B Research and the University	67
4.3	**GROWTH OF THE MULTINATIONAL CORPORATIONS**	69
4.4	**MOVEMENT INTO FINANCE CAPITAL AND PROPERTY**	72
	4.4A Regional Financial Institutions	73
	4.4B Dickinson/Joicey Case Study	74
	4.4C Investment and Investment Holding Companies	77
	4.4D Wider Financial World	79
4.5	**RULING CLASS COHESION**	82

5
CONCLUSION
87

APPENDICES

1.	EIGHTEEN FAMILY TREES	90
2.	ESTATES (FOR PROBATE) OF SEVENTEEN FAMILIES	113
3.	SCHEDULE OF INDUSTRIAL DEVELOPMENT IN WEST NEWCASTLE IN NINETEENTH CENTURY	114
4.	NOTES ON SOURCES AND METHODS	121

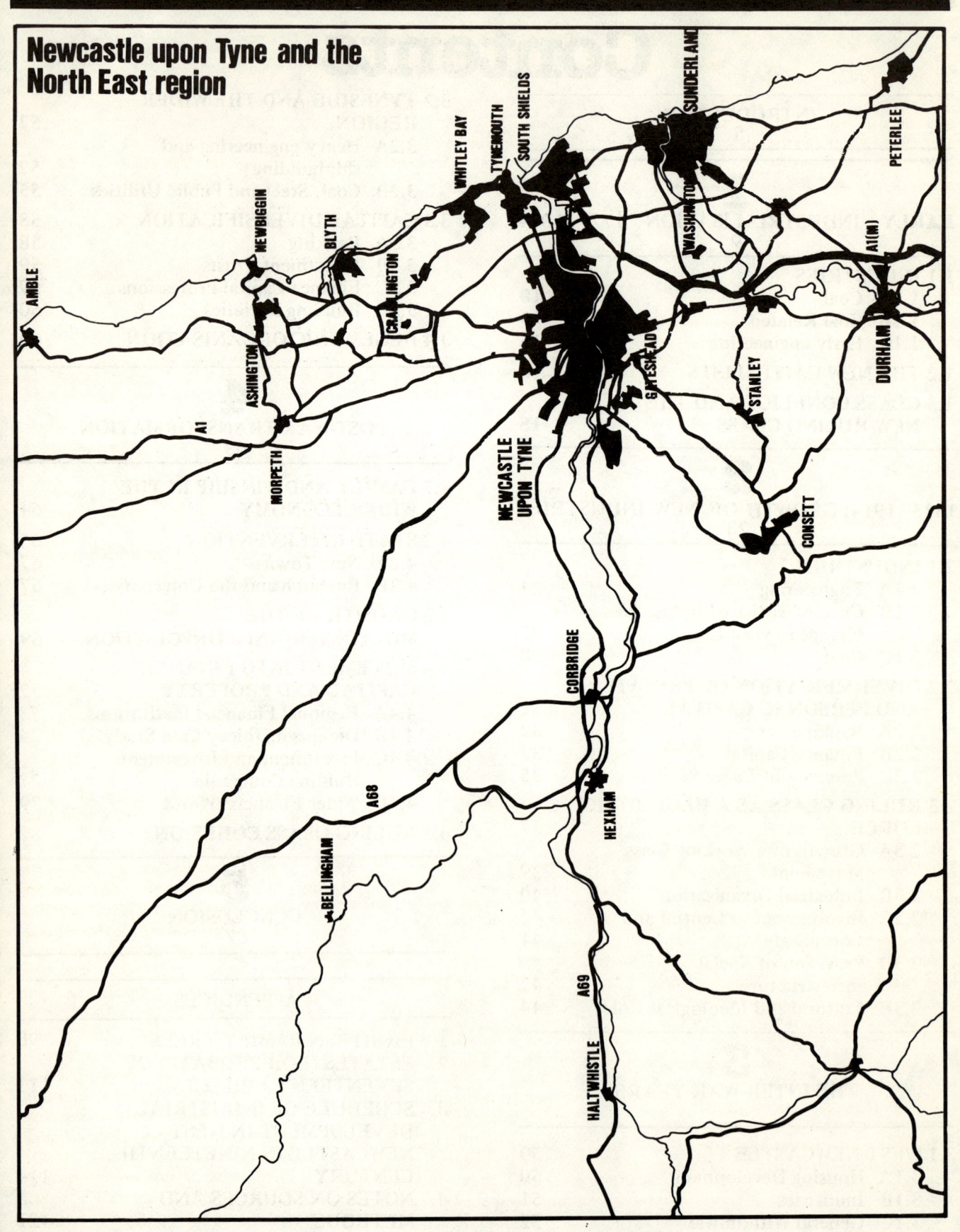

Introduction

THIS report is a study of economic and social power based on a historical account of the industrial development of Tyneside. It traces the emergence of a capitalist class in the nineteenth century, and examines the way in which this class has adapted in the twentieth century to maintain its control in the economic domain.[1]

In this respect the report does not fit neatly within the pattern of those CDP reports that have explored the present day decline of the inner city areas in terms of their poor housing conditions, high unemployment rates and changing industrial structure. In other respects however it is highly relevant to the changing emphases of the CDP teams as they have realized the need to develop a more systematic and rigorous analysis of the basic problems now facing the older industrial areas.

The CDPs were set up with the aim of encouraging 'disadvantaged' communities to organise themselves more effectively through the mobilisation of self-help and mutual aid. In this way, it was implied, it would be possible to achieve a re-allocation of resources and wealth to the poorest sections of the community. As the project teams began to work in their chosen areas, they increasingly rejected the early notions about the nature of the forces impinging upon these working class communities. As the Newcastle CDP Forward Plan[2] 1975-1976 put it:

> "The team has moved away from the original assumptions of the CDP programme that the causes of deprivation are to be found in the local community, and in the shortcomings of local policies and services. Our experience in Benwell convinces us that much of the disadvantage to be observed arises from structural causes. In other words, we would argue that the workings of the general economic and associated political system are inherently liable to create wide inequalities between groups in society."

Much of the work of the Benwell CDP has therefore concentrated on industrial change on Tyneside, for it is the basic economic processes that underly the present day problems of the inner city. The major feature to emerge has been the control exercised over the regional economy by a relatively small number of multinational corporations whose Tyneside operations often represent only a small part of their overall activities. Yet this concentration of control — itself a reflection of changes throughout the economy — has not led to the eclipse of the early industrial and coalowning families who had achieved a dominating influence on Tyneside by the First World War.[3] Several studies of contemporary industrial and financial organisation in the North East have pointed to the important role of a relatively small number of men in the economic and social transformation that has taken place in the region over the lasty thirty years.[4]

It has generally been argued that the changes and industrial restructuring taking place — the rundown of the old traditional industries, and the growth of new industries in the new towns and outlying industrial estates — are not only unavoidable, but also are in the best interests of all sections of the population. CDP work, both nationally and on Tyneside, has demonstrated that this is clearly not the case with the older industrial areas like West Newcastle. The decline in the local economy has brought for the working class population high unemployment, only a few low-wage jobs, and a high dependency on Social Security.

This leads us to a key question. In whose interests have these changes been occurring? If it can be shown that consistently a small number of men from an earlier capitalist class have become both integrated in key positions in the major financial institutions and large multinational corporations, and have been instrumental in promoting new policies and new investment in the region, this has important implications for some of the political debates now taking place on issues like nationalisation of the leading companies and banks and proposals for industrial democracy. Indeed, Tony Benn has recently argued that:

> "The debate about industrial democracy will highlight the real issue of Britain's unchanged power structure. The influence and control over national affairs exerted by an Establishment which depends on patronage has remained dominant."[5]

The identification of this 'establishment' or 'elite', and the interests it represents is central to developing an informed discussion of this question that goes beyond mere political rhetoric and dogmatic assertion. Yet, despite this, there have been remarkably few studies that have attempted to examine the exercise of economic power in a systematic manner using empirical material collected on a historical basis. Those that have tackled the question tend either to be at a very theoretical level, or contain a mass of contemporary detail unrelated to a general theoretical or historical framework.[6]

Giddens explains this state of affairs and the assumptions it has generated in this way:

> "In Britain, in particular, elite studies have been remarkable by their absence . . . This situation is in striking contrast to the relative proliferation of research concerned with the lower levels of the class structure. The contrast is not accidental. The meliorist tradition in British sociology, largely uninfluenced by marxism or revolutionary socialism generally, has naturally served to direct attention primarily towards the working class rather than the upper class, towards poverty rather than wealth. In spite of the lack of systematic research, however, it is commonly asserted that, over the past half-century,

fundamental changes have taken place "at the top" in British society. There is no longer, it is argued, a distinctive "upper class", still less a "ruling class" in contemporary Britain. Elites are no longer drawn from a background of minority privilege, and they are no longer cohered by the common social and moral ties which were once created by the gentlemanly ethos of the 'Clarendon' schools (i.e. the top nine public schools) and the ancient universities."[7]

This report challenges these assertions, and the assumptions upon which they are based, by examining early industrial development on Tyneside and by tracing the careers and activities of later generations of the early industrialists and financiers right through to the present day.

The adoption of this historical approach has been quite deliberate because as Gramsci puts it:

"It is not enough to know the ensemble of relations as they exist at any given time as a given system. They must be known genetically, in the movement of their formation. For each individual is the synthesis not only of existing relations, but of the history of these relations. He is a prècis of all the past."[8]

The main focus of the report is at the economic level and on the economic struggle, between a ruling class and a working class under capitalism since we argue with Poulanzas that "in the complex organisation of a class, it is the economic which holds the dominant role, in addition to determination in the last instance."[9] In explaining the need to distinguish the different levels in order to understand them, Poulanzas goes on to make an important point: "The isolated examination of economic, political and ideological class practice presupposes the concept of class as covering the unity of these practices ('struggle' between classes)." While from a theoretical point of view it is important to analyse the relative separation of the economic and political spheres that has occurred since the nineteenth century, our basic argument is that power within a capitalist society ultimately resides with those who control the uses to which private capital is put; and these people in the nineteenth century were, to put it crudely, the big industrialists and bankers, and now in the 1970s are the men who control the large corporations and major financial institutions.

The area chosen for the initial study of industrial development is West Newcastle. Although the choice of the area was made for very different considerations — for it was typical of many of the declining inner city areas with severe housing and employment problems — it fortuitously provides an ideal case study for looking at the historical development of capitalism in Britain.

While the development of the cotton industry in Manchester in the last quarter of the eighteenth century is roughly seen as the start of the Industrial Revolution, it was on Tyneside, and in particular in the West End of Newcastle, from the Close out to Newburn, that the heavy capital goods industries of coal, iron and steel, so essential for sustained economic growth, were to appear at the end of the eighteenth century and in the first half of the nineteenth century.

For a period of 150 years (1770-1920) the area was the location of two fairly distinct stages of capital accumulation that placed it at the forefront of the Industrial Revolution, the first based on coal-mining, the second on heavy engineering and shipbuilding. By any account it had an impressive industrial record: it embraced inter alia in the 1820s the largest glassworks in the country and the works where the Stephensons' famous Locomotion and Rocket railway engines were made; a factory producing in the 1860s the most accurate rifled guns in the world; the first factory to produce electric lamps on a commercial scale, (1881); and the world's first turbine-powered (alternating current) power station (1892).

In this sense, therefore, it is significant in its own right, but similar processes of capital movement and mass immigration based on the presence of coal and the river can be seen in other parts of Tyneside such as Jarrow and Wallsend. This suggests that the experience of West Newcastle is not only typical, but also should logically be studied in seeking to understand the way that in Britain the first industrial power, a capitalist system and its class relationships have changed and been adapted over time.

The particular method employed in the study has been to concentrate on the families or dynasties who originally played a significant role in the industrial development of West Newcastle in its growth period up to the end of the nineteenth century. While the report has this relatively small area as its starting point, it is inevitably drawn into consideration of events outside this defined geographical area. Most of the companies and the families controlling them in this early period had either left West Newcastle by the 1920s, or were operating at least on a regional level and often at an international level. For as George Harvey, the miners' checkweighman, writing in the First World War put it: "Capitalism knows no boundaries."

By studying individual companies and by tracing family fortunes and generational changes of directorship, it is possible to provide a clear indication of the mobility and diversification of private capital over time.[10]

Research into the role and nature of the family is by no means a new technique, but most studies have concentrated not on the wealthy and powerful but on the working class family suggesting by implication that it is in some way instrumental in continuing poverty, and seeking to understand it as a means of perpetuating social and cultural values.[11]

Here we have chosen to look at particular individuals and families, not solely for their own intrinsic interest, but because they represent certain class interests. What is significant is their response over time to a changing political and economic environment. Indeed, to test empirically any general theory of the development of a capitalist system, and the relationship between different classes, requires that we look at particular concrete examples and individuals.

In saying that the response of actors follows the logic of and therefore illustrates the development of capital, is not however to adopt a determinist position, nor to argue that they are consciously responding to that logic. As Ecker puts it:

> "All one can say is that individuals and groups within specific social formations tend to pursue their own interests, and that in a capitalist society these interests will be largely determined by the structure of the capitalist economic system."[12]

The task of tracing the rise of a ruling class, and its role in this process of economic development is ironically very much easier for the first 150 years than it is for the last 50 years and particularly for the period since the last war. In the former case, the existence of a relatively autonomous regional economy (at least in the earlier stages) makes it possible to identify important processes by concentrating on smaller areas — on West Newcastle initially and then, via the ripples of capital penetration, on Tyneside generally and the wider coalfield. Correspondingly, control of the means of production was far more obviously in the hands of easily identifiable capitalists, who played an overt role in the political and economic struggle that was seen to be taking place between capital and labour. Over the last 50 years, on the other hand, the picture has become more diffuse. The state has taken over functions previously performed by individual industrialists while members of the families have taken up important positions within the state apparatus; and the dynasties' economic activities have become spread geographically and between different sectors.

Moreover, as the ideology of democracy and equality becomes more deeply entrenched, the few who really exercise power prefer to keep their activities more discreetly hidden away. No longer do the obituaries eulogise about the wealth and enterprise of local and national "capitalists" as was common enough in the nineteenth century. It is true that newspapers publish the occasional article on the chairman of a public company or state-run industry, but for the most part nothing is heard about the figures who control the major financial institutions and multinational corporations.[13] How many people could even name the chairman of one of them? As this report shows, much information is of course available, but its inaccessibility makes the collation and interpretation of it a difficult and time-consuming job.

The empirical evidence that has been collected has been organised into four main sections. The first two cover the early period of industrialisation in West Newcastle and the subsequent development of the coal, heavy engineering and shipbuilding industries up to the First World War. The second two sections cover the transitional inter-war years and the post-war transformation of the region. The initial contextual work carried out by CDP on the historical development of the area revealed a remarkable build-up and concentration of economic power on Tyneside by the First World War. The first half of the report is concerned with describing and accounting for this. It shows that although there were large numbers of small entrepreneurs involved in a range of new industries, the major sectors, and especially coal and heavy engineering, were dominated from the start by a handful of wealthy, mostly merchant families. By the turn of the century this new ruling class not only exercised immense economic power, but also controlled many of the wider social and political institutions.

The first half of the report is not however intended to be merely of historical interest. It is an integral backdrop to the second half in which we examine how the social and economic power of these early capitalist families has developed and been transformed up to the present day.

With the growing concentration of control in the economy, there has been a significant diffusion of power; no longer do a few individual dynasties visibly control the factories, the banks and the local council. But what clearly emerges from examining the 1930s and the post-war years of state intervention is not an erosion of dynastic influence but rather a subtle accommodation to change, which has enabled individual family members to move into commanding positions within the region and within the wider national economy.

Footnotes

1. *The argument of the report rests primarily on detailed historical evidence. It does not deal at any length with the important theoretical questions raised — e.g. about the role of the state, and the nature of class relationships under capitalism.*
2. *Forward Plan 1975-1976. National CDP. Inter-project publication.*
3. *For a short and detailed account of the concentration of economic power in this period, see G. Harvey,* Capitalism in the Northern Coalfield, *Mimeographed. 1917. Newcastle Central Library. Harvey was a miners' checkweightman at Follonsby Pit, Wardley.*
4. *See J. Cousins.* The Cramlington New Town Company Structure. *(mimeo) 1973; Rowntree Research Unit. Aspects of Contradiction in Regional Policy: The Case of North East England. Regional Studies Vol 8 1974.*
5. *Sunday Times, p.53 January 30th, 1977.*
6. *See for instance Anthony Sampson,* The New Anatomy of Britain. *Hodder and Stoughton, 1971. A more interesting development of this kind of work can be found in:* Elites and Power in British Society, *Eds. P. Stanworth and A. Giddens 1974. Cambridge University Press. But its unconnected studies of wealth holding, and the social backgrounds of MPs, company directors and bishops etc. still provides only a partial picture of the wider exercise of power.*
7. *A. Giddens. New Society 16 November 1972, p.391.*
8. *A. Gramsci, Selections from the Prison Notebooks p.353, Lawrence and Wishart, 1976.*
9. *N. Poulanzas. Political Power and Social Classes pp.75 and 83. New Left Books. 1975.*
10. *The specific details drawn from a range of archival and other records are given in 18 family trees (see appendix), which show the industrial, financial and other interests of succeeding generations up to the present day. For ease of reference, each family tree has a number. When a person is referred to in the text, the name is followed by a reference to the schedule of family trees, e.g. W.G. Armstrong (FT2).*

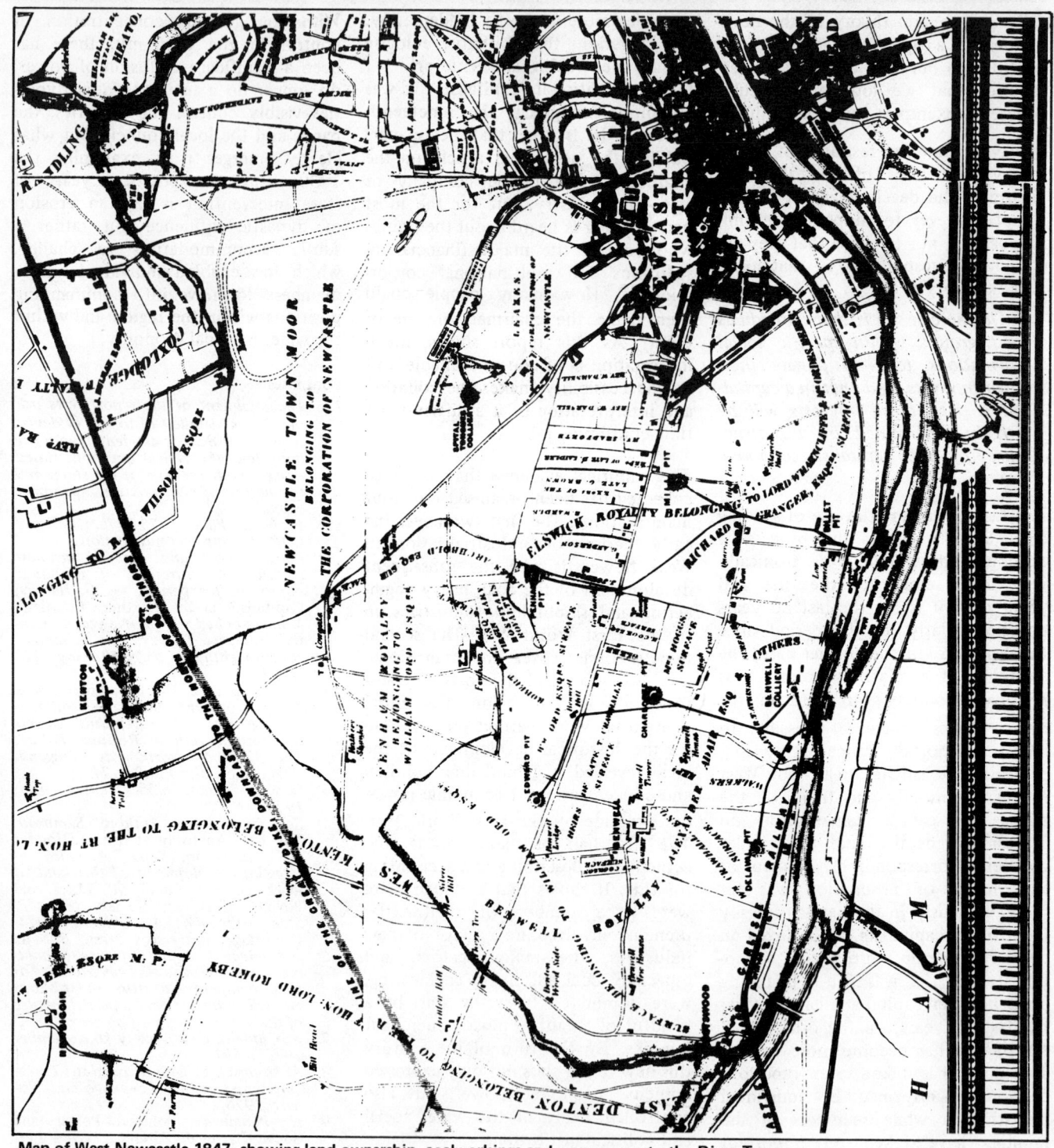

Map of West Newcastle 1847, showing land ownership, coalworkings and wagonways to the River Tyne.

Because of intermarriage the name of the person in the text is not always the same as that of the family tree e.g. C.J. Pumphrey see Priestman (FT12).

11. See for instance M. Young and P. Willmott: Family and Kinship in East London. *Routledge and Kegan Paul, 1957.* P. Townsend: The Family Life of Old People, *Routledge and Kegan Paul, 1957.* By way of contrast see R.M. Titmus, Income Distribution and Social Change, *1962, Unwin University Books,* where the family is correctly analysed as a unit for distributing wealth and income over succeeding generations.

12. T. Ecker, Capitalist Planning, the State and Regional Policy. *Working Paper 16. Studies in Regional Policy Implementation. Polytechnic of Central London. 1974.*

13. This state of affairs is in marked contrast to the spotlight that is constantly trained on major politicians, about whom the media transmit a daily flow of detailed and often personal information.

1
1780-1844 Early Industrialisation

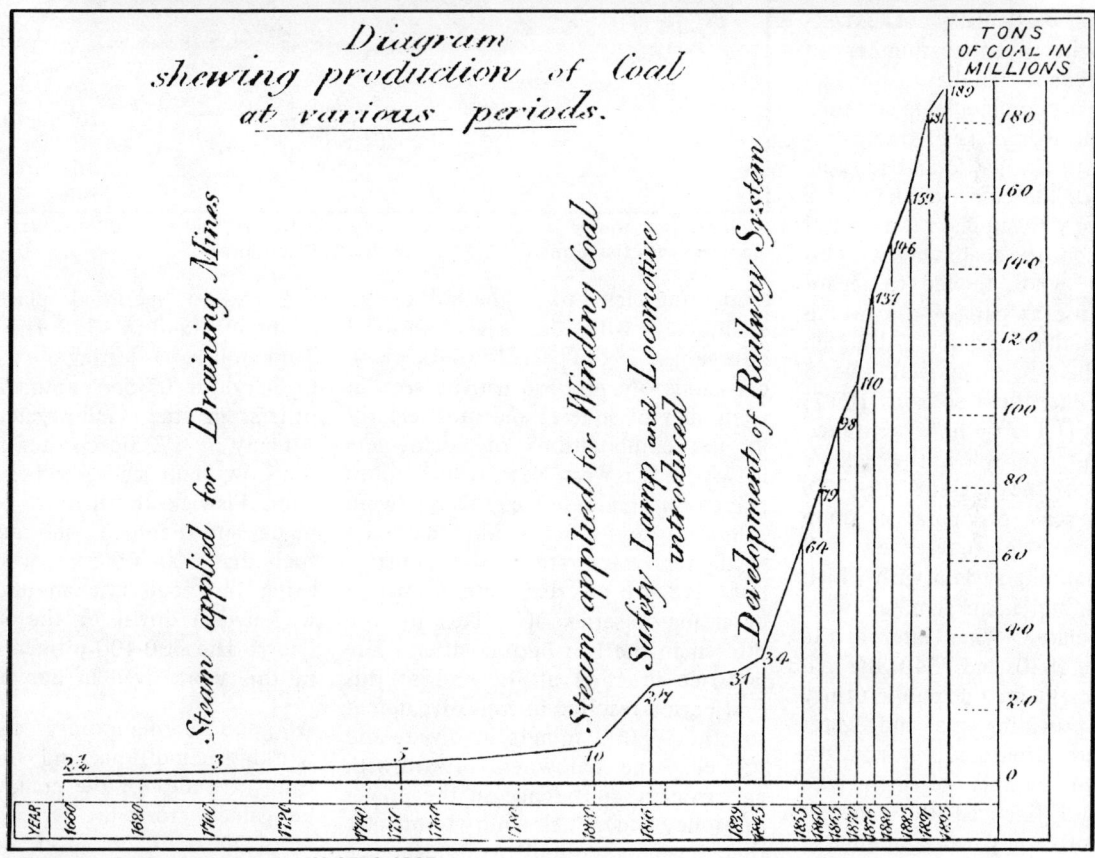

Diagram: Coal production in UK 1750-1895

ALTHOUGH many conventional accounts begin the history of industrial development in West Newcastle with the establishment in 1847 of Armstrong's Elswick Works, the previous 60 years provide an essential key to understanding the remarkable period of economic growth that occurred on Tyneside in the latter half of the nineteenth century. The most important industry was coal mining, made possible by the easily accessible seams beside the river. By the 1800s there were pits and shallow workings throughout the area employing hundreds of workers.

The abundant supply of coal and the proximity of the river Tyne provided the conditions for the development of other important industries also, such as glass, iron and lead manufacture. Even at this stage these industries required large initial capital outlay, but there were plenty of other low-capital industrial activities that were attracted to the area, all of them dependent on cheap coal. Dotted along the river, sometimes clustered beside a small burn, were brick manufacturers, glueworks, colour works, copperas[1] works, and paper factories. There were others also including two engineering and locomotive works Robert Stephenson & Co. and R. & W. Hawthorn and Co. They were to become familiar names throughout the world, and were the forerunners of the heavy engineering sector that was to dominate the area at the end of the century.

In some forms of manufacture, like brick-making the financial thresholds were low enough to allow entry to men from an artisan background, but the opportunities for future expansion were for the most part very limited. With the high-capital industries on the other hand, it was a different matter. Since the sinking of new pits and the opening of new metal and glass factories were so expensive only a privileged and wealthy few were able to participate. Control of these industries, therefore, and particularly coal extraction, lay with a small number of mostly merchant families who had been able to accumulate large amounts of capital through years of trading on the Tyne with the Baltic and Europe. In the case of the collieries they were able effectively to supplant the typical eighteenth century coalowner who, as a large landowner, tended to regard coal extraction as part of the overall business of land management. Although not all of them have survived, a good number — like the Cooksons (FT7) and Strakers (FT17) — have continued to play a dominant role in the region's affairs up to the present day. To achieve this scale of operation there was already existing a relatively well developed banking system with which these same merchant families were closely associated. When later in the period in the 1830s and 1840s the railway companies and the public utility companies providing gas and water supplies were promoted, it was the same limited number of men who organised and financed the schemes using the profits they had accumulated from their earlier industrial and mercantile enterprises.

The new forms of industrial production and the wealth that was being accumulated by this new capitalist class brought few advantages to the working class. A pattern of mass migration to the cities became established, but housing and living conditions were far worse than in the areas which the migrating workers had left behind them. To combat the social and political unrest that was associated with the growth of radicalism and chartism amongst the working classes, a new ruling class began to emerge,

Denton Hall, home of Mrs Montagu; the coalowners' living conditions were in stark contrast with the pitmen's. Picture: Newcastle City Library.

combining elements of the old landed aristocracy with the new industrial bourgeoisie. Concerted and class-conscious organisation can be seen in a number of spheres and most clearly in the combinations of coalowners in which the West Newcastle families played a major role. These were primarily and successfully designed to depress wage rates in the industry, but were also of crucial importance in defeating a series of strikes by the pitmen in the Northern coalfield. The last one in 1844 at the end of this first period resulted in a massive defeat for the 40,000 miners involved, and propelled the coalowners forward with an arrogant confidence in the power of money and in their ability to manage their business without the interference of their workers.

1.1 INDUSTRIES

1.1A COAL

The increased demand for coal that came with the beginnings of the Industrial Revolution brought a flurry of activity to West Newcastle. Coal workings were everywhere with pits at Gallowgate, Elswick, Benwell, Delaval, Fenham, Scotswood and further out at Walbottle and Throckley. But the expression "coals from Newcastle" has much older origins, for coal was mined in Benwell in Roman times — the earliest recorded place in the country — and in 1330 The Priory of Tynemouth was letting out the Elswick Colliery for £5 per annum as well as others in the Gallowgate vicinity. Already by 1725 according to Dunn,[2] the Low Main seam was being worked from Elswick through to West Montague and Fenham, and output was such that 600-700 carts were used to bring the coals (via an underground wagonway) down to the Scotswood Quay. The 300-400 pitmen employed in this work lived in Benwell village.

A good contemporary account of working conditions and the patronising attitudes of the coalowners can be gained from the writings of Mrs Montagu, who took over the management of the Denton Estates of her husband, Edward Montagu (Lord Rokeby)[3] when he died in 1775.

"As to Denton, it has mightily the air of an ant-hill; a vast many black animals for ever busy. Near fourscore families are employed on my concerns here. Boys work in the colliery from seven years of age... I had fifty nine boys and girls to sup in the courtyard last night on rice pudding and boiled beef; tomorrow night I shall have as many. It is very pleasant to see how the poor things cram themselves, and the expense is not great. We buy

rice cheap, and skimmed milk and coarse beef serve the occasion. Some have more children than their labour will clothe, and on such I shall bestow some apparel. Some benefits of this sort and a general kind behaviour give to the coal-owner, as well as to them, a good deal of advantage. Our pitmen are afraid of being turned off, and that fear keeps an order and regularity amongst them that is very uncommon."

Nor was this the only advantage to the coalowners. There was a great deal of money to be made from coal as a friend's reply to a letter of Mrs Montagu makes clear:

"(Thank you) for your kind communication of the great advantages which you have so good a prospect of deriving from your colliery. You may depend on my not mentioning any of the particulars. God grant you long life . . . to enjoy this new-found treasure . . . "[4]

The Coalowners

The Montagus were typical examples of coalowners in this early period, for up to about 1800 the capital for mining was put up generally by the big landowners themselves. Thereafter as the necessary level of investment and engineering skill rose to match the growing demand for coal, the landowning aristocracy increasingly preferred the more secure position of rentiers drawing a lower, but still substantial income from royalties and way leave agreements.[5] The Montagu's Denton Main colliery for instance, which extended under Lemington and Benwell, was worked very profitably from the Montagu Pit at the bottom of Scotswood Dene from 1765 to 1807 when it was leased to Messrs Cookson, Cuthbert & Co. (FT7).

In Benwell, William Ord,[6] from a wealthy landowning family that can trace its ownership of the Whitfield Estate in Allendale back to the 12th century, bought five farms in 1757, and worked the Fenham Colliery himself until about 1820 when it was leased out to John Buddle (FT5) and John Straker (FT17). Further West the Duke of Northumberland earlier had sunk pits at Walbottle and Flatworth, but relinquished all personal involvement by 1799. By the 1840s Walbottle was being worked by a company formed by Addison Potter (FT2), whose other interests included a substantial brewery at Forth Banks. Although a few of the great aristocratic landowners, like the Londonderry family in Durham continued as coalowners for a great deal longer (in the Londonderry case right up to nationalisation in 1947), the trend of selling out was very marked by the 1840s. In the wider coalfield the 4th Baronet Sir Matthew White Ridley (FT14) whose family had been closely involved in Newcastle banking and in the Lemington Glass Works leased out Cowpen Colliery in 1838 rather than raise fresh capital, and the Marquess of Bute who had won the Tanfield Colliery in 1829, sold out his interests finally to the Joicey family (FT3) in 1847. Already though by 1830 John Buddle (FT5) was able to tell a committee of enquiry into the coal trade that only five out of 41 collieries on the Tyne were worked by the landowners, the remainder being leased by adventurers.[7]

The old landed coalowners were then selling off their colliery interests because of their limited supplies of ready capital, and because of the risks involved. But as Dunn[8] observes there was another equally important factor — the pressure of eager buyers.

"The monopolists were seeking to get rid of their distant bargains and the whole state of matters foreboded an unlooked for revolution, arising partly from the increasing desire of large capitalists to invest their money in the high-priced coal of the deep collieries."

Before looking at the origins and activities of these "large capitalists", a few general points about the coal industry need to be made.

The Economics of the Coal Industry

The costs of colliery operations have always been considerable and involve the risks of low returns and even total loss. By 1860 up to £500,000 had been invested in some of the larger undertakings in the Durham coalfield where the seams were much deeper than in the earlier pits. But the tendentious complaints made vociferously by many of the colliery owners that the returns on mining investment were inadequate need to be treated with some scepticism. John Buddle giving evidence before a Committee of the House of Lords in 1829 stated: "Although many collieries in the hands of fortunate individuals and companies, have been perhaps making more than might be deemed reasonable and fair profit, according to their risks, like a prize in a lottery; yet, as a trade, taking the whole capital employed, it has certainly not been so". His argument though that "by no means 10 per cent had been made without taking into account depreciation of capital" has to be compared with the much lower 3.4 per cent yield that an investor would have obtained from public stocks at the time.

Joseph Lamb (FT9) makes a similar point privately in 1824 in a letter to a friend about his coal interests:

"The funds are splendid. Don't sell. Europe is and will long be tranquil. If you sold out where would you invest? No, you have good interest, and when you want your money, high profit is sure."

As we shall see later Buddle played a key role in organising a combination of coal owners on Tyneside to reduce the pitmen's wages, and had therefore every reason to understate the profitability of the coal trade. But the wealth that he himself amassed as a colliery viewer[9] and coalowner places further doubt on the reliability of his evidence, for his estates and coal interests at Benwell and Wallsend were valued at £150,000 when he died in 1843.

It was these "golden dreams of the coal trade" that had a significant influence on investment decisions throughout this early period, and in the second half of the century as the deeper pits away from the river began

Benwell Staith 1839; from here the coal was transported downriver.

to be opened up. Between 1830 and 1860 the capital invested in collieries on the Tyne and Wear increased from £2 million to £14 million. At different points in time the attractiveness of mining investment varied in line with the general state of the economy, but the overall growth in demand for coal is clearly illustrated in the diagram showing U.K. coal production figures up to 1895. In this first period there is a steady growth in the years 1800-1845 from 10 million per annum to 34 million tons, but it is in the second half of the nineteenth century that production really accelerated with output increasing almost sixfold in 50 years.

The New Coalowners

The new coalowners, who so systematically took over the running of the collieries both in West Newcastle and on Tyneside generally, had the large amounts of capital that the old coalowners lacked. Typically they were old established Tyneside families trading as merchants in corn, timber, wine, linen and the like or involved as shipowners or pioneer industrialists in the early eighteenth century glass chemical and lead industries. Several of them were also members of the merchant adventurers' guild or of the hostmen society incorporated by royal charter in 1600 as a guild for controlling the coal trade on Tyneside. Through these business and trading activities they were in an ideal position to seek out profitable outlets for new investment. Although, as we shall see later, they were involved in many other industrial enterprises, coal was the most important and lucrative.

Seven main families were involved as coalowners in West Newcastle in this period, many of them acting in partnerships with each other to work particular pits. The Benwell Colliery was worked by the Surtees (FT18) around 1805. They were then joined by John Buddle, who by 1825 had become the owner of the South Benwell Estate. Buddle, known on Tyneside as "the king of the coal trade", had many other interests including a lease of Fenham Colliery in the 1830s with John Straker (FT17). As early as 1770 Isaac Cookson (FT7) was the owner of the North Elswick Pit, and extended his activities to the Montagu Colliery at Scotswood in 1807 in partnership with William Cuthbert (FT7). By 1843 the Elswick Collieries had been taken over by Joseph Lamb (FT9) who had added to his coal interests in 1850 by taking on the Walbottle Colliery from Addison Potter (FT2). On the south side of the Tyne the main coal interest of the West Newcastle families was the Stella Coal Company which was purchased in 1837 by a consortium including John Buddle and his nephew R.T. Atkinson (FT5), Addison Potter, and Humble Lamb (brother of Joseph Lamb).

Even at this stage however their activities were not solely concentrated on West Newcastle, for in 1824 a partnership was formed to develop the Cramlington Colliery between Joseph Lamb, William Potter, John Straker and two others; and in 1838 Joseph Straker of Benwell Old House established the coal company of Strakers and Love at Brancepeth, County Durham, which the family were to control right through until nationalisation. By coincidence this was only one year after the Joicey family (FT3), (whose connection with West Newcastle was via the engineering works of J. and G. Joicey) commenced their mining activities at Tanfield, County Durham; a start that was to make them the most powerful and wealthiest coalowning family in the Northern coalfield.

To these seven families should be added three more who shared similar backgrounds — although they did not strictly become coalowners until the second half of the century. These were the Bensons (FT4) who took over the lease of the Montagu Colliery in 1857, and the Stephensons (FT16) who recommenced workings at the Isabella Pit, Throckley in 1867 with John Bell Simpson (FT15), a leading partner in the Stella Company. The Spencer Family (FT1) were also partners in this Throckley Coal Company, primarily it would appear to secure coal for their own steelworks at Newburn.

Some details of these families are given in the schedule at the end, but a few examples of their backgrounds fill out this picture of a merchant and early industrialist class, a few of them owning small estates in Northumberland and Durham.

Although they dropped away from the industrial mainstream of Tyneside from the mid nineteenth century, the Surtees family (FT18)[10] is an interesting case. Aubone Surtees was admitted as a member of the Merchants' Company in 1737, and of the Hostmen's Company in 1757, inherited an estate at Ovingham from his mother's side and had a wine business in the Close and a timber business at Pandon Gate. He is best known now as the father of Bessie Surtees who eloped from the Quayside with a coal-fitter's son, later to become Lord Eldon and Chief Justice of England. But at the time Surtees had a reputation for considerable financial skills and was involved in 1768 in setting up Surtees and Burdon, one of the earliest banks in Newcastle. By the time he died in 1800, the family's network of industrial interests, largely orchestrated through the bank, was extensive. Two of his sons Aubone and John were partners in a lead-mining business in Arkendale and Derwent, with property assets valued at £330,000 and working capital of £70,000[11] and were also involved in the formation in 1797 of the Tyne Iron works at Lemington with an initial capital of £100,000. The family's affairs were dramatically affected by the collapse of the bank in 1803 with Aubone and John having liabilities in the Tyne Iron works alone of £148,000. But it did not break the family for in 1826 Aubone and his elder brother William took the lease of the Benwell Colliery, trading under the name "William Surtees & Co., Coal-owners".

Another family with a mercantile background were the Lambs.[12] The original Joseph Lamb died in 1800, with an estate worth over £30,000. His earliest business appears to have been as a linen-draper and by the 1770s he is listed as a soap-maker in the Close. Like Aubone Surtees he became involved in banking, as a founding partner in 1777 of the Tyne Bank. By his death he had extensive interests, including a partnership in the Northumberland Glass Works at Lemington and another in a calico-printing works at Carlisle, a copperas works at Willington, and large share-holdings in collieries at Shire Moor, Heddon and Percy Main.

While these and other coalowning families like the Cooksons and Strakers were originally involved as merchants and in early manufacture, others like John Buddle and William Benson came from a professional or smaller gentry stock. Buddle's father, for instance, was a schoolmaster whose mathematical skills won him an appointment as a colliery viewer; while Benson had had long connections with Tyneside, but no large amounts of capital from trading. His ancestors included a rector, land agent, and farmer, and his coal connections appear to have grown out of his land-related quarrying interests near Hexham.

1.1B COAL RELATED

Not only was coal an important industry in West Newcastle in this early period, but it also threw up a range of other industries. There were three main categories — firstly high capital metal and glass manufacture; secondly a wide range of ancillary industries where the barriers to entry were lower; and thirdly an incipient engineering industry, which by the end of the century was to become by far the most important of all.

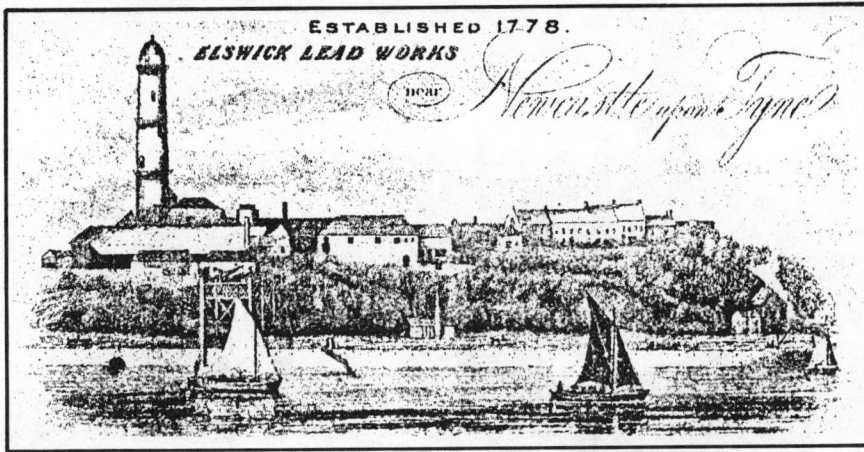

Elswick Lead Works about 1790. It is still in existence today. Below: Aubone Surtees' house on the Quayside. Both Pictures: Newcastle City Library.

Metal and Glass Manufacture

One of the earliest records of metal manufacture is in 1743 when Isaac Cookson (FT7), a leading member of the Goldsmiths' Company leased from John Hodgson, landowner of the large Elswick Estate, refining houses and an adjoining quay at Elswick for the refining of lead and extraction of silver.[13] As the road system was extremely primitive, the riverside belt provided an ideal site for the transport of raw materials — in this case from the lead seams of Blanchland — and finished product. Although there were several small foundries in the Close

Lemington Glass Works; the high cone still stands beside more modern buildings. Picture: Derek Smith.

area by the late 1770s, it was in the following 25 years that a number of large-scale enterprises were founded requiring large capital sums. The first, probably on the site of Isaac Cookson's refining house, was the firm of Walkers Parker & Co. established in 1778 for the manufacture of white lead, red lead and painters' colours.[14] The original partnership was between Samuel Walker, founder of a large ironworks at Rotherham who put up most of the original money and two Hull merchants, Richard Fishwick and Archer Ward. By 1802 the company had branches at Derby, Islington, London, Chester and Newcastle under Lyme. Although there is no record of the initial capital involved, by 1817 the total value of the property of the firm was £465,000 of which £128,000 related to the Elswick factory.

The second major company to be formed in 1787 was the Northumberland Crown Glass Works at Lemington. Some idea of the scale of the enterprise can be gained from the 130 ft. cone, which still stands today. Originally one of four, it was the largest ever built over a glass furnace. Writing in 1825, one year before the founding of the now famous St Helens Crown Glass Company by the Pilkington Brothers, the historian Mackenzie had this to say:

"In a short time there appeared four large scale glass houses, one of which is particularly lofty and beautiful, built of brick and of the most excellent workmanship. The warehouses and offices attached to the glassworks are very extensive; and the whole is allowed by travellers to constitute the most complete glass manufactory in England."[15]

The third large scale enterprise was the Tyne Iron works in which the partners were George Gibson a London architect and his son, P.J. Bulmer, a merchant from Hull, Richard Fiswick (now resigned from Walkers, Parker & Co.) and Aubone and John Surtees. The Surtees interest was probably an expansion of an earlier involvement in metal manufacture because in 1788 they are recorded as having an iron foundry at Skinnerburn. As we have seen the partnership in the Iron works collapsed in 1803 when the Surtees bank was closed down, but the company continued in reconstituted form until taken over by John Spencer and Sons (FT1) in 1869 and finally closed in 1876.

The Spencers Newburn Steelworks had by then become a major company employing more than 1,000 workers, but its origins and that of its founder, John Spencer, were much more modest than the three already mentioned. Spencer was an apprentice file cutter in Sheffield, who moved to Winlaton where he was employed for a while at Crowley's ironworks. He then started up on his own in 1810 as a file manufacturer in the Bigg Market, Newcastle, and expanded to the Newburn site in 1822. No details of the initial capital involved are available, but it is unlikely to have been great, since his first file grinding mill was in fact a water-driven corn mill.

As well as these larger enterprises there were two other small iron foundries, the one owned by Isaac Cookson at Close Gate and in existence by 1778, and the other owned by John and Isaac Burrell that was eventually taken over by Robert Stephenson and Co.

The characteristics of the entrepreneurs in this sector were then more varied than in the coal trade, which was dominated exclusively by long-established Tyneside based families. In the heavy metal and glass sector, these same families like the Cooksons and Lambs had considerable involvement, but there was also considerable penetration of the area by both immigrating entrepreneurs, and in the case of the Elswick Lead Works, large-scale external capital.

Ancillary Industries

Before 1800 there were a few manufacturing activities in the Close and Quayside area like the tobacco manufacturers Harvey and Davy, and the leather works of George Angus (FT1), which owed their position more to the role of Newcastle as a major port than to the presence of coal. Elsewhere there is a reference to John Losh and Lord Dundonald experimenting with the manufacture of alkali, at Bells Close in 1793 before moving to Walker to form a partnership with John and Aubone Surtees. But over the next 50 years — before the expansion of Armstrongs engineering works forced them out — a mass of small scale industries emerged along the whole riverside strip for which cheap coal was essential. Often clustered round a small burn, there were factories for the manufacture of colour, lamp-black, copperas, paper, glue,

Beam Engine, designed by George Stephenson and installed at the Forth Banks Works in 1823.

The Hetton Locomotive, built under the supervision of the Stephensons in 1822, the year before the opening of the Forth Banks Works. Picture: Beamish Museum.

firebricks and tiles. The technology, particularly for making something like a brick, was relatively simple, and the amount of capital required was often comparatively small. The barriers to entry were lower and it is likely therefore that some of the entrepreneurs in this sector were of artisan or humble origins with only very limited capital. But precisely because of their lowly origins and because many of these companies disappeared quite quickly, there is little detailed biographical information available.

Contemporary accounts tend only to show interest where these early pioneers were already well-known or where the firm was successful and became a major employer of workers. Thus in brick and crucible manufacture we know that William Harriman was a grocer and William Cochrane Carr was a man of humble origins who married the daughter of a market gardener. Of the other brick manufactuers we know virtually nothing, except where like Addison Potter they were also significant coalowners carrying out brick manufacture as a subsidiary activity.

Even if we assume though that all of the unknown entrepreneurs were from an artisan or similar background, there were still many of these companies that were set up by well-established men from a merchant or professional background. Again the difference from coalowning was that there was considerable involvement by entrepreneurs moving in from outside Tyneside. Familiar names like Cookson, Lamb and Stephenson appear, but there are a number of others from Yorkshire and further afield from London.

John Gibson, who started a colour works at Paradise, was the son of a London architect George Gibson, who was himself a partner in the Tyne Iron works; by 1818 the company had been taken over by Richard Hoyle, a chemist from Ripponden in Yorkshire. Other early entrepreneurs from Yorkshire included the Quakers Jonathan Priestman (FT12) and the Richardson family (FT13). Born at Malton, Priestman came in 1808 at the age of 21 to Newcastle and three years later had established a tannery at Newgate Street. In 1843 he moved to a greenfield site in Benwell to set up a new glue works and tannery, which the family continued to run until 1870s when they gave it up to concentrate on their coal interests. (See next section.)

A similar pattern was followed by Isaac Richardson, who came from a Yorkshire family that had originally diversified from farming into tanning in the 17th century. Without the contacts to enter the more profitable sectors like coal, he moved to Newcastle in 1785 to set up a tanning business and then in 1809 bought out the skinning and fell-mongering[16] business of Joseph Arrundale on Gallowgate. Although his two sons Edward and John did not move to the Elswick Leather Works site at Water Street until 1862, the family's interests had by then diversified considerably, for both brothers were large shareholders in the Northumberland and Durham District Bank, while Edward had an interest in the Derwent Main Colliery in 1843, and was one of the 12 original shareholders in the Consett Iron Company.

1.1C EARLY ENGINEERING

The story of coal extraction on Tyneside is also the history of the railways, as a witness to the Gauge Commission in 1845 made clear:

"We owe all our railways to the collieries in the North; and the difficulties which their industry overcame taught us to make railways and to make locomotives work them."[17]

Indeed one of the earliest significant advances was made locally for the Wylam Colliery when William Hedley in 1813 built the Puffing Billy and demonstrated that a toothed driving wheel engaging in a rack rail could be replaced by a smooth wheel. The development of the locomotive engine and the role of George Stephenson and his son Robert is sufficiently well-known that it needs little adding to here.

Only two years after the firm of Robert Stephenson and Co. was formed in 1823 on the Forth Banks, Newcastle, the country was to marvel at the opening of the Stockton and Darlington Railway when the Stephensons' new railway engine "Locomotion" pulled more than 30 wagons loaded with coal and passengers at speeds of up to 12 miles per hour. Between 1823-1831 the company built 37 engines including the Rocket and seven others that were displayed at the opening of the Liverpool and Manchester Railway in 1830. Renowned in his time and ever since, George Stephenson was the epitome of the self-made man. The son of a colliery fireman who succeeded to great prosperity by his undoubted self-taught engineering skills, he even had his biography written by that evangelist of self-help, Samuel Smiles.

What is less well-known is the extent to which the family company R. Stephenson & Co. was initially financed by outside money. The bulk of the initial capital of £4000 (split into 10 shares) was provided by Edward Pease (FT11), who took four shares and further made a loan of £500 to Robert Stephenson so that he and his father could each take two shares in the company. The remaining two shares were held by Michael Longridge, owner of the Bedlington Ironworks.[18] Pease was a wealthy woollen merchant, this time from Darlington, who played a prominent part in promoting and financing the Stockton and Darlington Railway. The investment was to give the Pease family a leading role in the company's affairs until after the Second World War, and proved to be highly profitable, for in 1848, Edward Pease is reported as saying that he had received £7,000 from the Forth Banks Works for that year alone.

Early engineering in West Newcastle was not however totally devoted to locomotive manufacture. Equally important as R. Stephenson, was the founding of R. and W. Hawthorn's Works on the Forth Banks in 1817. The Hawthorn brothers, Robert and William, were the sons of the engineer at Walbottle Colliery, but had very little capital to start the business. The initial workforce was only four, using machinery worked by a hand wheel, but gradually they expanded and introduced steam power in 1822. Initially manufacturing steam engines and general machinery, they built in 1831 the first of their locomotives, for which with their marine engines the company was to develop an international reputation. Together with R. Stephenson, these two companies were the forerunners of the heavy engineering industry that was to dominate the area by the end of the century and make Britain for a limited period the foremost industrial power in the world.

1.2 THE NEW CAPITALISTS

From this review of early industrial activity in West Newcastle, a number of important general points can be made, which in some cases conflict with commonly held views about the nature of early industrialisation. First, although Ashton is correct to argue that "Inventors, contrivers, industrialists and entrepreneurs — it is not easy to distinguish one from another at a period of rapid industrial change — came from every social class and from all parts of the country",[19] this obscures the extent to which on Tyneside the most profitable sectors, such as metal and glass manufacture and especially coal mining, had been firmly secured by a handful of families with long established connections with commerce and trade on Tyneside. Whilst the old land-owning aristocracy from the 1800s onwards played no significant part in this process of industrialisation, the role of a pre-existing merchant class was particularly important throughout the period. This is clear from the evidence of their considerable and direct involvement as entrepreneurs in the more highly capitalised sectors and suggests that the view that merchant capital did not play a progressive role in developing industrial capitalism does not hold for all areas and periods and needs some qualification. Marx argues that:

"Wherever merchant's capital still predominates we find backward conditions. This is true within one and the same country, in which for instance, the specifically merchant towns present far more striking analogies with past conditions than industrial towns."[20]

In discussing this question, Harvey suggests that merchant capital, whilst creating the conditions for the breakdown of the old feudal order, must be regarded as a conservative rather than a revolutionary force in bringing the new form of capitalist production. He states:

"The industrialisation that ultimately subdued merchant capital was not an urban phenomenon, but one which led to the creation of a new form of urbanism — a process in which Manchester, Leeds and Birmingham were transformed from insignificant villages or minor trading centres, to industrial cities of great productive might. In this process, it must be added, the once dominant trading centres, fashioned as they were by the peculiar ethic of merchant capitalism as well as by an economic function which was basically parasitic, diminished in economic and political significance."[21]

The significant omission is Tyneside for it was a major trading centre from mediaeval times — not only in coal but also for the Baltic countries — and then became a major industrial area by the end of the nineteenth century. The two most important sectors of the local mercantile class were the merchant adventurers and the hostmen, the former being incorporated in the fifteenth century as a guild of drapers (wool merchants), boothmen (corn merchants), and mercers (general dealers). The hostmen were so-called because they secured the right to "host" merchant strangers — in other words all sales by a visiting merchant had to be transacted through a freeman hostman. The participation of this same merchant class in the period of industrialisation up to 1845 is therefore the striking feature of the Tyneside experience. Nor was it simply a question of giving credit to the new industrialists and thus effectively investing in their stocks and stores as an extension of their traditional investment in commodities.[22] The Tyneside merchants were active pioneers and capitalists in the new industries, promoting partnerships, raising large amounts of capital and deriving great profit from the expansion of production that ensued.

This brings us to a second point. Although there were small-scale industries requiring only a little capital, by the beginning of the nineteenth century the major sectors of coal, metal and glass had already high thresholds that barred entry to all but the wealthiest. Hobsbawm may be right in saying in general that "the early phases of the Industrial Revolution (say 1780-1815) were limited and relatively cheap",[23] but it does not follow that all industries were relatively easy to enter. Exceptionally large amounts of capital were required for the metal works and coalmines, and even the £4,000 required for Stephenson's engineering works put the project far beyond the unaided reach not only of artisan capital, but also of a successful and well-paid professional engineer like Stephenson himself.

To raise this finance, large-scale capital organisation was essential, and in particular the existence of a well developed banking system. Crouzet describes the general position as follows:

"An important, though little investigated, phenomenon was the existence and development of a partly autonomous provincial capital market (or rather markets), centring on family resources and the activities of local business consortium with expert knowledge of local conditions and underpinned by the rise of provincial banking houses deeply involved in local trade."[24]

In Newcastle the first bank was opened in 1755 by Ralph Carr, a general merchant, in partnership with other merchants and hostman including John Cookson (FT7), and later this became known as Ridley & Co. for most of the period 1787-1839 when the second Baronet Matthew White Ridley and his son the third Baronet (FT14) were principal partners. Other West Newcastle industrialists involved in this early banking were as we have seen the Surtees (FT18) and the Lambs (FT9).

Banking was not however the only form of diversification in which the new industrialists were involved. Indeed banking at this stage involved considerable risks with many banks being forced to close. Two other main areas for investment were in land and in the public utility companies. A more detailed account of land-ownership in West Newcastle can be found elsewhere,[25] but a brief mention should be made of the three main estates, not only because the ownership structures played a crucial part in establishing the timing and type of residential development, but also because several of the dynasties played an important role in the process of development. The biggest estate in Benwell was that of South Benwell, purchased by John Buddle (FT5), and later to be developed at great profit by Lord Armstrong (FT2) and Sir B.C. Browne (FT5) as trustees for Buddle's grand-nephew.

Other industrialists also were involved in early long-term land speculation including the Crawhalls, rope-manufacturers from the East End who purchased parts of Delaval and Benwell, and Isaac Cookson (FT7) who purchased the Quarry House Estate in Arthurs Hill in 1826. The largest, and undoubtedly most important, estate in the West End was, however, the 700-acre Elswick Estate purchased for £114,000 by Richard Grainger in 1839 from John Hodgson Hinde, MP. This speculation was made possible through the raising of mortgages of more than £100,000 from local industrialists and financiers, notably the banker Edward Backhouse and Edward Richardson (FT13) of E & J Richardson Leather Works. Although Grainger's family eventually made a great deal of money from the estate, his high level of indebtedness would have almost certainly caused his bankruptcy in 1841, had it not been for the support and patronage of his solicitor and Newcastle Town Clerk John Clayton (FT6), who with his firm of Clayton and Gibson masterminded the residential development of Elswick right through to the 1890s.

The second main area for diversification came from the 1820s onwards, when large sums of money were raised for the railway companies and public utilities. Edward Pease (FT11) who provided most of the capital for R. Stephenson and Co. was with his brother the major shareholder in the Stockton and Darlington Railway Company, and other industrialists were involved in the Newcastle and Carlisle Railway Company. The two local public utility companies were the Newcastle and Gateshead Union Gas Light Company formed in 1830 with a capital of £30,000 and the Whittle Dene Water Company (whose name was subsequently changed to its present one, the Newcastle and Gateshead Water Co.) formed in 1845 with a capital of £120,000. More important than the amount of personal investment was the control exercised over the companies' affairs by the same limited number of familiar names. The list of main subscribers for the Gas Company include A.L. Potter (FT2) and Armorer Donkin — both to become partners sub-

How a recent brochure of the Newcastle and Gateshead Water Company portrayed the lawless anarchy amongst the water supply companies in the early days; since 1845 the Company has enjoyed the benefits of being a monopoly supplier.

Benwell Hall, home of the coalowner and industrialist W.I. Cookson and below, by way of contrast, typical pitmen's cottages of the period (at Slatyford Lane); for many working class families, living in one room only, even these were palatial.

sequently in Armstrong's Engine Works – Robert Hawthorn, A. Surtees (FT18) and J. Clayton (FT6). The provisional Committee of the Water Company included R. Hawthorn, Potter and Donkin, joined this time by the two other partners in Armstrong's, George Cruddas (FT8) and R. Lambert, Joseph Lamb (FT9), R.T. Atkinson (FT5) and J. Priestman (FT12).

1.3 CLASS CONFLICT AND THE NEW RULING CLASS

The new industries that came to Tyneside needed large amounts of capital, and brought great wealth to those who owned the means of production. Systematic details on family wealth during this period have not been collected because the system of central probate registration showing the value of the estate on death was not established until 1858. Two examples are known however. Matthew White Ridley (FT14), the banker and a partner in the Lemington glass works, left £10,000 to each of his 10 children so his total estate was probably substantially in excess of this,[26] while John Buddle (FT5) the coalowner had an estate valued at £150,000. Such sums represented very substantial wealth at the time. By comparison a pitman, probably the highest paid worker in the country, would be earning less than £1 per week.

The inequalities therefore were enormous between this new capitalist class and those who had only their labour power to sell; and the inequalities were reflected in their life-styles and living conditions.

While the industrialists like Aubone Surtees, the Cooksons, and R.T. Atkinson lived in the grand mansions of Benwell like Benwell Hall and High Cross House, or further afield in country estates in the Durham and Northumberland hinterland, the housing conditions of the working class became progressively worse. By 1841 the population of Newcastle had risen to 70,000, more than double the 1801 figure, but few houses were built for the new migrants. They were forced instead to live in the appallingly crowded tenements in the city centre.

There were other disruptions that the new forms of capitalist production brought to the established patterns of life. Not only was there substantial poverty, but in many cases there was a deterioration in living standards; on the northern coalfield wage levels dropped from a 5/- daily rate for pitmen to a general average of 3/9d from 1831-1844.

The former artisan producing goods at home, and the agricultural workers migrating to the town had to adapt to the routine and monotony of mechanisation and factory production. The results of these changes can be seen in the increasing class conflict that characterises the end of this first period both locally and nationally. The atmosphere is well caught in this description by Hobsbawm:-

> *"No period of British history has been as tense, as politically and socially disturbed, as the 1830s and early 1840s; when both the working class and the middle class, separately or in conjunction demanded what they regarded as fundamental changes . . . The most obvious evidence for this crisis is the high wind of social discontent which blew across Britain in successive gusts: Luddite and Radical, trade-unionists and utopian-Socialist, Democratic and Chartist. At no other period in modern British history have the common people been so persistently, profoundly and often desperately dissatisfied. At no other period since the seventeenth century can we speak of large masses of them as revolutionary."*[27]

Tyneside was no less affected than other areas and witnessed an upsurge in working class political activity, the growth of radical organisations and mass meetings and demonstrations. Arms were secretly manufactured and openly sold at a shop on the Side, and on one occasion on the Forth Banks the Riot Act was read four times before the troops were called in to disperse the crowds.[28]

An account of the general response of the owners to these threats to the new forms of capitalist production is beyond our scope here, for it would require an overview of political events as well as a discussion of particular industries. Some evidence of the emergence and social cohesion of a new ruling class can be seen in the formation in 1829 of the exclusive Northern Counties Club — an institution which is still important today — whose membership (see list) included many of West Newcastle's industrialists and landowners. Founded by the *"principal gentry of Newcastle and Northumberland on the plan of the club-houses in London"*, it was not of course a political organisation as such. It provides, however, an insight into the way in which the old landed and aristocratic class represented by the likes of the Duke of Northumberland, and William Ord, was becoming subsumed within — but not completely replaced by — a new ruling class whose power lay not in rank and landed interests, but in control of the factories and mines.[29]

Much of the new industrialists' time was taken up with organising their own businesses, but when their interests were under attack, from the government or from their workers, they were quick to respond. In 1811 for instance a temporary Act was introduced for charging duty on glass manufacture, which was distinctly advantageous to the manufacturers. When it was due to lapse seven years later, Sir Matthew White Ridley

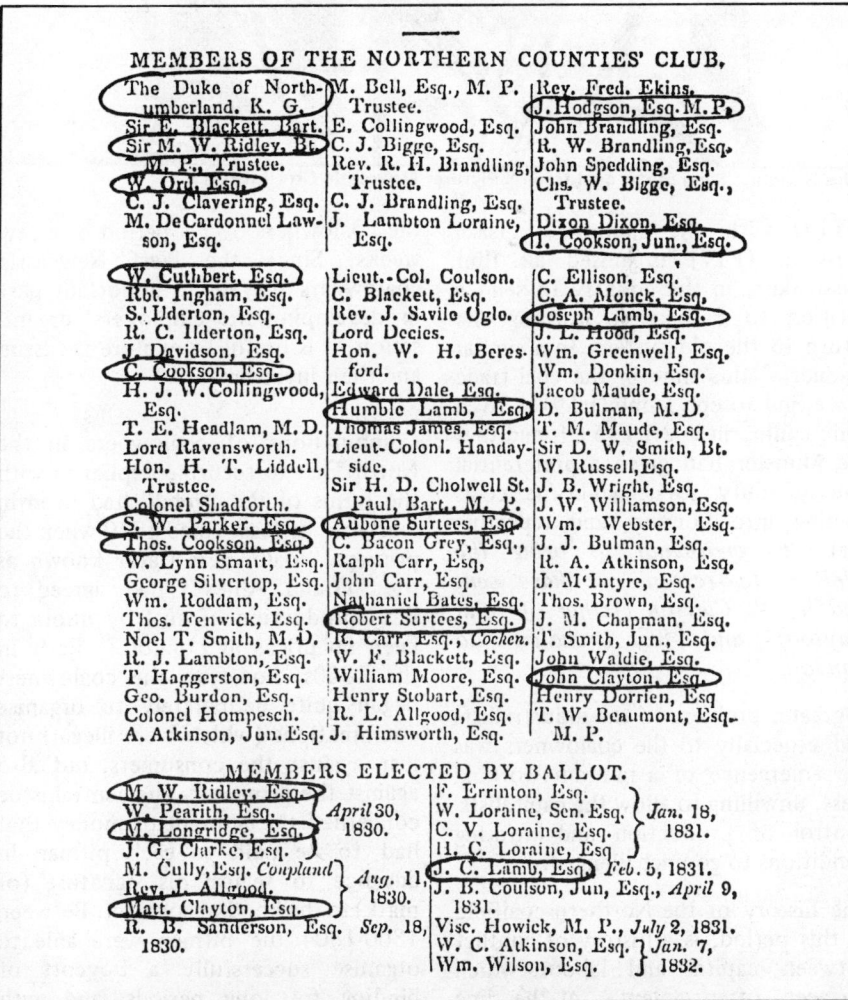

List of members of Northern Counties Club in 1833; those ringed are from the West Newcastle dynasties.

John Buddle, "King of the coal trade". Picture: Newcastle City Library.

(FT14) with the support of Isaac Cookson (FT7) organised all flint glassmakers in the country to send a petition to Parliament resisting the return to the old system. In a similar manner — this time in the coal trade — we find Joseph Lamb (FT9) in 1824 complaining in a letter to a friend that the Minister had given a preferential rate of duty for canal-borne coals coming into London, and reporting that *"to endeavour to bring the Minister to reason, we have sent Buddle, N. Clayton (father of John Clayton) and W. Brandling to London."*[30]

A greater problem to the industrialists and especially to the coalowners was the emergence of a militant working class, unwilling to allow the capitalists' control of production and working conditions to go unchallenged.

The history of the Northern coalfield in this period, is a history of conflict between capital and labour which surfaced, often violently, at the time of the yearly bond when all the pitmen were simultaneously hired by the coalowners over a period of a few weeks. Since the West Newcastle coalowners played an important part in developing the employers' organisation, it is useful to explore the issue and their involvement.

Combinations of coalowners in the North East to secure compliance with the terms of the "vend" had been in existence at least since 1710 when the principal coalowners (later known as the "Grand Allies") had agreed to limit production of coal by quota to keep up prices in London.[31] Early in the 1800s, however, the coalowners began quite deliberately to organise combinations (which were illegal) not just against the consumers, but also against the pitmen.[32] The central issue concerned the amount of money that had to be paid to each pitman in advance to secure his signature (or mark) to the bond or contract. Between 1800-1804 the pitmen were able to organise successfully a boycott of binding for long periods, and with skilled workers in short supply, the binding money was pushed up as high as 12 guineas per man — about a quarter of his total annual earnings. While earlier arrangements over the vend were punctuated by frequent disputes and withdrawals, the combination of employers begun in 1805 was much more successful. The driving spirit behind it was the "King of the coal trade", John Buddle, who was not only the owner of Benwell colliery and viewer at Wallsend, but also mining consultant for Lord Londonderry's collieries, and secretary of the coal owners committee.

He was already writing in 1804:

> *"I have seen most of the trade individually and hinted the necessity of adopting a regulation ensuring binding, as I find the men have got extravagent ideas already. Everyone admits of the propriety of such a measure."*

The immediate results were a dramatic lowering in the cost of binding — reduced on the Tyne to two-and-a-half guineas in 1805 and one-and-a-half guineas in 1806 — and the withdrawal of subsidised corn; in the longer term it led to a series of general strikes on the coalfield, the first in 1810 when the coalowners attempted to move the binding time to the slack period at Christmas despite the inconvenience this would cause the pitmen whose change of job would often require moving house.

Buddle was not the only local coalowner involved in developing the employers' strategy for dealing with the pitmen, for in 1812 William Potter (FT2), a coalowner and brewer on the Forth Banks, was writing to Buddle recommending that a general relief fund be set up for disaster victims. Eligibility, he argued, should be conditional on good conduct since this would discourage *"emigration... would restrain those outrages which they have occasionally fallen into and dispose them to a more respectful and submission to the lawful commands of their masters."*[33]

The culmination of the long struggle between the employers and the pitmen was reached at the end of this first period in the 1844 strike which affected the whole of the Durham and Northumberland coalfield. Determined to gain fairer working conditions that would ensure payment by weight instead of by measure, abolition of the fines system, and a guaranteed four day week, all 40,000 pitmen struck on March 31 in support of their claim. John Buddle had died in 1843, but again the local coalowners played a prominent part in the unsavoury events of the next six months. Joseph Lamb (FT9) and Armorer Donkin, later to become a founding partner in Armstrong's Company, were members of the coalowners' committee that met weekly to review progress in the employers' campaign. John Clayton (FT6) was elected to the three man tribunal set up to consider any appeals that were made against revisions in the "vend" or quota system.

The ultimate sanction open to the coalowners was to turn the pitmen out of their tied cottages. From the records of the coal owners committee[34] it is clear that the question of a general turning out was under discussion in June, but was not finally acted upon until July. The minutes do not record a specific decision being taken by the committee, but it is likely to have been finally agreed at the meeting of July 1, when Mr A.L. Potter (FT2) another founding partner in Armstrong's company *"attended the committee and stated that he had received information that there was to be an attempt made this week by the unemployed workmen to stop the pits at work".* As early as June 1 however the minutes record that "Mr Surtees (FT18) called at the meeting and reported that this day he had turned out 12 families at Benwell Colliery". The scene though was as nothing by comparison with the events that were to follow:-

> *"In July, notice to quite was served the workers, and, in a week the whole 40,000 were put out of doors. This measure was carried out with revolting cruelty. The sick, the feeble, old men and little children even women in childbirth were mercilessly turned from their beds*

PITMEN'S STRIKE.

THE following Statement shews the Number of Hewers at present employed, the Number of Workmen who have left the Union and resumed Work, together with the Quantity of Chaldrons raised per Day:—

	Hewers.	Men left Union.	Chaldrons per Day.
TYNE	2697	659	3638
WEAR	2231	1197	2926
TEES	1232	652	1746
TOTAL	6160	2508	8310
Return to Aug. 3,	5528	2009	7630
Increase this Week	632	499	680

Coal Trade Office, Newcastle upon Tyne,
10th August, 1844.

Wm. Heaton, Printer, 96, Side.

Coalowners' handbill; part of a well-organised propaganda campaign to demoralize the striking pitmen. Picture: Northumberland Record Office.

and cast into the roadside ditches. One agent dragged by the hair from her bed, and into the street a women in the pangs of childbirth. Soldiers and police in crowds were present, ready to fire at the first symptom of resistance, on the slightest hint of the Justices of the Peace, who had brought about the whole brutal prodedure."

The ruthlessness of the employers was matched by the sophistication of their public relations and propaganda campaign. Aware from the start that it would be a protracted struggle and that evictions were likely, they saw the danger of being too closely identified in the public mind with the army. When therefore in April the coalowners committee received a letter from Major-General Brotherton, general in command of the Queen's Troops in the North East District, offering to mediate between the parties, they were quick to decline on the grounds that:

"No good can possibly arise from any attempt to interfere between the masters and their men in a dispute about the prices and terms of labour; and that is more especially desirable that the military authorities, **who may eventually be required to act in support of the civil power, should be kept altogether unconnected with the disputes."**[36] *(our emphasis).*

Secure in the knowledge that the civil

and military authorities would support the "rule of law" and implement any eviction orders, the committee printed thousands of handbills every week to demoralise the strikers showing the numbers of hewers who had resumed work and the numbers who had left the union. On June 8 the *Newcastle Chronicle* reported that 1386 hewers had returned, and 215 had left the union.

By the 10 August, with the strike nearing its end, it was claimed that 6160 were at work, and that 2508 had left the union. Nor were the owners slow to scotch rumours, detrimental to their case for having heard on the same day that there were reports that some coalowners had made concessions to get their pitmen back to work, the Committee recorded without any attempt to check the facts that "they think it right to state that in no instance has any such concession been made."

Despite all this and being forced out of their houses — many of which were now occupied by "blackleg" foreign workers brought in by the coalowners — the pitmen still hung on. But finally in September they were forced to give in and return on the employers' terms. Richard Fynes in his account of the strike sums up as follows:-

> "The strike is over. Arbitrary power and immense wealth proved stronger than the courage excited by a good cause. In fact justice itself was trampled underfoot by aristorcratic tryanny, aided by unlimited riches. Thousands and thousands of unfortunate men were driven by a stern necessity back again to a condition of abhorent slavery."[37]

The might of capital had prevailed, bringing to those who controlled it a sense of power and destiny. The parallels with the social transformation that had taken place a century earlier are remarkable:

> "A double revolution was in progress in the North in the first half of the eighteenth century — the disappearance of the old gentry on the one hand and the rise of a new ruling class on the other — a change none the less revolutionary because its processes were silent as leaven.
>
> For, thanks to the profits to be made in coal-mining and satellite trades, the social progress which transmitted yeomen into merchants, and merchants in gentry was here greatly accelerated. Before 1745, the new men were completely in the saddle."[38]

A new ruling class was indeed in the saddle by the end of this first period but this time its hold was to be far more tenacious and its influence far greater. The power and technology of the new industrial capitalism was to transform West Newcastle and Tyneside in ways undreamt of even by the new capitalist class, but there was little doubt that it was they who controlled it — and controlled it to their own advantage and profit.

Footnotes

1. Ferrous sulphate or green vitriol, used in a wide range of chemical manufacturing processes.
2. M. Dunn. View of the Coal Trade of the North of England 1844. See also S. Middlesbrook. Newcastle upon Tyne, 1950 for references to early coal-mining in West Newcastle.
3. Edward Montagu was the grandson of the 1st Earl of Sandwich. His father Charles Montagu was a large coal-owner in the North of England and was one of the "Grand Allies", a coalowners' cartel first set up in 1721 to limit production at their collieries to keep prices up in London.
4. Letters quoted in W.W. Tomlinson, Denton Hall and its Associations. 1894.
5. F.M.L. Thompson. English Landed Society in the Nineteenth Century, pps.263-266. Routledge and Kegan Paul. 1963.
6. The name Ord was changed to the present-day family name of Blackett-Ord when in 1842 a niece of a later William Ord married a Reverend J. Blackett.
7. Quoted in F.M.L. Thompson, op.cit.
8. M. Dunn, op.cit.
9. A viewer was the manager of a colliery.
10. See R. Welford, Men of Mark Twixt Tyne and Tees Vol.3, 1895.
11. L.S. Pressnell, Country Banking in the Industrial Revolution, p.234. Oxford 1956.
12. See E. Lamb, Some Annals of the Lambs: a Border Family. Privately printed. 1925.
13. W.P. Hedley and C.R. Hudleston. Cookson of Penrith and Newcastle upon Tyne. Privately Printed.
14. A.H. John (Ed). Minutes relating to Samuel Walker & Co. Rotherham and Walkers, Parker and Co. Lead Manufactures. 1951.
15. E. Mackenzie, Historical View of Northumberland, Vol.2, p.382. Newcastle-upon-Tyne. 1825.
16. A fell-monger was a dealer in skins and hides.
17. Evidence of Captain J.M. Laws.
18. L.T.C. Rolt, George and Robert Stephenson, London 1960.
19. T.S. Ashton, The Industrial Revolution, p.13. 1948.
20. K. Marx, Capital, Volume 3.
21. D. Harvey. Social Justice and the City, p.260. Edward Arnold 1973. See also M. Dobb, Papers on Capitalism, Development and Planning, pps.5-16. London 1960.
22. See S. Pollard, Fixed Capital in the Industrial Revolution, p.156 in F. Crouzet (Ed) Capital Formation in the Industrial Revolution, Methuen, 1972.
23. E.J. Hobsbawm, Industry and Empire, p.75. Pelican 1975.
24. F. Crouzet, op.cit., p.51.
25. Private Housing and the Working Class, Benwell CDP Final Report series. 1978.
26. F.M.L. Thompson, op.cit. p.101.
27. E.J. Hobsbawm, op.cit., pps.73, 77.
28. T.J. Nossiter, Influence, Opinion and Political Idioms in Reformed England, Harvester Press 1975.
29. A further general discussion of this can be found in G.E. Mingay. The Gentry — The Rise and Fall of a Ruling Class, 1976. His reference (p.166-7) to "The Cooksons of Meldon Park, Cuthberts of Beaufront Castle, Strakers of Stagshaw House and Joiceys of Newton Hall and Ford Castle" as examples of a landowning class embracing the new industries, is however misleading. They were indeed major industrialists but their large country estates came later in the second half of the nineteenth century after the profits from the pits piled up.
30. E. Lamb, Some Annals of the Lambs, op.cit., p.74.
31. E. Hughes, North Country Life in the Eighteenth Century — pps.166-71 O.U.P. 1969. One of the first complaints came in 1712 when it was alleged that Mr Montagu's Hutton and Benwell pits were exceeding their quota.
32. P.E.H. Hair, The Binding of the Pitmen of the North East 1800-1809. Durham University Journal, 1965, provides a detailed account of the arrangements, and the role played by John Buddle.
33. Letter to John Buddle, 8 June, 1812. Northumberland County Record Office.
34. Joint Coal Trade Minutes 1840-1844. Northumberland County Record Office.
35. F. Engels. The Conditions of the Working Class in England in 1844, p.256. George Allen and Unwin. 1968. See also for a full account of the strike R. Fynes, The Miners of Northumberland and Durham, pps.56-106, 1873.
36. Joint Coal Trade Minutes, op.cit., 2 April 1844.
37. R. Fynes, p.105, op.cit.
38. E. Hughes, p.XVIII, op.cit.

2
1845-1914 Growth of New Industries

W.G. Armstrong's Engine Works, 1849. Picture: Newcastle City Library.

THE SECOND half of the nineteenth century was a period of massive change that was to enlarge the small central nucleus of Newcastle and its adjoining villages into a major industrial city. Just as coal provided the central thrust for the earlier development of West Newcastle, now it was heavy engineering and shipbuilding. To the two existing firms of R. Stephenson and R & W Hawthorn was added a third — W.G. Armstrong and Co. initially at the Elswick Works. Together these three firms employed nearly 20,000 men by the 1880s. They had not just *"put the area on the map"*, but had created the most important centre in the world for the manufacture of ships, armaments and locomotives.

The initial capital for Armstrong's Works came from a consortium of coalowners and there was a similar injection of large-scale coal capital into R & W Hawthorn in 1870 when the original owners pulled out.

The new industries were greedy for land — especially Armstrong, which by the First World War had virtually taken over an entire three-mile stretch of the riverside from Elswick to Scotswood. Smaller factories were either bought out or disappeared through lack of competitiveness. The successful companies and entrepreneurs either moved from the area to expand or concentrate production elsewhere, or were taken over by larger companies to continue production on the same site.

Since many of these new capitalists had family and business ties with each other, close working relationships were common between "competing" companies. In the larger engineering works especially this was paralleled by a vertical integration of production processes so that a firm like Armstrong could be wholly self-reliant in building a warship.

As the coal seams near the Tyne began to be worked out, the profits from these early workings and other industries were reinvested by the early coalowners in the new deeper pits in Durham and Northumberland. By the end of the period a handful of families, who had been involved in the earlier industries of West Newcastle, controlled a very substantial part of coal production in the whole of the northern coalfield. Some of the older pits like those at Benwell were taken over by smaller-scale entrepreneurs.

There was a diversification of personal capital as well. Several of the second and third generation entered banking establishing links with the finance capital sector that remain important today. And since the banks of the time tended to lend short-term only, much of the families' capital was used in the way that insurance companies' funds are used today — to provide finance for land speculation, for new developments like the electricity supply companies and for overseas speculation in commodities and mining. The other main investment — which added nothing to production — was in the purchase of large estates accompanied by extravagent spending on castles and mansions.

The wealth of the families reflected the expansion in production. Armstrong and Cruddas, directors of W.G. Armstrong, became millionaires, and more than 20 members of the families died with estates valued at more than £250,000. But the power of this ruling class cannot be measured simply in terms of wealth. Through a network of interlocking directorships and family ties they dominated many of Tyneside's major industries. Furthermore they were able to establish control over many of the wider social and political institutions. They became not simply a ruling class, but a hegemonic class. An example of this dominance in the industrial field can be seen in the role played by the directors of Armstrong in forming an engineering employers' association to counter growing trade union militancy after the successful 1871 Engineers' strike had won the right to a nine-hour day.

As councillors and holders of aldermanic seats the local bourgeoisie exercised substantial control too over local politics and the machinery of local government. This is not to say that there was no active working class movement in the city. Indeed there was, but the criterion of a hegemonic class is that it successfully imposes a world view of its own shaping. This incorporation of the working class had in Newcastle both a physical and ideological element. Not only were the schools, churches, parks, houses and libraries that the working class used provided by the big industrialists, but it was largely the latter who created and controlled the forums — the debating societies, the university extension movement, the local Press and others — in which the major political issues were discussed and interpreted.

2.1 INDUSTRIES

2.1A ENGINEERING

Victorian historians chose to describe the founding in 1847 of Armstrong's Works (now part of the Vickers Group) as the breaking of a sylvan peace. A writer at the turn of the century for instance had this to say:

> "The Elswick of 60 years ago was . . . considered to be a spot of great natural beauty, with green fields sloping pleasantly from the heights of Benwell to the river Tyne . . . The Elswick Works were reached by a country walk along the Scotswood Road . . . Another feature of the neighbourhood was the abundance of game to be found in its meadows and hedgerows."[1]

By omitting to mention the industries (including R. Stephenson and R&W Hawthorn) and coal workings already existing, they implied that it was the birth of a new era, a breakaway from the past. William Armstrong, later to become Lord Armstrong (FT2), was portrayed as the romantic hero whose inventive mind and practical skills tore the city from its mediaeval past, and transformed it to a major industrial centre. The reality was however very different, for Armstrong a qualified solicitor and the son of a Newcastle corn merchant, came from exactly the same mercantile and professional class as was predominant in the first phase of Tyneside industrialisation.

His financial backers moreover were already major coalowners and at least two of them — A.L. Potter and Armorer Donkin — had been heavily involved as members of the coal trade committee in crushing the 1844 pitmens' strike.

Armstrong and his four partners had been instigators two years earlier of the Whittle Dene Water Company, formed with a capital of £120,000 to suppy water to Newcastle and Gateshead. The chairman of the company was Armstrong's uncle A.L. Potter (FT2) while Armstrong himself was Secretary. The following year they formed the Newcastle Cranage Company to manufacture hydraulic cranes and in 1847 formed a partnership to establish the Elswick Works of W.G. Armstrong and Co.

Of the original £43,000 capital required in the first year, the bulk was provided by the partners with coal interests. George Cruddas (FT8), a linen draper and shipowner from North Shields with interests in the Oxclose Colliery, put up £12,000 and a further £2,500 towards the share of Richard Lambert, a solicitor and wine merchant; Armorer Donkin, senior partner in the solicitors' firm where Armstrong worked, and a representative of the Walbottle Colliery on the Coal Trade Committee contributed £12,000; and a further £5,000 came from A.L. Potter, senior partner in the Walbottle Colliery and one of the founding partners in the Stella Coal Company. Armstrong's contribution was limited to £2,000 and his patents valued at £3,000.

The history of the development of W.G. Armstrong is familiar enough that only the broad outline needs to be given here. From originally building cranes, the company soon diversified into the manufacture of bridges. Armstrong then successfully patented a new gun which was superior to all existing field ordnance, and he was appointed engineer to the War Department. From then on the company grew rapidly. In 1859 the Elswick Ordnance Company was formed and in 1867 an agreement was reached with C.W. Michell and Co. of Low

Walker to develop naval work jointly — Michell building the ships, and Armstrong supplying the guns. Seventeen years later the two companies amalgamated to form a new company with issued capital of £1.5 million. The following year a new shipyard was opened at Elswick that enabled the company, with its adjacent steel works, engineering and ordnance departments, to build and equip an entire warship from raw material to finished product.

Over the next 30 years the company was to record 84 launches and become the most successful exporter of warships in the world. Competition was, however, already fierce, and in 1897 the company was forced to merge with the Manchester firm of Whitworth to keep abreast of the more modern Sheffield-based firm of Vickers. In 50 years the growth of the company had been remarkable. Its workforce had grown from 100 to close on 20,000 by the turn of the century. An age of large-scale, highly automated production was already under way as this description of Armstrong's Works by a Swedish traveller shows. The days of the independent artisan producer were indeed over.

> "After passing through two or three areas, we came to a yet bigger and darker room, in which over nine hundred workers stand around lathes, planes, drills and filing and burnishing machines of the most diverse shapes and give the small pieces which come from the foundries the sizes and shapes of those gun parts, which the complex, finished product must include. Here we see again the incredibly slow and meticulously careful manner of work by the automated machines and the extraordinary limitation in the workers' participation in the process. These quiet, neat men (who are all of a particularly intelligent type for engineering workers) have apparently nothing more to do than put pieces of metal into machines, see to it that they are in working order and watch them minute by

Assembling a bridge for India at the Elswick Works, 1857; Armstrong, standing above overseeing the work.

The Armstrong gun, built in 1855; it was the first rifled breech-loading gun to be made. Picture: Newcastle City Library.

Bird's eye view of Elswick Works, 1887. Picture: Newcastle City Library.

Lord Armstrong outside his country seat at Cragside.

Sir Andrew Noble (centre) and wife with Japanese naval delegation. Picture: Newcastle City Library.

minute, while the machines carry out that part of the work for which they were specially constructed. For each shape, curve or surface of every particular part of the gun or machine guns there is a special machine, and when it has cut a block of metal to exactly as marked on the blueprints, the piece is ready to move to another machine to have another curve or surface turned, planed or filed – and so on until the piece has the exact intricate shape that the gun mechanism needs. This is mechanical engineering to perfection; machines create machines while the worker's job consists of something strangely in between physical and mental work: a sort of waiting job in which well-trained powers of observation count for most."[2]

The profits from Armstrong & Co. did not all go to Armstrong himself although he became a wealthy man with an estate valued at £1.4 million at his death. Of the original partners only the Cruddas family retained an immediate connection, with George and his son W.D. Cruddas continuing as financial directors until W.D. Cruddas died in 1912, worth just over £1 million. From an early period, however, a number of young men, mostly of an aristocratic, landed or military background joined the firm either to go through an apprenticeship or in a management capacity. Several of them moved on to become chairmen of other major engineering companies including C.A. Parsons, Sir Benjamin Browne (FT5) (Chairman of Hawthorn Leslie & Co) and Sir T. Wrightson (Chairman of Head Wrightson & Co, Middlesbrough). Others stayed, the most notable being George and Stuart Rendel, Col. Dyer and Andrew Noble (FT10) who became chairman of the company when Armstrong died. Noble was succeeded by his sons until the company was merged with Vickers in 1927.

So great was the wealth accumulated by some of the directors that it led even to disputes within the board with the Rendels becoming highly critical of Sir Andrew Noble and his policies. A running feud continued until 1911 when a 'solemn treaty' was signed under which the executive directors promised that they would carry out various reforms *"provided the independent directors (the Rendels) would accept responsibility for the executive directors' irregularities for many years past in secretly appropriating to themselves exceptionally large remunerations, and would further sanction certain very liberal remunerations in the future".*[3] Some idea of the scale of these remunerations can be judged by the capital that Andrew Noble and his three sons Saxton, Philip and John had accumulated by the time they died – in all just over £2 million.

Other Engineering

Although W.G. Armstrong was the largest engineering works – bigger than the other two major engineering firms, R. Stephenson and R & W Hawthorn – there were other important new companies formed. In 1849 James and George Joicey (FT3) established the family firm, J & G Joicey of Forth Banks and began the manufacture of locomotives and winding engines – one of the earliest of which was supplied to the Beamish No.2 Pit. Few details are known of the setting up of the company, although it is likely that the initial capital came from the family's colliery interests – there were five brothers involved – which had commenced 12 years earlier at South Tanfield, Co. Durham.

The brothers' social background is also somewhat obscure, although it is known that their father worked at the Backworth Colliery, possibly in some overseer capacity. Although he earned enough to enable James to get a good education and become a mining engineer, his was not the rich mercantile background that was so typical of the other West Newcastle coalowners. Another largish firm was that of Thomas Clark which was employing more than 300 workers in 1871.

The other main intervention of coal capital into local engineering came when the firm of R. & W. Hawthorn was taken over in 1870 by a consortium headed by Benjamin Browne (FT5) who had judiciously chosen as a brother-in-law, Buddle Atkinson (FT5), the heir to John Buddle's fortune.[4] Browne's personal capital (provided by his mother) was £5,000 and a further £10,000 was put up by Buddle Atkinson. An even great contribution of £15,000 came from the wealthy Durham coalowner John Straker (FT17), whose father Joseph (of Benwell Old House) had commenced the family firm of Strakers and Love. As a result of this the Buddle family and the Strakers secured a substantial stake in what later became Hawthorn Leslie & Co. The exact value of the shareholding of the son F.B. Atkinson is uncertain, but it represented probably a considerable part of the £760,000 estate he left when he died in 1953. The Straker interest continued right into the Second World War, with John Straker's son and grandson becoming chairman of the company in succession in the inter-war years.

Outside the West End of Newcastle, the other main family diversification was that of John Wigham Richardson (FT13). He was the son of Edward Richardson the coalowner, banker and leather manufacturer, whose firm E. & J. Richardson had moved from the centre of the city to a site in Elswick in 1860. With £5,000 capital provided by his father, John Wigham Richardson established in 1870 a shipbuilding yard at the Neptune Works, Walker. The company was to amalgamate 33 years later with Hunter's yard to form Swan Hunter & Wigham Richardson (the basis of the present Swan Hunter Group). The amalgamated company launched the Mauretania in 1907 with the help of a substantial state subsidy given to Cunard, the purchasers of the liner. Richardson's son retained a seat on the board and was chairman from 1945-1949, while his grandson still alive today, remained until the 1960s when he appears to have left to concentrate on the shipping and insurance business established by the family in London.

A continuing reminder of early West Newcastle engineering; in the background the High Level Bridge completed in 1849 by R. Stephenson & Co, and in the foreground the Swing Bridge built in 1876 by W.G. Armstrong & Co. Picture: City Engineers, Newcastle.

Winding Engine at Beamish Pit, built in 1855 by J. & G. Joicey, of Forth Banks. Picture: Beamish Museum.

2.1B CHARACTERISTICS OF CHANGE

Not all the local industries were of the high technology, high capital type that the most advanced sectors of

The Mauretania, built by Swan Hunter and Wigham Richardson, leaving the Tyne, 1907. Picture: Newcastle City Library.

engineering represented. Moreover, the Swedish traveller's description of Armstrong's machine shop was not typical of all the jobs in the Elswick Works. Many more involved processes where the physical burden of hard, unskilled manual labour was immense. As Samuel argues: *"Mechanisation in one department of production was often complemented by an increase in sweating in others: the growth of large firms by a proliferation of small producing units"* and he cites the example of armaments where the Enfield Rifle was manufactured by machinery on a system of interchangeable parts, but the cartridges were packed by hand at Woolwich by some 800 children aged from eight to 12.⁵

While a similar process was no doubt occurring locally, it was complemented by growing concentrations of production and control, for the logic of capitalism requires that a firm continually strives to lower its unit costs to remain competitive. To do this it has to create larger units of production, develop more efficient production processes, and invest more capital to achieve higher levels of technology.

Indeed W.G. Armstrong is a good example of this, for their failure to reinvest was a major cause of their lack of competitiveness with Vickers who were in the words of one of the Armstrong directors: *"Modern if anything. They have all the dispositions we lack"*. The decision therefore of the directors to invest the profits from the company elsewhere in speculative foreign enterprises and large estates (see later) can be seen as part of the cause of the long-term decline of heavy engineering in West Newcastle.

Disappearance of Small Firms

Smaller firms were also affected by these wider processes of the economy. In several cases companies like the Elswick Copperas Works and the Benwell Fishery were purchased for their land early on when Armstrong was first established. A further two companies, the Delaval Brick Works and the Scotswood Shipbuilding Co., were bought out in 1899 when the company built its Scotswood works. Others, like the engineering firms of Thomas Clark and John Waterson, disappeared from the trade directories in the 1880s, probably caused by slumps in trade.

Expansion out of the area

For the successful companies and entrepreneurs, expansion out of the area was a more likely solution with the local works either being sold off or retained as part of a larger enterprise. W.G. Armstrong indeed had already become a multinational company by 1884 when it opened a new sixty-three acre armament works and shipyard in Italy. Robert Stephenson and Co. on the other hand removed all their locomotive works at Forth Banks in 1900 in Darlington, selling off the land to Hawthorn Leslie. A similar pattern occurred at an even earlier stage with two other companies that were to become major employers on Tyneside — W.I. Cookson and George Angus. The Cooksons (FT7) had, as we have seen, a variety of interests in West Newcastle in the first period of industrialisation. The first record of their local works at the Close is in 1855, and in the following year they purchased a large site at Willington Quay, where their lead interests became consolidated to form the basis of the present day Lead Industries Group.⁶ The Leather Works of George Angus and Co. (FT1) was moved from the Close in 1867 to premises in Grainger Street and subsequently expanded to Walker in the 1930s and to the Coast Road, Wallsend in 1956. Expansion in this case meant also diversification for by the Second World War the firm had already almost completely moved out of leather and into synthetic products. Details of other companies can be seen in the schedule in the appendix.

Close Working Relationships

An alternative response to the problems of competition was to adopt close working relationships with complementary companies, a process that was made easier by the family ties and interlocking interests of many of the major industrialists.

Just as W.G. Armstrong and C.W. Mitchell worked together over a long period, so Palmer's shipyard at Jarrow established close links with R. & W. Hawthorn who supplied marine engines for more than 50 of their ships. In their turn R. & W. Hawthorn (and R. Stephenson) received for a long time all their supply of springs for locomotive manufacture from the Spencers' Newburn Steel Works. The relationship was sometimes more in the nature of capital diversification as occurred with the Throckley Coal Company where the Spencer family (FT1) subscribed almost half of the initial capital.[7] The immediate intention of these arrangements was to secure a reliable supply of materials at a predictable and usually lower cost. They brought economic advantages to both supplier and purchaser. But additionally they created an interdependency between many of these large companies, and a sense amongst the industrial bourgeoisie who controlled the companies that their common economic interests needed to be defended against an increasingly militant labour movement — a point to which we will return later.

In a sense, arrangements of this nature were a form of concentration to which the logical conclusion was amalgamation or takeover. And just as there could never have been any final solution to the problems of competitiveness, so firms in the area remained attractive to external companies seeking to expand or close down unwanted competition. In this way now large companies first penetrated the area in the early 1900s — General Electric Company taking over the Lemington Glass Works, and Gallaher buying out the large tobacco manufacturers Harvey and Davy of Hanover Square. Other companies fared less well. The cement manufacturers, Addision Potter and Co. of Willington Quay founded by A.L. Potter's son (FT2) was taken over in 1912 by British Portland Cement Manufacturers and promptly closed down. The classic example, though, is that of Swan's Electric Lamp Company formed in Benwell in 1880 by Joseph W. Swan. The first commercial lamp ever manufactured was made there in 1881 and the following year the company opened a new factory in Paris. There was, however, an immediate problem facing Swan — legal action taken by the Edison Company for allegedly infringing Edison's patents. Rather than fight the case, Swan agreed to amalgamate with Edison and shortly afterwards production was transferred from the Benwell factory.[8]

An early casualty: the Elswick Copperas Works bought out by W.G. Armstrong & Co.

Swan's first commercial electric lamp made in Benwell in 1881. Picture: Science Museum London.

R&W HAWTHORN — Locomotive and Marine Engine Manufacturers.

1817	Company formed
1830-50	100 locomotive engines produced.
1870	Takeover by coalowners' consortium, Browne, Straker and Atkinson.
1871	Takes over T. & W. Smith, Walker Shipyard.
1882	All marine engine work transferred to Walker. Loco work remains at Forth Banks.
1900	Expands into part of adjacent site, vacated by R. Stephenson.
1937	Fuses locomotive interests with R. Stephenson.
1943	Sells all loco. interests to R. Stephenson.
1960	R. Stephenson closes Forth Banks works — 800 redundant.

Anatomy of takeovers and rationalisation; not just a phenomenon of the 1970s.

2.1C COAL

The focus so far has been on the changes taking place in West Newcastle. In mining the theme of concentration can be very clearly illustrated in the geographical extension of coal capital to the deeper pits of the wider coalfield, and in the development generally of the coal combines. Locally the relatively small pits were taken over by men with far more limited capital. J.O. Scott, owner of the Delaval Colliery is reputed to have been the son of a Longbenton labourer. William Cochrane Carr, a man of humble origins married the daughter of a market gardener and took over the Benwell Colliery after starting as a brick manufacturer.

At the more profitable pits at Scotswood (Montagu) and Throckley, more substantial entrepreneurs moved in from the mercantile background that was common in the early period. And these pits were certainly profitable, for the owners of the Montagu, the brothers Thomas Walter Benson and Walter John Benson died at the end of this second period with estates valued respectively at £321,000 and £483,000. The other main local workings were those of the Stella Coal Company on the south side of the River Tyne, which continued as a very successful private company under the control of the Simpson (FT15) and Buddle/Atkinson (FT5) dynasties until nationalisation.

The centrifugal movement of capital into the wider coalfield was generated by the enormous increase in demand for coal that occurred in the second half of the nineteenth century. The diagram (p.9) shows the effect on national output which increased in the 50 year period up to 1895 from 34 million tons to 189 million tons annually.

Of this final figure 21 per cent (39.8 million tons) came from the Northumberland and Durham coalfields. The increases in output did not, however, come from any major technological changes such as mechanisation which was transforming the engineering industry; they came instead from the investment of massive amounts of new capital, and from a huge expansion of the workforce. For only a few were the "golden dreams of the coal trade" to become a reality; for these lucky few coal brought immense wealth, fabulous by the standards of the day, and even more so when the effect of price inflation is taken into account.[9] By 1870, the main pattern of control and ownership of the whole coalfield had been laid down with a few families who had been closely associated with earlier industrial development in West Newcastle playing a dominant role in the future of the region's most important industry right up until nationalisation in 1947. An examination of this process is best carried out by tracing the fortunes of particular families.

a. The Lamb Family (FT9)

Joseph Lamb's connection with Cramlington Coal Company had commenced as early as 1824 but in the period up to 1850, his interests were by no means exclusively centred there. He was the owner of the Elswick and Walbottle Collieries in the 1840s, and from 1806-1852 appears to have been the major executive partner in the Lemington Glass Works.[10] By his death in 1859 Lamb had become chairman of the Northern Coalowners' Association, and the Cramlington and Seaton Delaval collieries appear to have become the family's major interest, with the two sons inheriting a major share in the company. The younger son, R.O. Lamb, succeeded his father as chairman of the company – a position he held for the rest of his life. By his death in 1912, the seven pits at Cramlington and the Seaton Delaval Colliery were together producing almost two million tons annually and employing a workforce of about 2,800 men. The company gained a reputation for its steam coal from the West Hartley Main seam, and was a major supplier to the British Admiralty and several foreign navies. The family's involvement in the company was somewhat eclipsed after the First World War, because of the early death of Lamb's son Edward, but his brother's son and then grandson remained as directors of the Hartley Main Collieries (as it became known) until nationalisation.

b. The Straker Family (FT17)

The Strakers played a similarly influential role amongst the Durham coalowners. By his death in 1867, Joseph Straker, the founder of the firm Straker and Love, had already amassed a fortune of £300,000, while in the same year his son John Straker was elected chairman of a committee *"to form an association of colliery owners in Northumberland and Durham".* The family's main interest were pits and associated coke-ovens at Brancepeth, Co. Durham and Willington which by 1932 formed part of a private company with an issued share capital of £1.2 million. John Straker himself, who had purchased a 25 per cent shareholding in the firm of R. & W. Hawthorn, was also a director of the North Eastern Railway Company and a large landowner. The capital of £919,000 left when he died was to provide the base for later generations to diversify their interests across a wide range of financial and industrial sectors.

c. The Cookson Family (FT7)

John Straker's contemporary was William Isaac Cookson, who died only three years later, again with a massive fortune of £592,000. The firm W.I. Cookson & Co, a partnership between William Isaac, his brother John, and his brother-in-law William Cuthbert, was principally a lead manufacturing company, but the partners were equally active developing their coal interests. In 1870 they headed the list of 12 co-partners (another of whom was John Straker) in the Cowpen and North Seaton Coal Company that was taking a lease of the Lynemouth Mines, and were probably members of the original partnership formed in 1858. By 1892 the family was also involved in the Mickley Coal Company — the other main company that was to form the basis of the large Cookson combine that emerged in the 1930s — and were partners (with the Strakers, Spencers (FT1), J.B. Simpson

(FT15) and others) in the newly formed Wallsend and Hebburn Coal Company.[11]

d. The Pease Family (FT11)

The Pease family's initial connection with West Newcastle was Edward Pease's backing of R. Stephenson's locomotive works. As we shall see later, his brother's grandson John William Pease became a major Newcastle banker in the 1860s, but the family's coal interests in Yorkshire and Durham were developed by the firm of Pease and Partners as an integral part of a wider industrial empire centred in Teesside in ironstone mining, iron and steel.[12] In 1908 for instance, 70 per cent of their coal output was used in iron making. Local collieries worked by the Peases included those at Waterhouses, Esh Winning and Ushaw Moor, near Durham City.[13] Pease and Partners became a public limited company in 1898, and increased its capital substantially after the war to £1.5 million in 1918, and £3 million in 1920. Control, however, remained firmly in the hands of the Pease family for in 1923, seven of the nine directors of the company, and of Henry Stobbart and Co., a wholly owned coal subsidiary were members of the Pease family.

e. The Joicey Family (FT3)

George Joicey (d.1856) was managing director of the family engineering business on the Forth Banks, but his son James (later Baron Joicey) concentrated on developing the family's Durham colliery interests. By the turn of the century, having bought out in 1896 the Earl of Durham's collieries for a reported £300,000, the Joiceys had become the largest and wealthiest coalowners in the coalfield. By 1917 the company owned 25 mines in Durham, three coke-ovens and 50 steamers, and was producing six million tons of coal per annum bringing an annual estimated profit to the family of £¾ million.[14]

While James looked after the coal business, the older brother, J.G. Joicey, concentrated on the Forth Banks works, making a modest fortune of £32,000 by the time he died in 1899. His daughter's marriage however to Robert Dickinson (FT3), a Newcastle solicitor, was to set the seal on an alliance between the Joicey and Dickinson family that has been of major importance in the post-war period in channelling coal capital and compensation monies into property and the finance capital sector (see pages 74–77).

f. The Priestman Family (FT12)

The Priestmans were an exception to the general pattern for not only did they break into the small band of big time coalowners in this second period without an earlier involvement, but they were also immigrants to Tyneside without the business and trading links that most of the coalowners had established. The reason for this was largely a mixture of luck and speculation. Jonathan Priestman (senior) had been a tanner and like the Richardsons (FT13) had seen the attractiveness in investing his money in the Northumberland and District Bank.

When the bank collapsed in 1857, it was found that it had lent almost £1 million to the Derwent and Consett Iron Company. During negotiations a large number of shareholders, including Priestman, agreed as a settlement to take over the Consett Works and its associated colliery interests provided it was freed of all calls from the bank, and appointed Jonathan Priestman (junior) as managing director. This step brought the Priestman family into direct contact with the coal trade, and 12 years later Priestman left to become managing partner in the new Ashington Coal Company, in which William Milburn, the shipowner, was the major shareholder. Over the next 20 years, it grew into the largest colliery company in Northumberland and by 1898 had a share capital of £600,000 – of which £200,000 was held by the Priestman family, and £270,000 by the Milburns of Milburn House, Newcastle.

In addition, the Priestmans – in conjunction with the Peiles (FT12) part of the wider extended family – owned the entire share capital of Priestman Collieries, which controlled pits at Rowlands Gill, Blaydon and Axwell Park in Co. Durham. They were also pioneers in the use of Waste Heat Plant in the North East, forming in 1907 the Waste Heat and Gas Electrical Generating Stations Limited – later to be transformed into the Carliol Investment Trust, an important regional financial institution.

This focus on an emerging pattern of dynastic domination in the coalfield sheds light on the very important role of a few coalowning families within the new industrial bourgeoisie, but it has also to be remembered that similar structural changes were occurring within the industry as elsewhere. Not only was there concentration of ownership, but typically companies were diversifying their interests by developing ironworks, coke-ovens, waste-heat disposal plans and brickworks, and creating vertically integrated structures which enabled them both to transport the coal to the loading points via their own railway lines and to ship it abroad with their own steamers.

2.2 DIVERSIFICATION OF PRIVATE AND PERSONAL CAPITAL

Although the organisational changes that we have already described – the processes of concentration, integration and diversification – were steered through by the individual entrepreneurs who controlled the companies, they were doing so within the wider logic of a capitalist economy. This framework largely determined the available courses of action open if the company was to continue growing and competing successfully in the wider market. There were, however, other outlets for the investment of profits made from coal and heavy-engineering which were sought not because they fell within the pattern of a logical expansion of an entrepreneur's existing commercial ventures, but because they offered higher returns on capital, or the social status that comes with landed estate and high levels of conspicuous consumption. Many of the companies in this period were private (and thus controlled by a few family members) and even where they were public, as the case of Armstrong demonstrates, the directors like autocratic Czars could appropriate large sums for their own use. There was a huge potential therefore for shifting capital from one productive sector into other — often non-productive — sectors and activities. The decisions made were to influence profoundly the subsequent fortunes of a number of Tyneside dynasties. The three main areas of diversification were:

a. Banking.
b. Finance capital for industry and land speculation.
c. Purchase of agricultural land and large estates.

2.2A BANKING

In the earlier period there was a substantial involvement of merchant and industrial capital in banking. But there were considerable risks involved and at least two local banks collapsed, including the Commercial Bank (1793) and the Exchange Bank (1803). The collapse of the Northumberland and Durham District Bank in 1857 had even greater consequences not only for families like the Richardsons (FT13) who lost a lot of money, but also in fracturing business confidence in banking generally. For our purposes it had a further importance for it led to the establishment two years later of two new banks, Hodgkin, Barnett, Pease and Spence, and Woods and Co. with which the West Newcastle families were closely associated.

At the turn of the century both banks were to be taken over, the first by Lloyds (1903) and the second by Barclays (1897) as part of the amalgamations that created the system of today's big centralised clearing banks. Jonathan Priestman (FT12) was instrumental in the formation of the Hodgkin, Barnett bank, for he had opened a new bank following the collapse of the District Bank, and wrote to Thomas Hodgkin (FT12) a fellow Quaker and others with capital, in the hope that they would take over the business.[15] Of the initial four partners only Spence had local knowledge, as a former manager of the Union Bank, while the others were young men, bringing in family capital. Hodgkin and Barnett (FT3) came from London, the sons respectively of a solicitor and stockbroker, while John William Pease (FT11) was the grandnephew of Edward Pease who had earlier put up capital for Stephenson's locomotive works.

None of the West Newcastle families was initially involved in Woods and Co., but in 1868 John Clayton's nephew Richard (FT6) became a partner and was followed a decade later by John Coppin Straker (FT17) and later still by his brother Frederic. For both these families and those involved in the Hodgkin bank, the partnerships provided access for later generations into regional and national banking and into insurance and finance capital generally. It was also a diversification that brought financial rewards, as the *Newcastle Weekly Chronicle* of 1913 pointed out:

> "It would seem that banking is one of the most profitable occupations. One great concern has just declared a dividend of 18.5 per cent and others have approached that figure. With the growth of trade there is very naturally more demand for credit and with that profit is enlarged."[16]

Generally speaking, the role of the banks was to provide short-term capital and overdraft facilities — a role that was particularly important at times of recession. Indeed, both John Wigham Richardson (FT13)[17] and Sir Benjamin Browne (FT5) refer to the support given to their companies by Pease and Hodgkin, and imply that they might well have collapsed without it. Browne describes it thus:

> "Not only were they ready to give us their advice and assistance, but they behaved with the most extraordinary liberality in the matter of financial accommodation and overdrafts. We could not possibly have got on if they had not allowed us the most liberal accommodation for long periods — and that for many years after we had begun. I can only say for myself that, like two or three other large manufacturers on Tyneside, I was entirely made by the bank."[18]

Partners in the Barnett, Hodgkin and Pease Bank, 1894 including John William Pease (seated centre) and Thomas Hodgkin (seated right).

2.2B FINANCE CAPITAL

Once a company had become successfully established, capital for new investments and expansion tended to be internally generated from the profits of the company. But for new enterprises, it was the big industrialists and coalowners who played the role of finance capitalists, as the example of W.G. Armstrong and later the takeover of Hawthorn illustrates.

The public utilities are another case, for the two electricity companies formed in 1889 were largely the creation of two of the West Newcastle families. The smaller one, the Newcastle and District Electric Lighting Company, was closely associated with the Simpson (FT15) and Buddle/Browne (FT5) families, directors of the Stella Coal Company. Also included on the board of directors in 1911 was W.M. Angus (FT1) and Sir G.S. Milburn from the Ashington Coal Company.

In a sense, electricity undertakings were a logical form of diversification for the directors of coal companies, since control ensured a captive market for the collieries' output. In the period 1913-30, consumption of coal for electricity manufacture was nationally by far the greatest area of growth rising from 3.3 million tons to 10 million tons, representing an increase from two per cent to six per cent of the total.[19]

Similar links appear to have been established by the much larger concern, The Newcastle-upon-Tyne Electric Supply Company, for one of the early directors was Sir Lindsay Wood director of two other large coal companies, John Bowes and Partners and Harton Coal Company. The promotion of the Electric Supply Company was however mainly the work of two men who had married into the Richardson family (FT13), John T. Merz, a manufacturing chemist, and Robert Spence Watson a solicitor and important figure in the Liberal Party. By 1911 Merz had been joined on the board by J.H.B. Noble (FT10) with Viscount Ridley (FT14) acting as the debenture holders' trustee. Evidence of the close business and social connections between the various families, all members of the new industrial ruling class, can be seen in the amicable arrangement agreed as to areas of influence. *"Instead of fighting each other, these two companies agreed to divide the prospective spoils, the District Company taking the West of Newcastle, the Supply Company taking the East."*[20] This monopoly arrangement worked ideally for the Supply Company, for by the 1920s it had grown with its associated companies into a huge combination covering most areas between Tyneside and Cleveland and supplying power to the majority of industrial works. It

Interior of the Forth Banks power station, owned by the Electric Lighting Co; the first in the world to be equipped with turbine-powered (AC) generators. Picture: Science Museum, London. Below: Spreading power and influence; map showing areas covered by the Electric Supply Co in the 1920s.

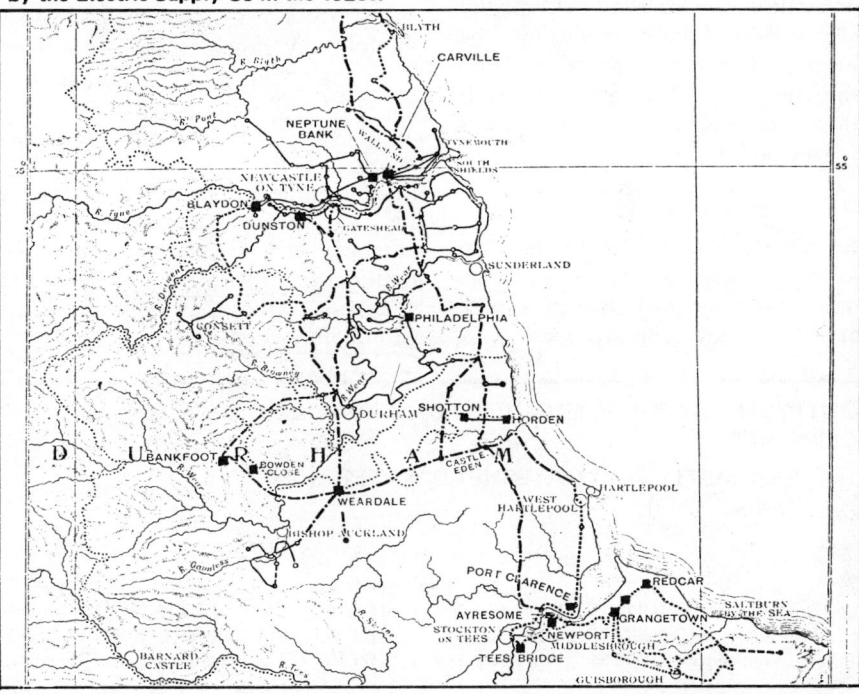

was also of benefit to other family members, for a good deal of the company's generating equipment was supplied by Merz's brother-in-law J. Wigham Richardson (FT13).

Electricity undertakings were not the only areas into which the families' influence spread. Another was the Tyneside Tramways and Tramroads Company[21] whose first subscribers in 1901 included John Wigham Richardson (FT13) and C.J. Potter (FT2). Again there was a link with the Electric Supply Company, which had a £13,000 shareholding in the Company. Two of its directors, J.T. Merz and J.H.B. Noble were on the Tramways board which was chaired by William H.A. Armstrong (later the second Lord Armstrong) (FT2).

Family influence continued with the older companies formed in the first period. Members of the Potter family (FT2) remained directors of the Newcastle and Gateshead Gas Company until nationalisation, while for the Newcastle and Gateshead Water Company continuity of dynastic control is almost unchanged up to the present day (see table).

Export of Capital

The 50 years leading up to the First World War were also a period of intense investment of British capital abroad. As new opportunities arose,

RATEPAYER:— "Grand New Gas Works, Sir. Whose are they?"
DIRECTOR:— "The Newcastle and Gateshead Gas Company's."
RATEPAYER:— "Who'll pay for them?"
DIRECTOR:— "YOU."

Contemporary cartoon; the director is Sir W.H. Stephenson, chairman of the company.

with the prospect of higher returns, companies and individual industrialists diversified into far-flung enterprises around the world — public utilities and railways, mining syndicates, and commodity speculations. From 1865 to 1914 new British portfolio investment abroad rose from an annual figure of £20 million to a peak of £200 million, and in the great boom (1911-1913) twice as much was invested abroad as at home. Significantly, the emphasis was placed on the development of facilities which increased the capacity of primary producing countries to export surpluses to Europe, rather than their ability to manufacture goods themselves.[22]

The extent to which the export of Tyneside capital postponed much needed new investment in coal-mining and heavy engineering is impossible to judge accurately without detailed figures; but the active involvement of some of the big bourgeoisie is quite evident. The second Lord Armstrong (FT2) was a director (with Lord Joicey as colleague) of the Waterston Gold Mining Company of Mexico, the Cairo Tramways and Heliopolis Oasis Co, and of the Langhorn North Borneo Rubber Company; Lord Joicey himself was a director of the Great Northern Coal Company of New South Wales, Australia as well as being a landowner in Canada and Australia. The Noble family also were involved with Sir Andrew Noble a director of the Mond Nickel Co and the Mountain Copper Company, while his son J.H.B. Noble became a director of the Jerusalem Electric Corporation.

Finance for Land Speculation

Other significant areas of diversification were the purchase of land for speculative development and the provision of finance capital for smaller operators. Examples of the former were George Cruddas (FT8) who purchased 48 acres of the West Elswick Estate in the 1860s, on which his overall profit was probably in the region of £40,000; and Thomas Hodgkin (FT12) the banker, who bought a 13.5 acre site at Delaval Road in 1882, selling it 18 years later for £10,300 at a profit of £3,800.[23] The more normal practice however for the big industrialists was to lend money on mortgage for speculative owners and developers. Thus by 1885 at least two of the early coalowning families were important sources of mortgage funds for Grainger's children who had inherited the Elswick Estate. William Cookson had lent £46,000 on one son's share, and £23,000 on a daugher's share; and Joseph and Henry Straker had a further £22,000 advanced on another daughter's share.

The best example, however, of nineteenth century finance capital can be

CONTINUITY OF DIRECTORSHIPS FOR TWO PUBLIC UTILITY COMPANIES

(1) NEWCASTLE AND GATESHEAD WATER COMPANY (formed 1845)

1911		1939		1976	
W.D. Cruddas (Ch.)	(FT 8)	B. Cruddas, MP	(FT 8)	H.H. Peile	(FT12)
Lord Armstrong	(FT 2)	Lord Armstrong	(FT 2)	E.G. Angus (FT1) (1975)	
Sir Andrew Noble	(FT10)	Lord Joicey	(FT 3)	M.I.B. Straker	(FT17)
Sir W.H. Stephenson	(FT16)	W.E. Stephenson	(FT16)	J.S. Stephenson	(FT16)

(2) NEWCASTLE AND DISTRICT ELECTRIC LIGHTING CO. (formed 1889)

1911		1944	
J.B. Simpson (Ch.)	(FT15)	F.R. Simpson	(FT15)
F.R. Simpson	(FT15)	E.G. Angus	(FT 1)
Sir B. Browne	(FT 5)	Sir L.J. Milburn (Ashington Coal Co)	
H.I. Brackenbury	(FT 5)	R. Boys-Stones	(FT15)
W.M. Angus	(FT 1)		
Sir C.S. Milburn (Ashington Coal Co.)			

seen in the record of John Clayton (FT6) Town Clerk of Newcastle, who masterminded the development of the Elswick Estate. Most accounts underplay the financial interest that Clayton personally had in the development of the estate, but the deeds show considerable involvement for he lent more than £40,000 on separate occasions as a mortgagee. Elswick was not of course his only interest; he was an active adviser in Grainger's city centre developments, and derived much of his capital from coal royalties. The spirit and style of the man is well described in this newspaper article:

> "It is difficult to discover more diligent success in acquiring money over a space of 30 years . . . Mr John Clayton never speculated. He never threw dice. He never sunk a pit. He never founded a bank. Slow, sure, regular and passionless, like a Laplander trudging and toiling over a waste of snow, Mr John Clayton has pursued the even tenor of his way; but instead of his feet being clogged like a Laplander with snow, they are clogged with yellow dust, unalloyed gold on sure and most indubitable accumulation . . . The commerce and population of Newcastle extend. The treasury of the Town Clerk swells grandly in the like proportion; the world smiles on Mr John. Mr John smiles on the world. There is no display of accumulated gold. The same steady, quiet, unimpassioned growth in opulence appears in the second epoch of 30 years as in the first. Money doubles itself in 14 years, interest and compound interest. In 1835 Mr John is nearly double in wealth as compared with 1825 . . . He is positive on nothing but principal and interest."[24]

That was in 1855. Over the next 35 years the same laws of accumulation continued to apply for when he died in 1890, his estate was valued at £713,000.

2.2C PURCHASE OF LARGE ESTATES

A more conspicuous form of spending — similar to the present-day trend of investment by pension funds in agricultural land — was the purchase of huge estates, particularly in Northumberland and Durham, but in other areas as well.

An indication of the scale of this can be seen from the list below of large landowners from the West Newcastle families.

John Clayton, solicitor and Town Clerk; masterminded the development of Elswick. Picture: Newcastle City Library.

Detailed information on land-holdings is not known, but the purchases involved large sums of money. In 1873, John Straker (FT17) purchased 4,370 acres in the Fourstones and Allerwash area of the Tyne valley (west of Hexham) at a cost of £146,000; the remaining 1,400 acres of the Greenwich Hospital Estate was auctioned on

LARGE LANDOWNERS 1883

Name	Acreage	Annual Rental	Area
Sir W.G. Armstrong	2,265	£ 6,606	mostly Northumberland
John Clayton	11,004	£13,213	mostly Northumberland
John Cookson	6,463	£ 6,506	Northumberland
Edward Joicey	7,854	£ 7,563	mostly Northumberland and Durham
Joseph W. Pease	2,500	£ 2,075	Yorkshire, Cornwall
Viscount Ridley	10,152	£12,189	mostly Northumberland
John Straker	12,376	£12,156	Northumberland and Durham

Source: John Bateman. Great Landowners of Great Britain and Ireland 1883.

W.D. Cruddas, a director of W.G. Armstrong & Co; he left over £1 million.

Top: Stagshaw House at the turn of the century; it is still in the hands of the Straker family. Picture: Newcastle City Library. Below: the extra wing added to Chesters by N.G. Clayton in the 1890s; the house is now the home of J.E. Benson (FT4). Picture: Ian Harford.

the same day to John Clayton for £79,000. The figure for Armstrong may have been an underestimate, for by 1900 he had increased his holdings to about 16,000 acres. His fellow director W.D. Cruddas also became a major landowner for his will listed major estates and 20 named farms to be left to his daughters.

It was not simply, though, a question of investments and returns. A large estate accompanied by a fine mansion or castle brought the social prestige befitting the members of the new ruling class. Families like the Ridleys of Blagdon Hall and Claytons of Chesters had already established large country seats by the end of the eighteenth century, and the new industrialists followed suit. One of the earliest was Joseph Straker who purchased Stagshaw House, Corbridge shortly before his death in 1867. The Joiceys (FT3), now one of the largest landowning families in Northumberland, also built extensive mansions such as Newton Hall, Stocksfield (John Joicey) and the "summer resort" of Blenkinsopp Hall, Haltwhistle — where John Edward Joicey the great grandson of Edward Joicey now lives.

The cost of this extravagant life style was immense. The scale of the work involved can be judged by the labour costs alone; when Nathaniel George Clayton inherited John Clayton's fortune, the addition of an extra wing and stables to Chesters took four years to build with up to 200 workmen employed at one time. None could surpass the excesses of the directors of W.G. Armstrong though. For those who first manufactured mass-produced modern weapons of war, only an ancient castle made an appropriate seat of residence. Haughton Castle overlooking the River North Tyne was the one chosen by W.D. Cruddas (FT8) and only transformed from a near ruin to its present state after a massive outlay of money. Lord Armstrong himself, not content with Jesmond Dene House and then a mansion built for him at Cragside, Rothbury, in 1893 added to his list Bamburgh Castle, upon which he spent £1.25 million in modernisation works.

Top: Haughton Castle, W.D. Cruddas' residence overlooking the River North Tyne, and below, Bamburgh Castle, modernised by Lord Armstrong at a cost of £1¼ million.

MEMBERS OF WEST NEW‑CASTLE FAMILIES DYING PRE 1914 WITH ESTATES VALUED AT MORE THAN £500,000

Lord Armstrong	£1,400,000
John Clayton	£ 713,000
W.I. Cookson	£ 592,000
W.D. Cruddas	£1,042,000
Sir A. Noble	£ 734,000
Viscount Ridley	£ 535,000
John Straker	£ 919,000
Joseph H. Straker	£ 982,000
John Joicey	£ 710,000
Edward Joicey	£ 700,000

The transformation of a new ruling class based on industrial and finance capital into one with a substantial landed interest was complete by the end of the nineteenth century. But it would be quite wrong to see this as a turning away from the everyday business of industry and commerce. Rather it was a base, as we shall see in the next two sections, from which the families were able to extend their interests still further into the contemporary world of multinational corporations and international banking and insurance.

2.3 RULING CLASS AS A HEGEMONIC FORCE

We have traced in this section the widening industrial and economic interests of the West Newcastle families, because these formed the basis of the power they exercised over the region's affairs. As Poulanzas puts it:

> "When we speak of dominance by the level of economic organisation of a class, as distinct from the level of its strictly political organisation, it does not mean that this class is absent in its 'pertinent effects' from the level of political struggle. It means simply that, in the complex organisation of a class, it is the economic which holds the dominant role, in addition to determination in the last instance."[25]

By the 1920s, substantial control of many of the large heavy engineering, coal and public utility companies in the North-East, and in particular on Tyneside, was in the hands of 17 or so family dynasties that had been actively involved in West Newcastle over the previous 150 years. The interconnected needs of the different sectors were secured by a framework of interlocking directorships, family and friendship ties, close business associations and links with a developed banking system. Nor was this concentration atypical of the region generally as Harvey demonstrates in his account of "the coal kings and their ramifications" in the northern coal field.[26]

The wealth that this concentration of economic power brought to the ruling class was incredible (see Appendix 2 for probate returns). By the war as the list above shows ten family members

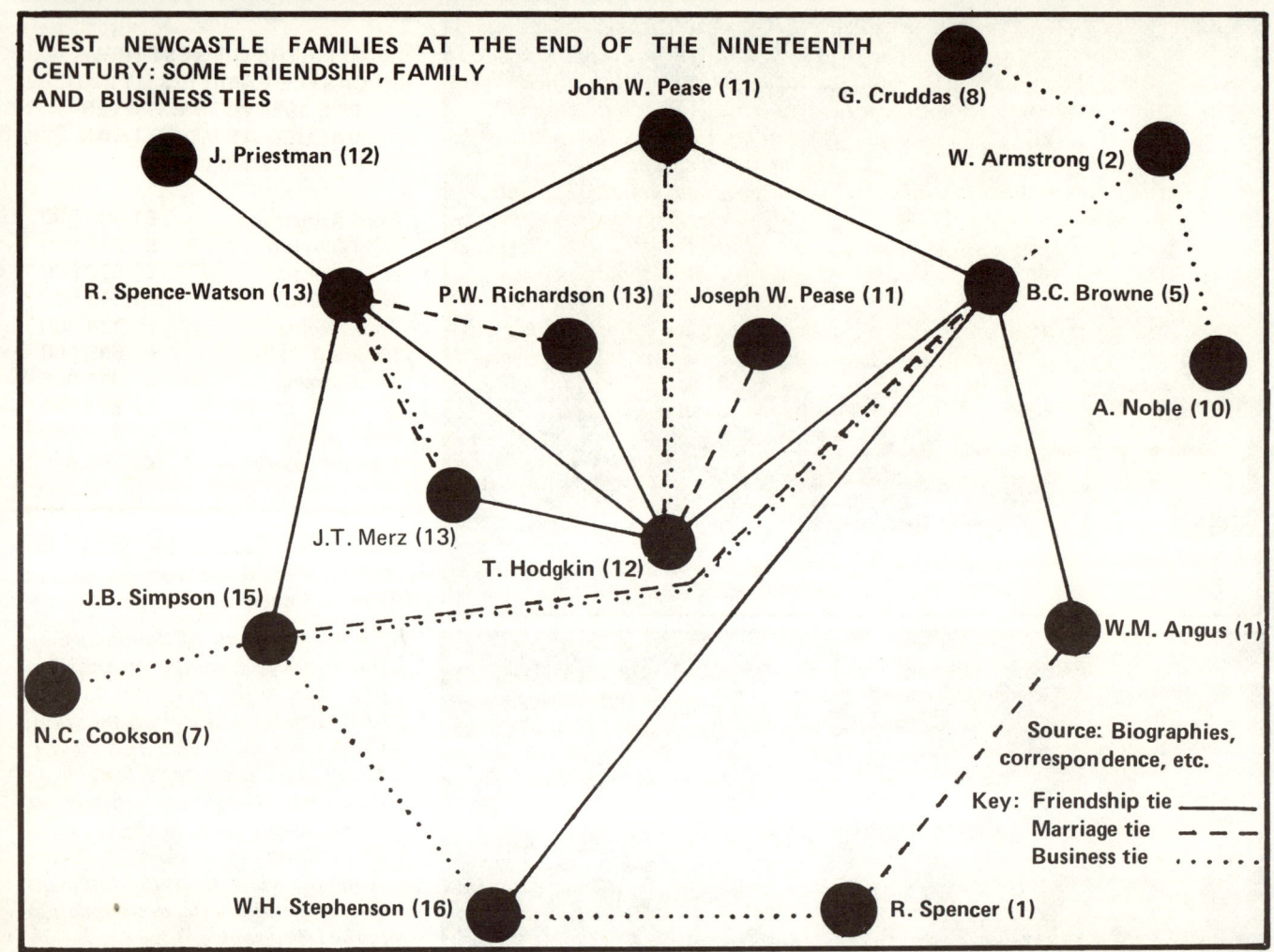

WEST NEWCASTLE FAMILIES AT THE END OF THE NINETEENTH CENTURY: SOME FRIENDSHIP, FAMILY AND BUSINESS TIES

Source: Biographies, correspondence, etc.

Key: Friendship tie ———
Marriage tie – – –
Business tie ......

had died worth more than £500,000 and more than 20 had estates valued at more than £250,000.

Money brought also a sense of shared values and common class interests; it brought a social homogeneity that for the most part overrode political and religious differences.[27]

Many of the men in the families were members of gentlemen's clubs, especially the Northern Counties Club and the Union Club, and from the 1880s onwards most of their sons were sent to the four most prestigious public schools — Eton, Harrow, Winchester and Rugby (see family trees). Biographies and contemporary reports of funerals and individual careers show the extent to which the families moved in closely overlapping social and business circles; and since many of the big industrialists lived in Benwell and the West End, close proximity brought further friendship and "neighbourhood" ties. The discreet cohesion of the bourgeoisie can be seen too in the patterns of intermarriage, particularly amongst the big coalowning families — a practice that continued at least into the 1930s.

The domination of the bourgeoisie under capitalism cannot however be explained simply in terms of its social cohesion and in terms of its economic power. It has to be related to the wider social and political institutions that mediate that power. An important concept in helping to understand how this takes place is that of 'hegemony' — a term first used by Gramsci. Anderson[28] explains it like this:

> "Hegemony was defined by Gramsci as the dominance of one social block over another, not simply by means of force or wealth, but by a total social authority whose ultimate sanction and expression is a profound cultural supremacy. The hegemonic class is the primary determinant of consciousness, character and customs throughout society . . . a hegemonic class can be defined as one which imposes its own ends and its own vision on society as a whole, a corporate class is conversely one which pursues its own ends within a social totality whose global determination lies outside of it . . . A hegemonic class seeks to transform society in its own image, inventing afresh its economic system, its political institutions, its cultural value, its whole mode of insertion into the world. A corporate class seeks to defend and improve its own position within a social order accepted as given."

Anderson was making a somewhat crude distinction between a corporate class and a hegemonic class, but the definition serves well to illustrate the process in which a ruling class becomes a hegemonic class, its position of pre-eminence dependent not simply on crude force — as for example occurred in the earlier 1844 strike when 40,000 pitmen were evicted from their houses — but on popular support. As Boggs points out in describing the Italian situation at a similar period, this transformation did not always take place.

> *"Civil society lacked the cohesion that had developed in England, the United States, and even France, where a sense of national 'spirit' had accompanied the bourgeois revolution. The Risorgimento of the 1860s and 1870s, whatever its pretensions and goals as the prime mover of Italian unification, failed to establish an ideological bond between elites and popular strata that would make possible an extensive national community. The new ruling class, based mainly in the Piedmont, set out to 'conquer' Italy and managed to 'dominate' its political life, but it was never able 'to lead' or mobilize consent, as such Northern liberalism became a 'dictatorship without hegemony.'"*[29]

2.3A GROWTH OF A WORKING CLASS MOVEMENT

None of this is, however, to suggest a final static position was achieved by the new ruling class on Tyneside. Their dominance by the end of this period was the result of a continuing class struggle, in which the West Newcastle families were playing an important role. A good description of the general climate of political and social unrest of the time is given by Price:

> *"There is one additional factor that must be mentioned . . . the rise of an aggressive working class movement. With the revival of social unrest in the 1880s, all discussion of social problems and poverty revolved around the working classes. The beginnings of the active involvement of the state in social questions, the official investigations into the structure of working class life, the campaign for Old Age Pensions and the like, all had as their reference points the potentially dangerous labouring classes. Furthermore, the spread of socialist and labour societies that rejected the class mutuality of mid-Victorian political and economic convention, the fierce battles on the industrial relations front, all served to draw attention to the working classes."*[30]

Locally, this upsurge of working class militancy was reflected politically in the growth of the Liberal Party, which until the Labour Representation Committee was formed in 1900 was the most successful party in attracting working class voters. The Liberal Party was not, however, a working class party. Even after 1885 when Spence-Watson (FT13), chairman of the Newcastle Liberal Association, introduced a new procedure allowing the various districts of the city to nominate executive members, the Executive remained in the hands of big industrialists like Sir Charles Palmer, Sir Christopher Furness and Walter Runciman. The basis of Liberal support lay in advocacy of free trade (hence cheap food), and in the party's willingness to support legislation aimed specifically at pleasing the "labour interest".

Whilst the Trades Council was willing to co-operate in this way, because the electorate preferred Liberal candidates to Labour ones, its ultimate determination to secure independent representation was reflected in the decision in the mid 1890s to set up funds to support candidates and pay expenses for attendance at council meetings. Partly this was a result of the composition of the Trades Council itself, for by the 1890s its membership (wavering in size between 5,000-11,000) included substantial representation from the "new unions" for the less skilled workers like dockyard labourers and gas workers. Possessing less industrial muscle, such unions were concerned to secure advances via legislative and municipal means, and had locally an influential proportion of socialist leaders who were prepared to stand as candidates, albeit unsuccessfully.

The issues that the Trades Council representatives were pressing included greater municipal powers, municipalisation of facilities (like gas electricity and water, in which the big industrialists had major stakes), power to procure more land for building, cheap tram travel, and recognition of trade union rates — all demands that ran counter to the notions of a free market economy and which in some cases challenged directly the interests of the big bourgeoisie who controlled the factories and land in the city.

There were other, explicitly socialist, political organisations also active in the city such as H.M. Hyndeman's Social Democratic Federation (SDF) that by 1883 had a Newcastle branch and a programme of demands including municipal housing and an eight-hour day; the Socialist Labour Party (SLL) set up in Newcastle and District to capitalise on the discontent caused by the 1887 Northumberland miners' strike; and the Central Socialist Institute formed by SDF and SLL followers to support the candidature of Fred Hamill as MP in 1895.

The development of a working class and labour movement in Newcastle cannot be adequately described here, but the above examples provide the background to the emergence of a hegemonic ruling class on Tyneside. The reforms introduced by the local bourgeoisie (see later) were largely a response to growing working class pressure, but they were a part only of the armoury of weapons used to head off the "potentially dangerous labouring classes" and more importantly the labour aristocracy of skilled artisans and mechanics that had become such a key force in the development on Tyneside engineering. To get an overall view of the role played by the West Newcastle dynasties, and the way their new social authority was achieved it is useful to examine four different areas:

a) Industrial organisation
b) Involvement in the Central and Local State
c) Provision of Social Infrastructure
d) Cultural and ideological role.

2.3B INDUSTRIAL ORGANISATION

A central question to which a number of the West Newcastle bourgeoisie addressed themselves in their writings was the relationship between "Capital and Labour", as they sought to justify the valuable and necessary role of the capitalist. Sir Benjamin Browne (FT5), a voluminous writer of national reviews and articles had this to say:

> *"I believe the real fallacy lies in the confusion of the wealthy class with the employers of labour. There are a few wealthy employers of labour, some millionaires, but they form a very small fraction of the whole, and the bulk of the large fortunes of this country are not made by direct employment of labour. I must also say that I cannot think it fair to assume, as people do, that employers are either the enemies of the working classes, or that they are hard in taking advantage of them. I believe the employers, as a class, are at least as unselfish, and quite as anxious to improve the conditions of those they employ, as either the trade union leaders, MPs or even the clergy."*[31]

Cartoons provided a subtle vehicle for putting forward anti-trade union views; an example from Punch 1889 ridicules the Tyneside pitman.

This kind of propaganda, though important for developing a 'world view' that underplayed the power and wealth of the ruling class, did not however distract them from the equally important task of organising against the growing power of the working class. Just as in the earlier period there had been unrest on the coalfield, similarly there were major strikes in Northumberland with two of the most important at collieries controlled by West Newcastle families — Strakers and Love (FT17) colliery at Willington in 1863, and the Lambs' (FT9) Cramlington Collieries in 1865. Here again there were evictions of the pitmen by the "candymen" — supported by the police and militia — and the importation of scab labour by the coalowners; and eventually on both occasions the pitmen were decisively beaten, despite widespread public support for their case.[32]

The most important confrontation between capital and labour was however the protracted 1871 Engineers' Strike which achieved a national significance and heralded a nine-hour day for the rest of the country. Of the 7,500 men involved, 4,300 came from the West Newcastle works of W.G. Armstrong, R. & W. Hawthorn, J. & G. Joicey and T. Clarke.[33] Opposition from the employers was total and uncompromising, with Armstrong (FT2) Andrew Noble (FT10) and B.C. Browne (FT5) playing a central role. Although the culmination of the four-month strike was a crushing defeat for the employers and their old-style confrontation tactics, they were not slow to learn the lesson.

The strike led first to the formation of the Associated Employers and later in 1895 to the setting up of the Engineering Employers' Association, an influential and powerful national organisation with representatives from Barrow, Belfast, the Clyde and the North-East. Here again the local dynasties had strong representation with Noble (Armstrong) and Browne (Hawthorn Leslie) elected as two of the three North-East members. By 1897/8 when the Amalgamated Society of Engineers struck for more than seven months in support of a reduction in working time to eight hours per day the outcome was very different:

"This conflict was fought out under far different conditions from 1871, for in the 1897 strike, the employers under the admirable leadership of Colonel Dyer (a director of Armstrongs) proved to have become a fighting body of the most tremendous strength."

The 1871 Strike marked an important new phase in the struggle between local capital and labour. Confrontation and crude opposition to the trade unions was replaced by negotiation and compromise as the unions and their leadership were encouraged to participate in structures designed to make the existing system of industrial production work more efficiently. Indeed, only two months after the end of the strike, the Coal Trade Association after meeting a deputation of pitmen, agreed a reduction of hours for boy workers to eleven, and in 1873 a joint committee was formed — with J.B. Simpson (FT15) one of the six coalowners' representatives — to settle all disputes. Sir Benjamin Browne, a much changed man since his early blooding in the 1871 strike, had little doubt of the effectiveness of this new strategy in containing working class demands as he revealingly explains in *The Times* of 1906:

"It is often considered that trades unions are organisations existing mainly for the purpose of quarreling with the employers, but this is a very unfair view to take of them. Where one thousand or one hundred thousand workers have common interests, it is far better that they should act together, under trained and experienced leaders, than that each man should act separately, or that the whole should be swayed by mere passion or prejudice, which is always liable to be fermented by ignorant and unscrupulous agitators ... Since the working classes were better organised, their demands have been, as a rule, far more moderate and their action far more thoughtful than in olden times ... I have no hesitation in saying that the North Country coal trade has worked far better and more smoothly, under the firmness and tact of half-a-dozen leaders — most of whom happen to be also MPs — than it would have done had the two counties been entirely unorganised."[34]

Another key figure in promoting the new rapprochement between capital and labour was Robert Spence Watson (FT13) the Newcastle solicitor and Liberal reformer whose brother-in-law was J. Wigham Richardson, the shipbuilder. According to his biographer, Spence Watson acted as arbitrator in about 100 industrial disputes covering the iron trade of the North of England, the coal trades in Durham, Northumberland and Cumberland, the Durham coke trade and the North Eastern Railway[35] — the principal industries in which the West Newcastle dynasties were involved. He also had his own commercial interests in the Electric Supply Company and the Electric Light Company and died a man of considerable wealth (although not on the coalowning scale).

It would be wrong simply to describe Spence Watson as representing the interests of a capitalist class, for he had the support of the trade unions in all the cases in which he acted as arbitrator. He epitomises rather the ambiguous role of the Liberal Party in this period in trying to reconcile the inherent conflict between a capitalist class and the working classes. His sympathetic attitude to the labour movement and his support for trade union organisation of unskilled workers like the dockers, was very different from the position taken by men like Lord Armstrong and Sir Andrew Noble.[36] But his underlying philosophy and support for the continuance of the profit motive was little different, as is shown by his advocacy of the "sliding scale", by which wages varied according to the price of the goods that were sold. If adopted, he argued:

"It does not settle labour disputes, it avoids them. It is no doubt a distinct step in the direction of industrial co-partnership. It forms in a certain sense a quasi partnership between employer and employed, between capital and labour. It is partnership in production ... the question of profits is not for them."[37]

The sliding scale system gave significant advantages to the employers — especially in coal mining; for not only could the coalowners, by transfer pricing sell coal and coke to their associated or subsidiary iron, electricity and gas companies at a cheaper rate (thus reducing wages), but they could also underbid competitors with the confidence that wages would drop.

Spence Watson's frame of reference both as a politician and as a solicitor was the expansion of trade and industry, the growth of the empire, as he described himself in his opening address to young law students in 1880:

"Every day new fields of practice are opened out. Mines in Spain; villas in Switzerland, railways in Sicily; estates in America; islands in the South Pacific; mineral concessions in France."

Objectively, therefore, the role of Liberals like Spence Watson was a reformist one, which while bringing some gains to the working class was primarily directed at stabilising the relationship between employer and employed.

In no way did the Liberal Party substantially challenge the powers and privileges of the ruling class — a point that is underscored by the support given to the Liberals by industrial capital. James Joicey (FT3), who later became the first Baron Joicey, is the best example of this. For a long period he was a Liberal MP (1885-1906), and owner of his own Liberal paper, the *Newcastle Daily Leader*. At his death in 1936 he was worth more than £1.5 million, but even 50 years earlier when he first became involved actively in politics the family's fortunes were large, for both his uncles died with estates of £700,000 each.

2.3C INVOLVEMENT IN CENTRAL AND LOCAL STATE

Close involvement in government, both national and local, was a feature of the growing influence of the West Newcastle families. As well as Joicey, six other dynasties had members, sometimes several, who became MPs — Cochrane (FT2), Clayton (FT6), Cruddas (FT8), Pease (FT11), Richardson (FT13), Ridley (FT14). In the case of the Ridleys it was more a question of maintaining a tradition for the fifth Baronet, Matthew White Ridley who was Home Secretary from 1895-1900 was the fourth successive generation to enter the House of Commons. Several also were elevated to the peerage, both for political work and as major industrialists — Lord Armstrong (and his grand nephew at a later date), Lord Joicey, Viscount Ridley, and the three members of the Pease family, Lord Gainford, Lord Daryngton and Lord Waddington.

Just as men like B.C. Browne and Andrew Noble had become by the First World War, national figures in employers' organisations and spokesmen for British industrial capital, others either combined these roles with political activity — Lord Joicey was also President of the Mining Association of Great Britain in 1904 — or concentrated on the political side. In this can be seen not only the consolidation of a local ruling class, but also its infusion within a wider national bourgeoisie. It represented a process of industrial and political integration that provided an important base in the inter-war period for opposing coal nationalisation, and gaining State support for industrial combinations and price fixing arrangements (such as that organised in the iron and steel industry through the Import Duties Advisory Committee), all of which were entirely protectionist in nature rather than aimed at increasing output or efficiency.

Political involvement was not limited however to the national scene. Throughout the second half of the nineteenth century, which witnessed an all-time record in the city's geographical and population expansion, control of Newcastle Corporation rested largely in the hands of big to medium-sized industrialists supported by larger numbers of professionals, shopkeepers and merchants — although the former group was declining in significance towards the end of the period. Early on John Clayton, as Town Clerk, had a decisive influence; later, Sir Benjamin C. Browne (FT5), twice Mayor of Newcastle, and Sir William Haswell Stephenson (FT16) (1836-1918), were two important figures. Stephenson was described in his obituary as *"the epitome of the history of Newcastle for the corresponding period."* Stephenson's main business interest was the Throckley Coal Company, but by his death he had a string of other directorships to his name. Elected first as a councillor for Elswick in 1869, he was chairman of the Finance Committee for more than 20 years, seven times Mayor of Newcastle and was on five separate occasions offered a safe seat as Tory member of Parliament.

LOCAL NATURAL HISTORY.

THE FINANCE BIRD.

The Finance Bird is a somewhat rare fowl in Newcastle. The one we depict feeds chiefly on coal. Although tame, it is not easily caught. It has a proud, reserved bearing, and its plumage of the peacock genus, proclaims how much it likes to be admired. It is a deadly foe to the social parasites which are bred amongst us. At certain seasons it builds for itself little mounds, in front of which it is fond of sunning itself. An intelligent fowl, it has never been known to stray. Several times it has basked in the light of Royalty. Its Latin name is "Gulielmus Stephensonius."

2.3D PROVISION OF SOCIAL INFRASTRUCTURE

By comparison with today, State involvement in the provision of social infrastructure and social services was minimal. The 1870 Education Act enabled local councils to finance elementary education through the rates, but it did not become free until 1891. Virtually no housing was built by councils until the collapse of private house building immediately before the war led to the introduction of state-subsidised housing in the 1920s. Health and recreation facilities were few; and yet all of these services were part of the broad demands of the labour movement, and all were of vital interest to the big industrialists

Elswick Mechanics Institute, provided by W.G. Armstrong. Picture: Vickers Ltd.

Hodgkin Park, given to the council by Thomas Hodgkin, the banker, when he left Benwell Dene House. Picture: Newcastle City Library.

who required a healthy and educated workforce.

The provision, therefore, of a range of institutions and facilities by the West Newcastle families must therefore be understood as part of a wider programme of reforms designed to buy off or incorporate the more militant and politically active sections of the working class. The form that this "social control" took was not so very different from the cheap rice and milk described by the Scotswood coalowner Mrs Montagu 100 years earlier, but the description of the process was now more subtle. As John Wigham Richardson (FT13) put it in a lecture to the Economic History Society:

> "Now, if we think it necessary to study incessantly the perfecting of our railways, our steamships, and our factories, how much more should we strive to perfect our citizens! By wise poor-laws, we can make each man intelligent and skilful. By sanitary reforms, we can make his body stronger and his valid life longer. By just laws, and just administration, we can secure to him the due enjoyment of the fruit of his toil . . ."[38]

Local examples of this social engineering by the big industrialists are numerous and revealing. Lord Armstrong (FT2) was one of the first in the field by establishing the Elswick Mechanics Institute in the early 1850s, and later by starting a school in 1866 for the technical education of his workmen's children. His motivation can be seen clearly in his opening speech:

> "Children left to themselves will not only grow up in ignorance, but will almost infallibly fall into vice . . . In school education, the impressionable minds of children are acted upon by precept and example. Habits of industry are acquired.";

Another speaker stressed that education "must have an important influence on the workmen in relation to their employment" (Newcastle Daily Chronicle). In a similar manner, the Spencers (FT1) provided a Working Men's Institute at Newburn, and W.H. Stephenson (FT16) libraries at Elswick, Walker and Heaton. Another favoured act of munificence was the provision of parks, usually when the family moved away from the area and the large estate: thus Hodgkin Park (FT12) and Cruddas Park (FT8) were established in the West End, and Armstrong Park in the East End — all names that have survived today.

The provision of housing was more complicated.[39] A few of the coalowners and industrialists in the early part of the period built houses for their workforce, but in the main the mass housing built between 1870-1910 for the labour aristocracy of skilled workers and for the white-collar proletariat of service sector workers was erected in smallish plots by builder/developers, not by the big industrialists themselves.[40] They did, however, play an important role in the laying out of estates, and thus in the determination of the kind and size of housing that could be built. This can be seen most clearly with the South Benwell Estate, which was put onto the market in 1883 by William Armstrong (FT2) and B.C. Browne (FT5), as trustees for Buddle Atkinson's estate. Plans for the estate show a clear intention to surround and contain the smaller working class housing with higher status houses on the main grid roads (like Buddle Road and Armstrong Road).

The big bourgeoisie meanwhile lived in their mansions and estates in Benwell Village and on the West Road,

The social distance between different streets and types of house reflected the status accorded different jobs at factory level... foremen at Spencer's Newburn Steel Works, 1908 (left) and smelters at Spencer's Newburn Steel Works, 1909. Pictures: Newcastle City Library.

and the professionals and middle classes remained in the large terraced houses of Elswick. It was in short a pattern of separate but adjacent residential development that helped to reinforce notions of class mutuality and equality whilst very distinctly separating off the most militant sections of the working class from the "residuum" of labouring classes in the crowded city centre.

Religion, too, was seen as an important method of maintaining control of the working class. As a speaker at the local branch of the National Education Union put it:

> "Educate him (the poor man) as high as they could; but don't educate him without religion. If they did, they create a deadly monster before them, whom they would not be able to quell. They would have danger perpetually in their path and would never be free from apprehension that the individual they had framed might not some day turn upon them with all the talents that he had gained, and guided by no particular morality, be the means of their destruction."[41]

Churches therefore became a popular form of endowment with the Cruddas family building the large St Stephens Church, Elswick, and G. Angus (FT1) and B.C. Browne contributing substantial sums of money to other local churches. The largest benefactor of all was again Sir W.H. Stephenson (FT16) who was a major contributor to most of the Methodist churches built in West Newcastle, giving £2,500 to the Elswick Road chapel and more than £3,000 to the Bond Chapel at Benwell.

Institutions — whether they be churches, schools, working men's institutes or libraries — which provided education for the working class, could of course be double-edged in their effect, as the speaker at the National Education Union had pointed out. That is to say that far from incorporating the working classes they could open up new avenues for advancement, new opportunities for extending the class

Sunday School Demonstration on Adelaide Terrace, 1910; religion, encouraged and financed by the big industrialists, was regarded as a safe outlet for the working classes.

struggle. Indeed, by 1887 at a conference on technical education, Armstrong — in the face of increased demands for comprehensive free education — was coming down strongly in favour of limited vocational education only for the working class. As the *Newcastle Daily Chronicle* (November 28th 1887) reported: *"Long experience has taught him what may be got out of the average mechanic and he is not disposed to indulge in any Utopian dreams as to the magical influence of certain forms of knowledge... On the contrary he pronounced the present education system unquestionably wasteful."* A point that was echoed in remarks made by B.C. Browne:

> "As regarded the general training of young children, he had always thought it possible that they might have too much of what they commonly called headwork. It might be better if they were more practised with the eye and the hand."

2.3E CULTURAL AND IDEOLOGICAL ROLE

For the higher forms of education, on the other hand, and the wider cultural institutions, the enthusiasm of the ruling class continued unabated, for it was in these forums that the dominant ideas of a hegemonic class could be expounded and propagated. This general process of creating an ideology or world view has been described as follows:

The opening of the Newburn Methodist Sunday School in 1906; much of the money came from the coalowner, Sir W.H. Stephenson. Picture: Newcastle City Library.

Advertisement for the opening of the Bond Methodist Chapel in 1881; as the main benefactor Stephenson could use it for public meetings as well.

"The ideas of the ruling class are in every epoch the ruling ideas, i.e. the class which is the ruling material force of society, is at the same time its ruling intellectual force. The class which has the means of material production at its disposal, has control at the same time over the means of mental production, so that thereby, generally speaking, the ideas of those who lack the means of mental production are subject to it. The ruling ideas are nothing more than the ideal expression of the dominant material relationships, the dominant material relationships grasped as ideas."[42]

On Tyneside, members of the West Newcastle dynasties played a seminal role not only in creating a range of institutions whose influence can still be seen, but also in formulating an analysis of class relationships that bears a striking resemblance to the stratification theories of class that dominate the mainstream of sociology today.

From an early period the Literary and Philosophical Society acted as an important centre for the discussion of literary and economic questions and for the encouragement of scientific enquiry. Lectures given for instance on Stephenson's safety lamp, Armstrong's hydraulic power and Swan's electric lamp marked major breakthroughs in new technologies. The Society was also instrumental in two new initiatives: firstly the setting up of the North of England Institute of Mining Engineers, a powerful organisation in the development of the coalfield; and secondly the establishment of the College of Physical Science in Newcastle (subsequently renamed Armstrong College) which later was to become Newcastle University. Backing and money for the scheme came from a roll-call of familiar names — including Armstrong, B.C. Browne, Thomas Hodgkin the banker, J.B. Simpson and a number of other coalowners — but the key figure was again Spence Watson, whose aim was the provision of *"higher middle-class education, more specifically of a scientific character."*[43]

Spence Watson's interests were not however restricted to the College, for he was a pioneer in 1879 of the University Extension movement, which was commenced with the backing of the Lit. and Phil. with a course of lectures on 'Political Economy'. Designed *"to bring the very best teaching that the country can afford, through the hands of the most thoroughly competent men, within the reach of every class"*, the scheheme was an immediate success. As Spence Watson put it *"I doubt whether there has ever been anything to compare with the numbers, especially of working*

Armstrong College, 1916 (now part of Newcastle University).

Arthur Henderson (centre seated) with fellow workers at R. Stephenson & Co in the 1890s; he was to become Leader of the Labour Party in 1931 after Ramsey MacDonald.

men, who came forward eager to learn. At one time there were more than 1,300 students in a colliery district boasting a population of 19,000."

Equally influential was the Tyneside Sunday Lecture Society over which Spence Watson presided for 26 years, and which according to his biographer *"brought thousands of citizens, week after week during the winter months in contact with some of the leading thinkers of the day".*

A glimpse of the kind of ruling ideas — about 'equality' and 'freedom' and 'class' — that were put foward at these seminars and meetings can be gained from a lecture given to the Society by Spence Watson himself:

"There is much nonsense talked about the capitalist, as though he was worse than the average of men . . . . Enact what laws you will; make the hours of labour what you please; divide the land and the capital of the country as you choose; revolutionise everything and everybody; and you have only done unmitigated mischief, and put the old world clock back to midnight. Money is not the principle thing. The real question is how we are to lead truer and nobler lives. It is a moral revolution, an entire change of ideas, a complete alteration of our mental standpoint, that we need, and for which we must labour. We must abandon the idea of force and welcome that of freedom. We must get rid of the idea of class as conferring special honour of privilege, and regard it only as denoting particular sympathies. We must insist upon equality of opportunity for all men alike, whilst we guard jealously against any state interference with the individual further than is imperatively required to insure such equality of opportunity."[44]

One interesting product of the social and educational milieu that the bourgeoisie created in Newcastle was Arthur Henderson, who later became leader of the Labour Party in 1931 on the resignation of Ramsay MacDonald. A moulder at the Locomotive and Foundry Works of R. Stephenson and Co. Henderson became an active member and lay preacher of the Elswick Road Methodist Church, a protégé of Spence Watson's as the *"coming man among the workers",*[45] and was elected in 1892 as Liberal Councillor for Westgate North. His transference to the Labour Party came in 1903 when he became Labour MP for Barnard Castle.

The particular reformism that characterised the leadership of the Labour Party from its earliest days can therefore be very clearly traced back in Henderson's case to the climate of ideas that the local bourgeoisie so effectively nourished. As Miliband puts it in comparing Henderson with Ramsay: *"There was little, in ideological terms, which separated him from MacDonald. If anything, Henderson was the more consistent representative of a Labourism, not substantially different on most counts, from progressive Liberalism."*[46]

The growth of the Labour Party, which took place at the expense of the Liberal Party and its supporters like

Spence Watson and Lord Joicey, brought important advances for the working class. But it has to be understood also as an integral element in the wider ideological incorporation of the working class, for more than any other single institution, it generated the expectation that fundamental and irreversible changes could be made to the capitalist system through the system of Parliamentary democracy. As Anderson puts it in discussing the question in a more general context:

> "The peculiarity of the historical consent won from the masses within modern capitalist social formation is . . . that it takes the fundamental form of a belief by the masses that they exercise an ultimate self-determination within the existing social order. It is thus not the acceptance of the superiority of the acknowledged ruling class (feudal ideology) but credence in the democratic equality of all citizens in the government of the nation — in other words, disbelief in the existence of any ruling class."[47]

The 30 to 40 years that led up to the First World War were a crucial period in this process of generating a consensus. They laid down the framework and imposed limits within which subsequent developments like the growth of the Labour Party and the trade unions took place.

The dominance that the big bourgeoisie had achieved in Newcastle and on Tyneside generally by the outbreak of war — a dominance reflected in their control over the factories and mines, the banks, the local press,[48] the local state and the main cultural institutions — was never again to be achieved in such a comprehensive and integrated form, for in the twentieth century, as the next two sections describe, the West Newcastle dynasties have become absorbed within a wider national bourgeoisie.

A summary of the spirit of the times and of ruling class ideology can be judged from the editorial in the *Newcastle Daily Chronicle* on the opening of the Elswick Library — a gift of W.H. Stephenson (FT16) — by Sir Matthew White Ridley (FT14), the then Home Secretary:

> "The great wave of industrial expansion is slowly but inevitably submerging our old landmarks, we have every possible and perplexing variety of opinion as to its further development. Agitation is everywhere. Change, transition are heard of on all sides . . . The way has been cleared, by the abolition of privilege and the granting to all a share in the Government of the nation and by the acknowledgement of the equal right of everyone to the highest culture . . . Our new democracy is practical but it is not brilliant, or romantic, or exhilarating. It drills the multitude into a pallid, idealless uniformity of purpose, but it makes no effort to raise it to the highest standard of individual excellence. The chief danger from it is the possibility of convulsive, headstrong, and unreflective action. The chief difficulty with it is to build up a citizenship animated equally by popular pliancy and patrician valour, insight, and restraint. Such functions as will take place to-day at Elswick will tend to create the desiderated spirit. The beneficence of Alderman Stephenson will help to weaken the prejudices which foster invidious social distinctions. It will aid too in

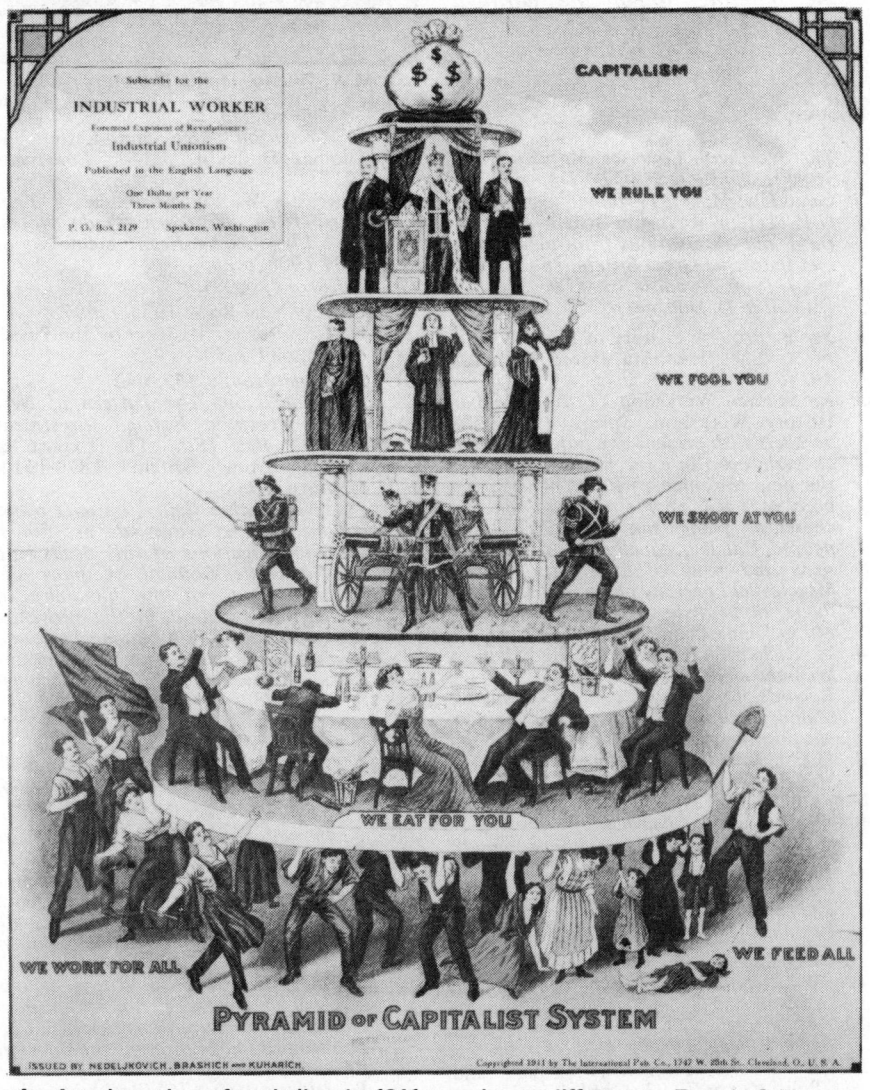

An American view of capitalism in 1911; was it any different on Tyneside? Picture: Workers Movement Library, Stockholm.

softening the differences between classes, and in fostering a sentiment of unity and solidarity in the community... Men like Sir M.W. Ridley who, with leisure and means, give their days and nights to the service of the nation, act both as a stimulus and an example. They cannot remain passive amid the revolution which is changing the face of society. And they know that any diversity of interest between the classes is as nothing compared with the interests which are in common. They are as much opposed to revolutionary disorder as to reactionary repression, and work hopefully towards the enlightenment of the national conscience and the building up of the national character."[49]

Sir M.W. Ridley, Home Secretary 1895-1900.

Footnotes

1. *The Northern Counties Magazine* Oct. 1900 p.7. quoted in D. Dougan. *The Great Gun Maker, 1970.*
2. G.F. Steffen. Roving in Britain – *descriptions and observations from picturesque and industrial Great Britain. 1895.* Translated from Swedish by L.W. Sheldon.
3. Quoted in D. Dougan, *p. 154, op. cit.*
4. See B. Browne. History of the New Firm of R. & W. Hawthorn. *Privately printed 1914.*
5. R. Samuel. Workshop of the World in History Workshop. *Spring 1977.* The parallels with present-day industry found an eerie echo in a recent interview with the new chairman of ICI: "When somebody says ICI, people tend to think of a chemical plant run by half-a-dozen people. But it is equally true to think of rows and rows of little girls (sic) in Macclesfield packing pharmaceutical products, or in Arderseir boxing up ammunition." Guardian, *1 April 1978.*
6. W. Richardson. History of the Parish of Wallsend. *1923.*
7. *Records of the Throckley Coal Company.* Memorandum of Articles. 1891, held at Northumberland Record Office.
8. M.E. Swan and K.R. Swan. Sir Joseph Wilson Swan – *Inventor & Scientist, pp. 71ff. Oriel Press. 1968.*
9. As R.O. Lamb, Chairman of Cramlington Coal company put it at a dinner to mark his 50th year as chairman "I have seen times when no profit could be made, but I have also seen most prosperous times beyond the dreams of avarice."
10. E. Lamb *pps.103-106, op.cit.*
11. W. Richardson. History of the Parish of Wallsend. *1923.*
12. A. Briggs. Victorian Cities *pps.243, 251. Pelican. 1968.*
13. R. Moore. Pit-men, Preachers and Politics, *pps.78-92.* Cambridge University Press. 1974.
14. G. Harvey, *op.cit.*
15. L. Creighton. Life and Letters of Thomas Hodgkin, *p.54-6.* Longmans 1917.
16. Newcastle Weekly Chronicle. *1 February 1913.* Northern Trade Notes.
17. See J.W. Richardson. Memoirs of 1839-1908, *p.205.*
18. B. Browne, *op.cit.*
19. Colliery Year Book 1935, *p.697.*
20. W. Richardson. History of the Parish of Wallsend, *p.341. 1923.*
21. W. Richardson, *p.355, ibid.*
22. See M. Simon. The Pattern of New British Portfolio Foreign Investment in A.R. Hall (Ed.) The Export of Capital from Britain 1870-1914. Methuen, 1968.
23. These and other figures on land transactions in West Newcastle are drawn from investigations of title deeds held by Newcastle Council. A more detailed account of the hierarchy of speculators involved in the provision of working class housing can be found in Private Housing and the Working Class, *Benwell CDP Final Reports Series, 1978.*
24. Sketches of Public Men of the North. *Northern Examiner 1855* quoted in L. Wilkes and G. Dodds, Tyneside Classical, *pp.53-4.* John Murray, 1964.
25. N. Poulanzas, *p.83, op.cit.*
26. G. Harvey, Capitalism in the Northern Coalfield, *op.cit.*
27. Benjamin Browne (FT5) for instance, a leading member of the Tory Party was quite prepared in 1883 to collude with the Liberals Joseph Cowen and Robert Spence Watson (FT13) in securing the election as councillor of a Liberal member of the Trades Council in order to undermine allegations that the Corporation did not represent the interests of working men.
28. P. Anderson and R. Blackburn (Eds) Towards Socialism. *Fontana, 1965.*
29. C. Boggs. Gramsci's Marxism, *p.50.* Pluto Press, 1976.
30. R.N. Price. Society, Status and Jingoism, *p.106* in G. Crossick (Ed.) The Lower Middle Class in Britain. Croom Helm, 1977.
31. B.C. Browne. The Ownership of Capital. *Economic Review, 15 October 1913,* in Selected Papers on Social and Economic Questions, by B.C. Browne. Cambridge University Press, 1918.
32. R. Fynes, *p.225 ff. and p.246 ff. op.cit.*
33. E. Allen and others. The North East Engineers' Strike of 1871, *p.115, F. Graham, 1971.*
34. B.C. Browne. Labour Problems. Times Engineering Supplement in Selected Papers, *op.cit., pp.101-2.*
35. P. Corder. The Life of Robert Spence Watson, *p.170, 1914.*
36. When asked in his evidence to the Royal Commission on Labour (1906), if he would permit his workers to have their trade unions present their case, Noble's reply was emphatic: "We refuse in all cases".
37. P. Corder, *p.177, op.cit.*
38. J.W. Richardson, *p.333, op.cit.*
39. See Private Housing and the Working Class. *Benwell CDP Final Report Series. 1978.*
40. It is interesting to note that only three weeks after the end of the 1871 Engineers' Strike, Armstrong and Co. were buying land from one of the partners, George Cruddas for the building for the first time of workmen's houses at Newcombe Street. Whether this was a direct response to the increased militancy of the workforce, or a pure coincidence remains an open question.
41. Newcastle Daily Journal, *29 March 1870.*
42. K. Marx and F. Engels. The German Ideology, *p.64.* Lawrence and Wishart, 1970.
43. P. Corder, *op.cit., pp.143 ff.*
44. R. Spence Watson. Labour: Past, Present and Future. *Local Tract, 1890.*
45. M.A. Hamilton. Arthur Henderson: a bibliography. *Heinemann, 1938, pp.7ff.*
46. R. Miliband. Parliamentary Socialism, *p.184.* Merlin 1972. One of the more well-known examples of this Labourism was the introduction by Henderson and three other Labour MPs in 1911 of a Bill which would make strikes illegal unless 30 days' notice had been given in advance. The move was unequivocally condemned at the TUC Conference later in the year. R. Miliband, *ibid., p.35.*
47. P. Anderson. New Left Review, *no.100.*
48. Of the two biggest newspapers, the Newcastle Daily Chronicle *was owned by Joseph Cowen MP, a leading member of the Liberal Party, and close associate of Spence Watson, while the* Newcastle Daily Journal *had been since 1867 in the ownership of the Northern Counties Conservative Newspaper Company. Its first chairman (1867-1895) was N.G. Clayton (FT6), and its second chairman (1895-1912) was W.D. Cruddas (FT8). Another Liberal paper, though not as large as the* Chronicle *was the* Newcastle Daily Leader, *owned by Lord Joicey (FT3) from 1885-1903.*
49. Newcastle Daily Chronicle, *26 September, 1895.*

3
The Inter-War Years

Spencers' Newburn Steel works; collapsed in 1926 throwing over 2,000 workers on the dole. Picture: Newcastle City Library.

THE INTER-WAR years were a period of transition, reflected locally in the gradual distancing of the families from the day-to-day activities of the city, and at a wider level in their further integration within a regional and national bourgeoisie that was both shaping a new role for private capital and marking out the parameters of State intervention in the region's affairs. The depression left thousands out of work on Tyneside. Worst affected were the export-oriented capital goods industries — heavy engineering and shipbuilding especially — that were now in decline, as the mass consumption based industries in the South and Midlands leapt forward.

All of the big industrialists and bankers had moved out of West Newcastle by the 1930s to larger estates and mansions, mostly in Northumberland and Durham, thus severing the political connections with the city that had been so evident in the nineteenth and early twentieth centuries. The estates they left behind, and a few undeveloped sites in Benwell and Elswick, provided a base for several emerging building companies, like William Leech and John T. Bell, but on the whole, with a few exceptions, the direct links between industrial capital and the builders and developers of working class housing was replaced by a system of finance organized by the growing building society movement.

All of the heavy engineering companies were affected by the slump; some closed, others laid off workers, and paid no dividends for several years. Although Armstrong-Whitworth remained the largest employer by far, its forced merger with Vickers in 1927 brought the end of any family involvement in the company. The coal industry retained a large workforce in the area throughout the period, and remained as in the wider coalfield, firmly in the hands of the original coalowners.

Indeed, with the growth of State-encouraged combines, concentration of the families' control of coal production in Northumberland and Durham became even more significant — covering directly and indirectly just under a half of the region's output. Amalgamations, restrictive agreements and cartels were however not only a feature of the coal industry. They occurred, too, in steel, shipbuilding and electricity supply. Again, as with coal, the families retained a close involvement with these large declining companies, but their overall strategy was one of minimal reinvestment, so that the large amounts of capital they had extracted from the industries could be redirected to more profitable sectors.

The forms of this capital diversification are difficult to pin down precisely. They can be seen implicitly in the general movement of later generations of the families into the finance capital sector generally — into banks, building societies, stockbroking, the law, insurance and property — and more specifically in the emergence of a number of investment trusts and investment holding companies, that were closely tied in to the families' other interests.

The development of links and influence within a wider national ruling class was of course already well established by the turn of the century by men like Armstrong, Ridley and Joicey. The inter-war period saw the consolidation of this process. Not only were the families playing a leading role in employers' organisations — helping to sink proposals for coal nationalization in 1919 and to defeat the 1926 General Strike — but also by their prominent position on various self-appointing regional policy bodies, they were able to impose their own views of the 'regional problem' and shape the nature and direction of State intervention in the period of tranformation following the Second World War. The extent to which these policies benefited the material interests of the regional bourgeoisie only became fully apparent in the next period.

3.1 WEST NEWCASTLE

If the 50 years that preceded the First World War had been years of 'engagement' by the local bourgeoisie in the economic and political life of West Newcastle, the 25 that followed were years of withdrawal. Most obviously this happened where the big houses in Benwell and on the West Road were taken over for educational or other institutional use. In the case of the Pendower Estate belonging to the Pease banking family (FT11) the house and grounds were sold to the Council at a reduced price on the condition that it was used *"for the purpose of housing the labouring classes"*. By the 1930s the process, started as early as the 1870s, was complete.

There was, too, a withdrawal from the political life of Newcastle. The last big titled industrialist to play a prominent part in municipal affairs was the coal-owner Sir William H. Stephenson (FT16), who died in 1918. From then on the business of the council came to be dominated instead by professionals, smaller businessmen and shop owners.

3.1A HOUSING DEVELOPMENT

All involvement in the business and commercial life of the area did not of course immediately come to a halt. While most of the Elswick and South Benwell estates had been developed by the war, there were a few peripheral estates, which provided some of the first sites for the speculative owner-occupier housing of the 1920s and 1930s.[1]

Two of them are of particular interest because they demonstrate the flow of coal capital into this newly emerging private housing market. The first is the Hodgkin Park Road estate which was bought and developed, via Milburn Estates, by the Milburn family who with the Priestmans (FT12) owned the Ashington Coal Company. Milburn Estates is also interesting as an example of the early diversification of coal and shipping capital into office property, for it was formed in 1905 by the Milburns to take over various parcels of land they owned and Milburn House itself, a huge office complex in Newcastle behind the cathedral, which had been completed in the same year, and still stands today.

The second is the Bilborough Gardens area (a fag-end of the South Benwell estate) where some of William Leech's first houses were built. Though now a millionaire and president of William Leech (Builders) Ltd., at the time Leech had virtually no capital of his own, since his previous job was as a window cleaner. Finance for the development as well as for other sites at Brunton, Gosforth and Sunderland was provided by the Junior Property and Investment Company — a company which was formed in 1933 by Robert Joicey Dickinson (FT3) and was an important vehicle for channelling the Joicey coal monies into the property sector (see next section).

Milburn House office complex on Dean Street; an early diversification of coal capital into property. Picture: Newcastle City Library.

3.1B INDUSTRIES

The pattern of industrial land use in West Newcastle on the other hand had been established by the turn of the century, so there was little room for new industries. The war had brought a short boom to existing firms like Armstrong-Whitworth, and Hawthorn Leslie, where increased output of ships, armaments and locomotives required a greatly expanded workforce. But soon after a drying up of demand brought slump conditions to the heavy engineering sector. The whole of Tyneside was affected. In West Newcastle the biggest single collapse was the closure of the Spencers' (FT1) Newburn Steel Works in 1926 throwing more than 2,000 workers onto the dole.

Another important engineering firm to close was J. & G. Joicey's Forth Banks Engine Works which, though always subsidiary to the family's (FT3) coal interests, had established a reputation for well-constructed locomotives and winding engines.

Armstrong-Whitworth never closed, but it was dramatically affected by the ending of the war. The Elswick factory had built a third of Britain's total production of guns, 47 warships, more than 1,000 aeroplanes, 14.5 million shells and 21 million cartridge cases.[2] Attempts after the war to diversify out of shipbuilding included the building of locomotives and motorcars, but neither were successful. The most costly mistake was a disastrous £10 million scheme for a Newfoundland Paper Mill which involved the building of a completely new seaport and power station. Overstretched and inexperienced, the company was soon in difficulties, and with a debt of £2.5 million to the Bank of England, was forced to merge in 1927 with Vickers to prevent bankruptcy. The construction of tanks proved the salvation of the Elswick Works in the early 1930s before rearmament brought increased demand, but thousands of workers had still to be laid off.

The major shareholders in the company did not however suffer so badly. On Lord Armstrong's death, the chairmanship had gone to Sir Andrew Noble (FT10), who with his two sons Saxton and John dominated the board of directors until Sir Andrew's death in 1915. Both his sons remained as directors until the merger with Vickers — with Sir John Noble (as he had then become) vice-chairman of the company — but by the 1930s their links with the company had been severed in favour of directorships in a number of public utility and banking companies. The switch of their capital from Armstrongs (and away from reinvestment that would have brought work to West Newcastle), was achieved with little apparent difficulty, despite the drop in share prices in Armstrong-Whitworth from a pre-war £3 to 2/6d. in 1926. At their deaths at the end of the inter-war period, Sir John's estate was valued at £639,000 and Sir Saxton's at £372,000. A similar pattern of early withdrawal from the company and diversification of interests can be seen with the other two families involved in the early days — Cruddas (FT8) and Armstrong (FT2).

Coal was the one industry in West Newcastle that remained firmly in the hands of the old coalowners — the Simpsons, Stephensons and Buddle Atkinson. Moreover, it was a major employer throughout the period as the table below shows:

EMPLOYMENT IN COAL MINING IN WEST NEWCASTLE (1935)

Elswick Coal Company	1,070
W. Benson & Sons (Montagu Colliery, Scotswood)	1,010
Stella Coal Co (Blaydon)	3,987
Throckley Coal Co	1,521
Total	**7,588**

Source: Colliery Year Book

The changes in ownership that did take place reflected the trend towards amalgamations that were taking place throughout the industry; the Benwell Colliery was sold by Cochrane Carr to the Elswick Coal Company (controlled by the Simpsons [FT15]) in 1931 and the Benson's (FT4) Montagu Colliery was taken over by the Mickley Coal company, part of the Cookson (FT7) combine.

Although the output of the local pits was a good deal smaller than those in the deeper coalfield — ranging from 250,000 tons per annum for the Elswick Company to 1.25 million tons

Bilborough Gardens, Benwell; one of William Leech's first developments, for which he obtained finance from the Joicey/Dickinson family. Picture: Ian Harford.

Scene of the Montagu Pit disaster in 1925; 38 men and boys were drowned. Picture: Newcastle City Library.

W.A. Benson, photographed recently outside his home, Newbrough Hall; a young coalowner of 20 at the time of the disaster, he remained a director until nationalisation.

for the Stella Company — the profits were still substantial (viz the £800,000 the two Benson brothers [FT4] left behind when they died). While most of the families could be counted on to make philanthropic donations for good causes, they were far less keen to part with their money where it was being demanded by their workers as a right or as compensation. After the Montagu Colliery disaster in 1925, when 38 men and boys were drowned, the union in one case — where a hewer whose weekly wage of £3.16s.0d. had provided exactly half the family's income — had to take proceedings against the owners to get an increase in compensation from the £90 offered to the £200 awarded by the Court.[3] Shortly after this, control of the company passed to the Mickley Coal Company, and the Bensons appear to have withdrawn from active management — although W.A. Benson remained a director right up to nationalisation.

3.1C GENERAL WITHDRAWAL

The withdrawal generally of the bourgeoisie from the area — both politically, as residents, and finally as entrepreneurs involved in day-by-day management — was important for it distanced the working classes from those who controlled the factories, and provided the churches, libraries and houses. As other CDP reports[4] have argued, increasing intervention by the State in these social and welfare fields after the First World War was caused by a number of factors. But it was not an entirely new phenomenon. The 1870s had seen a spate of legislation covering factory conditions, housing and health standards and education. They were provoked partly by the kind of labour unrest discussed in the last section, but they were also reforms that served the long-term interests of capital. Not only was it necessary to head off working class militancy, but it was also desirable to have a healthy and literate workforce.

In a similar way the development of council housing after the war was in part a response to industrial unrest and rent strikes in 1915, but also a consequence of the collapse of the private housing market in the decade leading up to the war.[5] The cumulative result of these changes was that the State gradually took over functions previously exercised by the bourgeoisie, and thus mediated the more direct class relationship that had hitherto existed. While no doubt proximity in the nineteenth century provided the ruling class with keener intelligence on the state of mind of the masses, it had the disadvantage that the masses could see all too plainly the discrepancies between their own life style and wealth and that of the ruling class. While the new castles and mansions may have been much grander and the life styles more extravagant, there is truth in the saying *"out of sight, out of mind".*

3.2 TYNESIDE AND THE WIDER REGION

A more precise understanding of the role of the regional bourgeoisie in the inter-war years has to be sought by spreading the search wider, by looking first at the wider Tyneside region and the industries that the families controlled or were closely associated with. The peak of the post-war depression came in 1931-1932, when 34 per cent of coalminers, 47 per cent of steel workers and 62 per cent of shipbuilders and shiprepairers were out of work.[6] The basic industries they had worked in were concentrated in the old industrial areas and particularly the North East; and they were the industries over which the West Newcastle families had substantial control. The problem for the regional bourgeoisie was that they were industries in decline.

3.2A HEAVY ENGINEERING AND SHIPBUILDING

In the case of heavy engineering and shipbuilding, that were particularly dependent on exports, they could no longer rely on the captive foreign markets that formerly existed when Britain was the main workshop of the world. By 1937, 35 per cent of workers in the North East were in the declining industries compared with seven per cent in the Midlands and only one per cent in London. It was becoming a country of contrasts; in the North-East and the other areas that had cradled the Industrial Revolution there was massive unemployment and declining profitability of the traditional industries, now up to 70 or 80 years old; in the South and the Midlands there was the growth of highly profitable high wage consumer goods industries and a new system of mass production that relied on domestic demand.

There were two basic options open to the regional bourgeoisie. They could either reorganise and modernise the old industries to make them competitive with their more recent and more capital intensive foreign counterparts — a policy that would not of course have dealt with the short-term problems of the depression but would have put them in a much more powerful position in the post-war boom years; or they could run down the industries by failing to replace obsolescent plant and equipment, and by diversifying their own personal capital into securer and more profitable outlets elsewhere. In general the response was of the latter kind, accompanied by the fostering of cartels, mergers and monopolies within the industries. This was aimed not so much at increasing efficiency and output as at protecting markets and reducing competition.

To effect these changes, a degree of State intervention had now become desirable, indeed necessary to protect the interests of industrial capital. The days of liberal capitalism and of laissez faire were over. As Hobsbawn puts it:

> "Between the wars, and especially during the 1930s, Britain turned from one of the least into one of the most trustified or controlled economies, and largely through direct government action. It achieved the amalgamation of the railways (1921), the concentration – indeed the partial nationalization – of electricity supply (1926), the creation of a government-sponsored monopoly in iron and steel (1932), and a national coal cartel (1936)."

The life-style of the coalowners did not visibly alter in the depression; J.L. Priestman (with bowler and moustache) driving his stage coach through the country lanes, 1934.

The example of Armstrong-Whitworth's forced merger with Vickers and the exit of family capital from the company showed this process occurring in the West End. In shipbuilding a consortium of shipbuilders formed National Shipbuilders Security Ltd (backed by the Bank of England and a 10 per cent levy on members) to buy up empty yards and sell them with a covenant forbidding future shipbuilding. By 1932 nine North-East yards had received this treatment and others followed including Palmers of Jarrow. The two shipbuilding firms that the West End families were most closely associated with — Swan Hunter and Wigham Richardson and Hawthorn Leslie (as well as Vickers) — gained considerably from this reduction in the industry's capacity particularly when naval orders picked up from the mid 1930s onwards.

But there was little new investment

Launch of the tanker Auricula during the war from the Hawthorn Leslie yard.

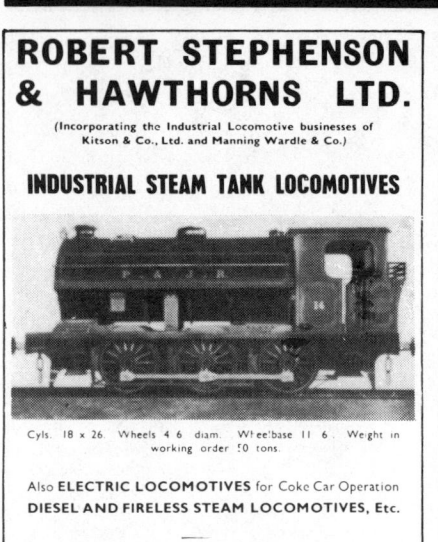

Advertisement for Robert Stephenson and Hawthorns, 1945.

The Elswick Leadworks in 1966, with the shot tower still in existence; already by 1939 it had become part of the Cooksons' group of lead companies. Picture: Newcastle City Library.

with the result that after a 10-year post-war boom, they found themselves, like other Tyneside yards, unable to compete with the modernised German and Japanese industries.

With both these companies, the families retained important links, a Straker father and son (FT17) holding the chairmanship of Hawthorn Leslie throughout the period until 1943; while with Swan Hunter and Wigham Richardson, two of the founder's sons were directors throughout their lives while the elder one, Sir Philip Wigham Richardson (FT13), held the chairmanship from 1945-1949.

In the case of both families, however, there is clear evidence of their interests widening away from the troubled shipbuilding industry. Sir P.W. Richardson's main concerns were a London-based steamship and insurance broking company (named after himself) and Armadores Finance and Investment Company. He was also involved, with his son G.W. Richardson as chairman, in the setting up of a typical growth sector company for the period, Airspeed (1934) Ltd, for the manufacture of aircraft. Formed with an issued capital of £290,000 to acquire an earlier business, it had a factory at Portsmouth airport and exclusive licenses to manufacture and sell within specified countries the Fokker and Douglas DC2 aircraft. On a smaller though highly successful scale the Straker family moved into the mass consumption market by opening up in 1937 a motor vehicle distribution company in Newcastle (selling Ford cars) — which was finally bought out by a London consortium in 1971.

A similar pattern is discernible with other related companies. Although Robert Stephenson & Co had moved to Darlington in 1900, they had continued to work closely with their former neighbours Hawthorn Leslie, whose locomotive works remained at Forth Banks. The decline in demand in the 1930s — Hawthorn Leslie built only four locomotives in 1933 from a peak of 47 in 1920 — led to a merger with the new firm, Stephenson Hawthorn, concentrating the production of industrial locomotives at Newcastle, and main line ones at Darlington. Again the older generations retained connections — E.C. Straker was chairman and Lord Daryngton from the Pease family a director — but on their deaths the direct links through the board were dropped.[7]

The Pease family interests by contrast continued to expand. By 1946 Lord Daryngton's brother, Claud Edward Pease, was chairman of the large Horden Collieries Group, a director of Barclays Bank and chairman of two regionally-based property and investment companies. The Owners of the Middlesborough Estate and The Cleveland Trust (see next section); and his nephew Sir R.A. Pease was a director of five coal companies and several other companies, including Carliol Investment Trust (see later) and Brush Electrical Engineering. Brush was an example of the rapidly growing new electrical sector doubling its issued capital to more than £1 million and acquiring three new firms in the period 1939-46.

Further insight into the process of family diversification can be seen with the Cooksons (FT7) and their lead interests. Built up by the family over more than half a century, the lead and antimony business of Cookson and Co was transferred in 1922 to Cookson Lead and Antimony Company, which became in 1930 part of a much larger group Goodlass, Wall and Lead Industries. While the Cooksons have remained closely involved in the development as a big multinational company of Goodlass Wall, and then Lead Industries Group (as it was renamed in the 1960s), it is clear from a comparison of directorships held in 1925 and 1936 that Clive Cookson was in other ways expanding his interests beyond local lead and coal. For he was chairman of three other companies, Northern Development and Finance, British and Foreign Metal and Chemical

Company, and Republican Mining and Metal.

An exception to the more general pattern of withdrawal from the traditional engineering industries is the case of George Angus. Originally started as a leather business in the Close, the company had always had an expansionist policy (unlike the more conservative Elswick Leather works of E. & J. Richardson), opening a large warehouse in Liverpool and branches in America and South Africa at the turn of the century. By the First World War it was involved in the manufacture of textile-based fire hose and machine belting. Although the 1920s saw a further expansion of the company's activities with the establishment of a gear cutting division, it was still only a smallish firm with a workforce of 500 when E.G. Angus (FT1) and his brother became joint managing directors in 1932.

The big leap forward came shortly afterwards with the development of a mechanical seal division — the result of a mixture of luck and good judgement. British industry generally had a very poor record in undertaking systematic scientific research and development (an essential requisite for industrial expansion) and compared badly with the record of American and German industry. Though more advanced than many, Angus was far behind on mechanical seal technology, but had the good fortune to have developed very friendly links with a German firm that had discovered that the seals could be made of synthetic rubber (Buna N) instead of leather. An agreement between the two companies gave Angus unlimited access to the technical information required and the process was quickly developed to meet the Royal Air Force demand for seals that could withstand high temperatures and pressures. By the end of the war, there were 2,000 people working at the Oil Seal Division instead of the original 40 — an indication of the importance of the German firm's synthetic rubber formula in making possible the extraordinary recovery and growth of George Angus from the depression of the early 1930s.[8]

3.2B COAL, STEEL AND PUBLIC UTILITIES

In the basic industries of coal, steel and the public utilities, it was a different picture. The process of fusion between these industries had already been well advanced locally and nationally by the end of the First World War. On Tyneside, as we have seen, the Newcastle and District Electric Lighting Company was controlled throughout its life by the directors of the Stella Coal Company and the Ashington Coal Company, while the North-East Electric Supply Company had links with the Easington Coal Company (J.H. Noble) and the Consett Iron Works (R.A. Cookson) as well as with major engineering companies. The Samuel Commission found that 23 per cent of all coal output in 1924 was sold to associated companies, and the 1928 Committee on Trade and Industry reported that pig iron manufacturers directly controlled 62 per cent of their coal and 55 per cent of their coke supplies. By the Second World War all the big steel plants were closely associated or combined with coal companies.

Examples of this close association in the North-East are Pease and Partners and the Consett Iron Company. The former owned collieries, coke-ovens and ironstone mines in Durham and Yorkshire and ironworks in Middlesborough. Although expansion of the combine in the 1920s and 1930s brought more outsiders in as directors — there were seven members of the Pease family (FT11) in 1923 on the 10-man board of Pease & Partners and its associated company H. Stobart & Co — the family remained closely connected through Sir R.A. Pease and Lord Gainford. The Consett Iron Company, with its steel works and extensive colliery interests in the Chopwell and Leadgate area of Durham, was never controlled by any one particular family, but had strong links with the Cooksons (FT7) and other family members for in 1939 its chairman Clive Cookson had as fellow directors Viscount Ridley (FT14) and Sir Cecil Cochrane (FT2).

This kind of vertical integration enabled the coalowners by a system of transfer pricing to sell coal cheap to associated companies in industries where prices could be maintained at high prices by government tariffs. Thus the Census of Production for 1935 shows that the selling price (in shillings) per ton of coal varied substantially from industry to industry; from 11.4s for coke, 12.7s for blast furnaces and 14.2s for electricity to 19.6s for motors and cycles and 24.5s for brewing.[9] While record profits could be maintained in this way in the steel and public utility sectors, wages in the labour-intensive mining industry — which were determined by price levels — could be kept depressed.

The consequences of this protectionist strategy were most serious for the mining industry in which the West Newcastle dynasties had come to exercise a dominating influence. Already by 1919 the Sankey Committee was pointing to the low levels of investment in the coal industry, and its limited mechanization when compared to foreign coalfields. Despite this there was little new investment throughout the whole of the inter-war period, and certainly not enough to replace the increasingly obsolete plant and equipment in the mines. So little had been done by the coalowners to modernize the mines — and thus make them more competitive — that in 1947 only 2.4 per cent of output was mechanized. It was not until the National Coal Board took over that important advances were made in raising this figure. Armoured face conveyors or 'panzers' were introduced which had to be imported from Germany, where mining technology was again considerably more advanced. In this way the shearer loader which can cut automatically a wide swathe of the coal seam, could be mounted on the 'panzer' and hauled across a 200-yard long face. Within a decade mechanized output had risen to 23 per cent and by 1967 had climbed even more dramatically to 85 per cent.[10]

Amalgamations

The other main feature of the inter-war period was increasing concentration of ownership. The Samuel

Commission had recommended in 1925 that the problems of the coal industry could only be solved by amalgamations and this became the keynote of State policy right up to the war. It was argued that this would bring economies of scale and that the larger combines would have the capital base to modernize and diversify into the by-products industry. To put the policy into effect a Coal Mines Reorganization Commission was set up which recommended various schemes for the different regions. Although progress was slower than the Government wanted, there were 56 voluntary mergers between 1926 and 1936 involving over 400 pits. The PEP Report (1934) summarized the position as follows:

> "In nearly every district it is probably true to say that three-quarters of the production is concentrated in less than half the total number of pits, and in the hands of less than a quarter of the total number of colliery owners."[11]

The Northumberland and Durham coalfield was no exception to the general pattern, although the extent to which control was exercised by a few families may have been for historical reasons more marked than elsewhere. The table opposite shows the coal companies where the West Newcastle dynasties had a major or controlling interest. There were in addition other companies where the families had sizeable shareholdings or held directorships. These included Horden Collieries (Pease family), Wallsend and Hebburn Coal Company (Simpson), Hartley Main Collieries (Lamb), and Easington Coal Co (Noble). From the details of the table, it can be seen that ten of the West Newcastle families were very closely linked with collieries employing a workforce of 60,000 and producing 20 million tons per annum or 45 per cent of the entire output of the Northumberland and Durham coalfield.[12] In several cases — for example the Lambton, Hetton and Joicey Collieries, Priestman Collieries, Strakers and Love, and Stella Coal Company — the families appear to have owned virtually the entire share capital of the companies concerned.

The two largest coal companies in the North East; Ashington Colliery, owned by the Priestman and Milburn families. Picture: Newcastle City Library. And (below) railway shunting yards at Sunderland owned by the Joicey Collieries.

State policy therefore had the effect of concentrating still further the control of the region's most important industry, but the avowed strategy of facilitating the modernization and efficiency of the mines was unsuccessful. This was not, however, the only support given to the coalowners by the State. Not only had there been political intervention by the Government in 1926 to help the coalowners impose wage cuts on the miners, but also under the Coal Mines Act 1930 centralised machinery at national and district level — run entirely by coalowners and their representatives — was set up to create a cartel for fixing the price and output of coal from each colliery; and following the threat of a national stoppage by the miners in support of a wage demand, central selling schemes were established in 1936 with government agreement for the expressed purpose of raising prices. Profits and dividends rose, but wages remained low, particularly in the northern coalfield, where average earnings per manshift (1938 figures) were between 9s/8¼d. and 9s/9d. compared with 13s/3d. in North Derbyshire and Nottinghamshire and 11s/2¾d. for the country as a whole.[13] Details of profitability in the 1930s are not available for the majority of the collieries listed in the table, since as private companies they were not obliged to disclose this information. Those that are available show the success of the 1936 scheme:

COAL COMPANIES IN WHICH WEST NEWCASTLE FAMILIES HAD A MAJOR OR CONTROLLING INTEREST: SIZE OF WORKFORCE AND OUTPUT, 1934

Name of Company/Group	Main West Newcastle Families involved	Total employed	Annual Output (tons)
1. PRIESTMAN GROUP	Priestman, Pumphrey Peile		
Ashington Coal		9,550	4,000,000
Priestman Collieries		3,140	1,000,000
Priestman Whitehaven Collieries		1,957	600,000
2. LAMBTON, HETTON AND JOICEY COLLIERIES	Joicey	13,636	5,000,000
3. COOKSON GROUP	Cookson Straker, Benson		
Cowpen Coal		3,733	1,300,000
Hazlerigg & Burradon Coal		1,659	600,000
Mickley Coal		1,083	320,000*
W. Benson		1,010	300,000*
4. PEASE & PARTNERS	Pease	4,581	1,500,000
H. Stobart & Co		2,910	850,000
5. CONSETT IRON CO	Cookson, Ridley	6,921	2,350,000
6. STELLA COAL	Simpson Atkinson	3,987	1,250,000
Elswick Coal		1,070	250,000
7. STRAKERS & LOVE	Straker	3,466	1,100,000
8. THROCKLEY COAL	Stephenson	1,521	450,000
		60,224	20,870,000

*These are estimated figures based on average output per man in Northumberland in 1938.

Source: 1935 Colliery Year Book and Coal Trades Directory.

	Average Ordinary Dividend	
Name of company	1926-36	1936-8
Consett Iron Co	0	8¾
Horden Collieries	4.6	10
Pease and Partners	0	7½

Other evidence of the wealth that members of the coalowning families were amassing can be found in probate returns (see appendix); Lord Joicey and his son the second Baron died with estates valued at £1,520,000 and £784,000, J.C. Straker, chairman of Strakers and Love left £560,000, and the two Priestman brothers, Francis and Lewis together left £511,000.

Popular memory of the 1930s is of a period of recession and crisis in British industry with hunger strikes and thousands unemployed. For the workers in the depressed mining and heavy engineering industries on Tyneside this was the reality, but for the regional bourgeoisie, the coalowners and big industrialists it was very different. They still had control of large accumulations of capital, but the coal industry like heavy engineering was no longer the glamour sector that it had been when the West Newcastle families first made their fortunes in the nineteenth century. As Margot Heinemann puts it:

> "The pits have been gutted and robbed, the assets wasted ... The coal industry today, especially in the older districts, no longer 'attracts' the big investor in search of quick profits. There is no lack of money in the City of London, but modernizing our basic industry is too long-term and unprofitable a proposition for rentier financial institutions."

Nor was it attractive for the old coalowning families. Instead they were looking to the new sectors where profits were high. The process of diversification particularly into the finance capital sector was to become much clearer in the post-war period, but the beginnings of the movement were already much in evidence in the 1930s.

Left: boys leaving Charlotte Pit, Benwell, 1929; the youngest (at the front) aged fifteen was earning 2/4d per day, the others aged seventeen received 3/4½d. Picture: J. Gartland.

3.3 CAPITAL DIVERSIFICATION

We have already noted the movement of some second and third generation family members (viz Richardson, Pease and Straker) out of heavy engineering into the new consumer goods industries. Other diversification — for instance into public utilities — was more a continuation of a traditional form as the coalowners sought to gain control of important outlets for their own commodity. Thus as well as the electricity companies, the Newcastle and Gateshead Gas Company had close ties with the big coal companies, the board including in 1944 J.L. Priestman (FT12) from the Ashington Coal Company, R. Lishman, who was chairman from the Cookson coal combine, and Lord Ridley (FT14).

The most notable change however was the movement of later generations of the families into the finance capital sector, into banking, insurance, investment holding companies, property companies, building societies and into professions — stockbroking and the law — that were money-management oriented. It was a movement that distanced them from the point of production, from the factories and mines, and created a group within the capitalist class — 'finance capital' — whose interests did not always coincide with industrial capital. Too crude a distinction between the two sectors is misleading — and certainly there were families like the Pendower Peases and the Claytons who had always represented finance capital rather than industrial capital — but the general trend is unmistakable, particularly in the post-war period, when the coalowners' capital, locked in the fixed assets of mines and machinery, became suddenly transformed under the compensation terms into highly liquid government bonds. In the transitional inter-war period, the conflict between industrial and finance capital found expression often in the same family and, as we have seen in the heavy engineering sector, was most often resolved by moving personal and family capital out of the older low-profit industries into the new high profit sectors elsewhere.

3.3A BANKING

In the finance capital sector there was both a national and regional dimension. The takeover of the two main Newcastle banks, by Lloyds and Barclays at the turn of the century marked the absorption of local banking into a national system in which the Big Five came rapidly to attain a commanding position. The number of joint stock banks was reduced from 38 to 12 in the decade 1914-1924 with Lloyds increasing its issued capital from £20 million in 1900 to £74 million in 1926.

The influence of the families that had been connected with the original banks spread in parallel. J.W.B. Pease (FT11), who later became Lord Wardington and was the son of the founding partner of the Hodgkin Barnett and Pease Bank, remained on the board of Lloyds throughout his career. He was chairman for 23 years (1922-1945), and chairman and director of several other banks and insurance companies. In the 1920s the other 'West Newcastle' members on the board of Lloyds were P.E. Noble (FT10) son of Sir Andrew Noble, and A.F. Pease (d.1927), chairman of Pease and Partners from the steel and coal owning side of the family. By 1946 Lord Wardington had been joined by Viscount Ridley (d.1964), whose uncle Sir J.N. Ridley (FT14) was chairman of Coutts Bank, and deputy-chairman of the National Provincial Bank.

John Clayton's grand-nephew F.G.H. Clayton (FT6) was on the board of Barclays Bank throughout the whole of the inter-war period (1911-1946) and by 1936 had been joined by Claud Edward Pease (FT11), the brother of A.F. Pease.

All of these men had either begun banking careers on Tyneside before the amalgamations, or were brought on to the boards for their industrial connections. But there were other third generation members who began banking and insurance careers as young men in the 1930s; R.L. Barnett (FT3) who joined Sun Alliance and London Insurance immediately after Eton and Oxford, and C.I.C. Bosanquet (FT12) (later to become Vice-Chancellor of Newcastle University), who worked for *The Economist* and Lazards, merchant bankers, before becoming assistant general manager of the Friends Provident and Century Life Office from 1933 to 1939.

At the regional level new financial structures and institutions were emerging, and old ones were changing — a process in which the West Newcastle ruling class were playing a formative part. They provided vehicles for the deployment of family capital, but equally important were competing with each other to attract — and thus to control — the largest share of savings.

Both the banks and the insurance companies set up local boards of directors to integrate their central operations with their activities in the regions. The functions of the boards appear to have varied. The most decentralised arrangements were those of Barclays Bank who from the original amalgamation of 20 local banks in 1897 had established local head offices which had responsibility for administering the branches in their area. Thus both the brothers F.G.H. Clayton and F.C. Clayton (FT6) were on the Newcastle board in 1925, the latter continuing as chairman into the early 1960s. Another example was the Bank of Liverpool and Martins (which subsequently was renamed Martins until taken over by Barclays in 1969); the chairman of the North-East district board was Francis Priestman (FT12) (also chairman of the Ashington Coal Company), and one of the directors was Sir J.H.B. Noble. Both Priestman and Noble together with a third coalowner J.C. Straker (FT17) were also on the local board of one of the larger insurance companies at the time, North British and Mercantile Insurance Company[14] whose head office was in Edinburgh. In this they were continuing a tradition of close industrial and coalowning links with the company, which were probably more important in the nineteenth century as a way of securing loans for industrial capital. Other links with local insurance boards can be seen with the Royal Insurance Group (Joicey), Northern Assurance (Simpson) and General Accident Fire and Life (Dickinson).

3.3B INVESTMENT TRUSTS

One interesting method of diversifying into finance capital can be seen in the development of investment trusts in the late 1920s and early 1930s. The history of three companies, which all commenced in the early years of the century, reveals particularly this change of direction. All three companies, Waste Heat Company, the Tyneside Electrical Development Company ("The Tyneside") and Industrial Plant were formed to develop and exploit new techniques for electricity generation, many of which had emanated from the work of the Merz family (FT13). They were backed by industrial and coal-owning capital, much of it associated with the West Newcastle families. The Tyneside formed in 1906 appears to have been primarily involved in financing and marketing the electricity made by Waste Heat. Its first subscribers included P.E. Noble (FT10), G.B. Richardson (FT13) and A. Wood (Harton Coal) while its first directors were all on the board of the Newcastle Electric Supply Company — including J.T. Merz (FT13) its chairman. Waste Heat, which owned several generating stations, had even closer links with West Newcastle capital for its directors included J.B. Simpson (FT15), and F. Priestman, H. Peile and Joseph Pumphrey (all FT12).

Since the electricity companies — Newcastle Electric Supply Company, and Newcastle and District Electric Lighting Company — were statutory bodies with restrictions on the amount of profit they could make, these specialist companies appear to have been formed with the intention of exploiting the new techniques as profitably as possible. They relied, however, entirely on the electricity companies for buying their output

Cross House, Westgate Road, offices of the Dickinsons' firm of solicitors; now known as Dickinson, Dees, they still operate from the same premises.

or renting their plant[15] so the interlocking directorships were the key to their profitability. By the 1920s there is clear evidence of the transforming both of this relationship and of the role of the companies. A new arrangement was entered into in 1922, under which the Electricity Supply Company was to pay in the region of £200,000 for the hire purchase of Waste Heat's plant — *"without independent valuation"* as one disgruntled shareholder aptly pointed out after describing the overlapping interests of the two companies' directors and the techniques of inter-company accounting that were employed to disguise the true financial and investment position of the company.[16]

For the remainder of the inter-war period, Waste Heat's connection with the industry did not entirely cease, but continued through an investment portfolio which included electrical undertakings amongst others.[17] The Tyneside on the other hand restructured its capital base in 1929 and became reconstituted as the Tyneside Investment Trust with a public share issue. In this it was following a general pattern of renewed investment trust formation in the late 1920s that was fuelled by a boom of international trading and financial transactions. By 1930 the Tyneside's net assets were valued at £290,000, but only 23 per cent of its investment portfolio was in North-East Industry — a trend that was to become much more marked in the post-war period following nationalisation of the mines.

3.3C FINANCE CAPITAL PROFESSIONS

As capital was flowing into the finance capital sector, so there were locally, as well as nationally, family members that entered the professions that were best equipped to handle the transfer. Shortly before and after the First World War, the only two stockbroking firms, that are now in existence in Newcastle — Wise, Speke and Co (FT17), and Boys-Stones, Simpson and Spencer (FT15) — were first formed. In the legal profession, solicitors like John Clayton (FT6), his partner William Gibson, and T.G. Gibson (d.1911) had always played a key role in the commercial and industrial development of Tyneside. William Gibson, for example, purchased the Willington Coal Royalty in 1913 and leased it to the Wallsend and Hebburn Coal Company, while T.G. Gibson was first chairman of the Newcastle Electric Supply Company, a director of Elswick Coal Co and a wealthy city property owner. Members of these and other 'legal' families continued this involvement, while others from coal and banking families also joined the profession.

From the West Newcastle families four men are of particular importance because of their connections with coal capital — R.J. Dickinson (qualified 1927), R.A. Barnett (1936), I.J. Dickinson (1947), all of whom are related to the Joicey family (FT3), and J.S. Stephenson (1949). As companies expanded or new ones were formed, and more complex legislation was introduced relating to personal capital (taxation, formation of trusts, estate duties etc), the provision of specialist advice on investment and accounting became both important and profitable for well-connected firms like Dickinson, Miller and Turnbull (now Dickinson, Dees) in which the Dickinsons and Barnett were partners.

3.3D BUILDING SOCIETIES

The most important growth area for solicitors was however the development of owner-occupation as an important tenure form, which generated a steadily increasing flow of fees for the conveyancing work it entailed.[18] The Dickinsons' firm undoubtedly benefited from this, but of more interest is their connection with the Rock Building Society (now Northern Rock), for it was as directors of the larger regional building societies — which have provided the finance for the dramatic increase in owner-occupation over the last 30 years — that several of the former coal-owning and industrial bourgeoisie began to emerge in the post-war period.

Building societies were changing between the wars like many other institutions. From their nineteenth century origins as mutual organisations, they had soon become dominated by property professionals (solicitors, estate agents and architects) builders, and small industrialists providing finance for a mostly petit-bourgeois landlord class. Even then though they were an attractive investment for big capital as well as the small saver. As the Northern Counties Report (1900) put it: *"Under a system, enlarged and consolidated by time, the capitalist no less than the artisan, has been afforded a safe means of investment"*. Robert Dickinson, the first solicitor to the Rock Building Society is a good example of early exchange professional involvement, but his grandson, R.J. Dickinson, who became a director in 1942 (his firm had remained as solicitors to the Rock throughout the period) had by then come to represent much wider financial, property and coal interests (see list, p.76 of R.J. Dickinson's changing directorships 1937-75). Although some of the smaller building societies have continued the limited style of operation typical of the early years of the century, the growing importance of owner-occupation was reflected in the steady growth of funds controlled by the societies, particularly the larger ones; Northern Counties and Rock for example both increased their assets from about £1.5 million to £4 million in the period 1925-1945. The major change in control of the building societies however becomes evident only in the early post-war years (see next section).

3.4 HEGEMONIC ORGANISATION

In the period leading up to the First World War it was possible to describe loosely the West Newcastle bourgeoisie as an area-specific ruling class, and to trace its emergence as a hegemonic force. Although the bigger names were actors on a national stage, links with the city and Tyneside were still close enough for the big industrialists and coalowners to maintain a strong personal dominance of the economic and political life of the area. The growth of the Labour Party, a world war and the withdrawal of the bourgeoisie from the area were all factors that led to a diffusion of the control that had once been exercised over the immediate local area.

By the beginning of the Second World War, the dynasties' economic and political interests had spread far beyond West Newcastle and Tyneside. To suggest therefore that the families acted as some kind of distinct area or regional force would be misleading, for it would imply the existence of an organized regional bourgeoisie that was acting to protect and pursue its own interests vis-a-vis a wider national bourgeoisie. The picture is however more complex than that, for many family members had interests outside the region altogether; in banking alone, as we have seen, the families were represented on the boards of three of the Big Five clearing banks, holding in one case the chairmanship and in another case the deputy chairmanship for most of the inter war years.

The spread of influence can be seen in other spheres as well. The last years of the war and the 1920s had seen a proliferation of trade and employers' organisations, which previously had existed mainly in iron and steel alone. By 1925 the Federation of British Industries (now the CBI), in existence for under 10 years, had 250 affiliated associations;[19] and just as the northern coalowners had been an important influence within mining generally — Lord Joicey (FT3) was President of the Mining Association of Great Britain in 1904 — so in the new bodies, the big industrialists from Tyneside held important positions. Clive Cookson (FT7) was Vice-President of the FBI from 1925 to 1957 and Lord Gainford (FT11) was President in 1927, as well as being President of the National Confederation of Employers' Associations and of the Radio Manufacturers' Association.

The extent of the coalowners' influence can be seen most directly in the successful sabotage of the Sankey Commission's proposals in 1919 for coal nationalisation, which seemed to most people a logical policy after the government had taken over control of the mines during the war. In statements in the House of Lords and elsewhere, members of the families trumpeted their objections. A.F. Pease (FT11), chairman of Pease and Partners, declared at a shareholders' meeting: *"Coal control should be removed at the earliest possible date, so that they (the mines) could be handed back to the owners on a commercial basis."* Lord Joicey was equally emphatic at the Newcastle Chamber of Commerce: *"We must have our hands free, the Government must not control or obstruct our operations"*. Lord Gainford (FT11) giving evidence before the Sankey Commission was quite clear in his threats to the Government:

> *"I am authorised to say on behalf of the Mining Association that if owners are not to be left in complete executive control they will decline to accept the responsibilities of carrying on the industry, and, though they regard nationalisation as disastrous to the country, they feel they would in such event be driven to the only alternative — Nationalisation on fair terms."*[20]

The propaganda campaign paid off. Despite an overwhelming ballot of miners in favour of nationalisation,

Armstrong-Whitworths naval yard at Walker in the 1920s; the problem was how to replace the declining traditional industries with profitable ones based upon mass-consumption. Picture: Newcastle City Library.

and a government promise to carry it through, nothing was done until after the Second World War.

With their prominent positions in major financial and industrial organisations, and with the ear of those in government, the West Newcastle dynasties had by the 1930s become closely integrated within the wider ruling class. Their financial interests were already diversified far beyond Tyneside's older coal and heavy engineering industries; and yet as we have seen the traditional links with these industries (and in many cases major shareholdings) continued.

There were therefore significant local (as opposed to national and international) interests that the regional bourgeoisie needed to protect. We have already seen the way in which the big coalowners nationally — including those from the North-East — gained State backing for a policy of amalgamations and price cartels. There is evidence also that the industrial and coal capitalists of the area organized at a regional level as well, although it is more difficult to pin this down than in the previous periods.

One very public demonstration of solidarity occurred at the time of the 1926 General Strike in support of the miners' claims, when the regional coalowners and others keenly supported the setting up of the voluntarily-organised strike-breaking force, the Organization for Maintenance of Supplies (OMS).[21]

Many prominent local industrialists and coalowners were on the committee including Sir G.B. Hunter, Viscount Allendale, Sir A.M. Sutherland (Bowes and Partners), Sir L.J. Milburn (Ashington Coal) together with eight members of the West Newcastle families (see list).

Family members on the 'OMS' Committee. 1926

H. Peile (V-Pres)
F. Straker (V-Pres)
Lord Joicey
E. Joicey
P.B. Cookson
F. Clayton (Treas)
G.B. Atkinson
T.D. Straker-Smith

Source: *Newcastle Daily Journal*, 12 April 1926.

The more interesting developments however occurred towards the end of the period and after the war, when a series of regional development bodies were set up to propose solutions to the run-down of the region's traditional industries. The depression had brought home the structural problems facing the region's industry, and in particular its poor performance in comparison with the mass-consumption industries based in the South. The first body to be set up to make proposals was the North East Development Board,[22] whose chairman was Lord Ridley (FT14).

At the outbreak of war, the Board was disbanded, but from the industrialists' point of view it had never been a satisfactory organisation. As Fogarty puts it: *"The constitution of the pre-war Board had proved to be overweighted on the side of the local authorities and the procedure followed in forming the North-East Development Agency (set up after the war) was accordingly designed to ensure a better balance between industrial and local authority interests."*

The method employed to obtain this 'balance' is revealing for in 1943 Lord Ridley assembled a small group of five or six people including Clive Cookson (FT7) and three other industrialists who produced an outline plan of proposals for the post-war development of the region. The outcome was the creation of the Northern Industrial Group. Of the West Newcastle dynasties, Lord Ridley was chairman, Clive Cookson was Vice-Chairman, and R.A. Cookson, and E.G. Angus (FT1) were members — an important section of a wider regional bourgeoisie whose connections could similarly be traced back to early industrialization in the region. Although trade unionists had been brought into the group, its objectives and direction clearly reflected the interests of industrial capital, and particularly those of the 'basic' industries of coal (five members), iron and steel (five) and public utilities (two), and of shiprepairing/shipbuilding (13) and heavy engineering (five). Apart from the 'West Newcastle' industrialists, other major figures included the chairman or managing director of several large companies — Ashington Coal, Dorman Long, Hawthorn Leslie, Head Wrightson, Richardson Westgarth, Cleveland Bridge and Engineering, North-East Coast Ship Repairers and Palmers Hebburn. As the Rowntree Unit puts it:

> "Supporting each long-standing figure (on the various regional bodies) lies an interest or constellation of interests, which give their recipient a specific and significant place within the social structure of the region . . . The pattern emerges. Regional policies are pursued consistently by a group which represents a unified elite within the North-East."[23]

No detailed examination of the various regional development bodies can be made here, but in general four main themes, which have remained to this day can be seen behind the new policies for the region:[24]

1. That the traditional industries — with which the regional bourgeoisie remained linked — were no longer a viable basis for economic growth.

2. That what was needed were the 'new' light industries and particularly those making consumer goods, which were expanding elsewhere.

3. That linked to the transformation of industry was the need to modernize the social and environmental fabric of the region.

4. That where the older industries had growth potential that could be easily developed, they, like the new industries, should be given maximum State assistance in the form of infrastructure provision and a permissive industrial location policy.

Tracing the pattern of diversification of family capital that had already taken place by the outbreak of war, has demonstrated why the industrial bourgeoisie who controlled the older declining industries should wish to promote the new mass consumption industries — instead of for example arguing for a massive state-supported reinvestment programme in industries like shipbuilding. In the next period, to which we now turn, we can see how their interests have been further advanced.

Footnotes

1. See Private Housing and the Working Class. *Benwell CDP Final Report Series. 1978.*
2. D. Bean. Armstrong's men. *The Story of the Shop Stewards Movement in the Tyneside Works. 1967.*
3. J. Davison. Northumberland Miners. *1919-1939 p.195.* National Union of Mineworkers, 1973.
4. See for instance Gilding the Ghetto. *National CDP. 1977.*
5. See Private Housing and the Working Class, op.cit.
6. E.J. Hobsbawn, p.209, op.cit.
7. The subsequent history of the company is interesting. After the post-war replacements had been completed, the production of steam locomotives dwindled as diesels took their place. British firms were underinvested and could not compete with US firms (especially General Motors) which captured the lion's share of the market. To deal with overcapacity in the industry, the Locomotive Manufacturers Association produced a rationalization plan to cut out the weakest members. By 1954 Stephenson-Hawthorn had become part of the Vulcan Foundry of Newton-le-Willows, Lancashire, and the following year was taken over by English Electric. In 1960 the Forth Banks site was closed, followed in 1964 by the Darlington works — with all locomotive production transferred to Newton-le-Willows where it continues today as part of GEC.
8. Details of the development of the company in this period are based on an interview with Col. E.G. Angus.
9. M. Heineman. Britain's Coal, p.113. 1944.
10. National Coal Board. Annual Report 1975/6. Table 2. This improvement, though largely the result of massive State investment, was also helped by the closing down of the older inefficient mines. In the period 1957-1967 the number of producing collieries was reduced from 822 to 438, while the size of the workforce fell from 703,000 to 419,000.
11. Quoted in M. Heinemann, p.108, op.cit.
12. The lower figure of 20 million tons excludes production from the Priestman Whitehaven Collieries and the Pease Yorkshire pits. Total output in the two counties in 1934 was 44.6 million tons.
13. Colliery Year Book 1945, p.664.
14. In 1888 the life assurance funds of the company stood at £3.77 million, as compared with the total funds of £5.67m of one of the largest insurance companies, the Liverpool-based Royal Insurance (1888 figure).
15. Waste Heat lent its plant to the power companies at a rental of 10 per cent, plus other charges.
16. A. Gemmell. The Syndicated Supply of Electricity on the North-East Coast. Published statement. 1923.
17. It did not formally become an investment trust until 1948 (see next section).
18. See Private Housing and the Working Class. Benwell CDP Final Series 1978.
19. By 1917 the following "family" companies were already members of the N.E. Coast Branch of the FBI: Armstrong Whitworth, Consett Iron, Cookson & Co, Cowpen Coal Co, Hawthorn Leslie, Pease and Partners.
20. This and other coalowners' statements quoted in: J Davison, p.16-17, op.cit.
21. For an account of the OMS, see A. Mason, The General Strike in the North East, pp.50-53. 1969.
22. For a good account of the regional development bodies of this period, see M.P. Fogarty. Plan Your Own Industries, *OUP 1947;* and Rowntree Research Unit. Aspects of Contradiction in Regional Policy: The Case of North-East England. *Regional Studies Vol.8, 1974.*
23. Rowntree Research Unit. 1974, op.cit.
24. The historical origins of regional policy and its contemporary relevance are discussed in Regional Capitalism: A Regional Solution for the North-East? *CDP Final Report Series.*

4 Post-War Transformation

Shaft of the old Elswick Colliery beside the Noble Street flats; few reminders are left of the area's former coal industry. Picture: Derek Smith.

IN THIS last section the focus changes entirely to the region and the links with the wider economy, for coal nationalisation in 1947 effectively severed the families' direct connections with West Newcastle's industrial base. The three main characteristics of the post-war period have been increasing State intervention in the management of the economy, centralisation and concentration of industrial power, and the growing importance of the big financial institutions. In all of these changes, family members have played, and continue to play, an important role.

Tyneside's old ruling class have, for the most part, not been in control of the elective machinery of local government in the region as was the case in Newcastle up to the First World War, for the North-East now and particularly Co. Durham is regarded as a Labour stronghold. But over the non-elected State machinery and other important regional institutions — through which large amounts of central state funds have been channelled — members of the old families have had a dominating influence. These include several official and semi-official industrial development bodies, the New Towns and Newcastle University. In this way Tyneside's old ruling class has been able to implant within official thinking its own definition of the problems affecting the region, and advocate solutions that best suit its own material interests.

The response to growing concentration within the economy has had two aspects. Where the families have been closely involved in companies which already had cornered a large share of British and foreign markets, the companies have been able to expand to become themselves large multinational operations with subsidiaries in many other parts of the world. Additionally the policies promoted by the former regional bourgeoisie have encouraged the penetration of the region of nationally- and internationally-based companies, to whom their interests have been sold.

The movement of later generations of the families into the finance capital sector is however the most marked feature. While this was not a totally new phenomenon, the extent to which it has occurred has been facilitated by nationalisation of the coal and power industries that took place immediately after the war. This freed the old coal-owning families of the ties of an industry that by then was chronically underinvested, and at a stroke gave them millions of pounds in compensation, which they could redeploy in more profitable outlets elsewhere. In a few cases the money was used to develop new small-scale enterprises, but for the most part it provided later generations of the families with tickets of admission into a wide range of financial and related institutions. At the regional level there was a rapid move to take control of the Rock (now Northern Rock) Building Society — which has since become via take-overs and amalgamations by far the largest in the region. With the phenomenal growth of owner-occupation this has enabled the families to exercise an important influence on the building industry. It has also provided a key into the wider property market, which is clearly demonstrated in the case of the Joicey/Dickinson dynasty. Another outlet for the families' accumulated capital and compensation monies has been investment and investment holding companies. Though they are based in the region and have provided capital for some local entrepreneurial activity, their main focus is outside the region on the wider stock markets of the world.

At this wider level also, family members have become closely integrated in key positions within the large banking and insurance institutions, providing links both back to the regional financial structure and into large-scale industrial capital.

4.1 FAMILY AND KINSHIP IN THE WIDER ECONOMY

In the post-war years the geographical links of the families have become still further attenuated from West Newcastle. The historical nature of this report has led us to describe the role and importance of 18 'West Newcastle' dynasties, but many of the present generation — whose power, influence and wealth is founded on the area's grimy industrial past — may well have never heard of Benwell, Elswick or Newburn, let alone visited the area. For the West End of Newcastle is typically regarded now as an area of 'inner city decay' and of industrial decline, where the State is left to pay for the social and other costs when private capital is withdrawn.

To trace the movement of this private capital and the influence it has brought to West Newcastle's ruling class, the focus of this last section turns to the North-East region generally and to the wider economy. By doing this it becomes possible to answer a central question, posed in the introduction — of how a local capitalist class has defended its interests over time in the face of increasing centralisation of capital.

There have been three major and interlinked changes that have occurred in the organisation of the economy since the last war. Each has its origins in earlier periods, but it is over the last 30 years that the tendencies have become most marked. Firstly, there has been growing State intervention in the management of the economy[1] — both through the provision of subsidy and support for private capital, and through the nationalisation of major sectors of the economy. Secondly, the growing concentration of production has been reflected in the phenomenon of the multinational corporation, which plans its operations on a global scale and shows loyalty to neither region, country nor continent. Accompanying the growth of these huge companies there has been, thirdly, the development of finance capital institutions which have become the major influence in determining the flow and pattern of new investment. Before the First World War only three per cent of insurance companies funds were invested in ordinary company shares, but by the 1960s this figure had risen to 42 per cent; and it is now estimated that financial institutions hold about 55 per cent of all shares that are quoted on the Stock Exchange.[2]

Recently these changes, and particularly the second and third have been more widely recognised, but the implications that are thought to flow from them are not substantially different from what academics and others were saying in the boom years of the 1950s and 1960s. An American economist describes the modern corporation as follows:

> *"No longer the agent of proprietorship seeking to maximise return on investment, management sees itself as responsible to stockholders, employees, customers, the general public, and, perhaps most important, the firm itself as an institution . . . From one point of view, this behaviour can be termed responsible: there is no display of greed or graspingness; there is no attempt to push off onto workers or the community at large part of the social costs of the enterprise. The modern corporation is a soulful corporation."*[3]

The growth of egalitarian and democratic values and pressures has, it is argued, been a further factor in the emergence of this new managerial breed of top executive. Schooled in a welfare state age the new executive has naturally considered social welfare objectives to be as important as, if not more important than profit maximisation. Within the state machinery also, it is argued, recruitment has become far more open, so that the senior civil servants who mastermind the complex detail of government policies, are no longer drawn from the select ranks of a few public schools but reflect the attitudes of a cross-section of the population.

As a corollary, these views imply the fading away of the old ruling classes, whose power was based on personal wealth and control of production. A few names may live on as reminders of an earlier period, but for the most part a once powerful ruling class is now, it is implied, no more than a dwindling interest group with a few titles and landed estates to its names. With estate duty and now capital transfer tax, even their remaining wealth has been stripped away, or will shortly become so.

Lord Joicey. Picture: D.M. Smith.

... and his residence, Etal Manor, with racehorse stables behind. Picture: Ian Harford.

Analyses of this kind, lacking a general theoretical and historical framework, fail to convince because they are partial, selecting arbitrary and limited data instead of proceeding holistically. Indeed, the material here could be treated in the same manner by selective examination. Lord Joicey (FT3) and Lord Armstrong (FT2) descendants of two of the richest men in the North-East — and to a lesser extent the Bensons (FT4) and Cooksons (FT7) of Meldon Park — do own large estates and appear to have few business connections. Management of the estates no doubt provides some work for them, but their main activities seem to centre on shooting, hunting and racehorses.

An examination of capital flows and wider family connections shows however that this is a very deceptive picture. For one of the striking features of the family trees (see appendix) — which is not apparent from a casual search of lists of directors and shareholders — is the extent of intermarriage between a handful of families. At first sight they may appear as a curious but not particularly remarkable coincidence, but as the alliances build up over the generations — see for example Barnett (FT3) and Priestman (FT12) — it becomes apparent that they are a major factor in explaining important linkages between different companies and sectors over time. Since women never appeared in any entrepreneurial or professional roles, a man who married into a dynasty might often receive or inherit substantial amounts of capital, although in some cases it was more a question of forging an alliance with an already well-established and wealthy family — as for example the stockbroker N.H.R. Speke (FT17) who married into the Straker family, or R.C. Bosanquet (FT12) from a banking family who married the daughter of the Newcastle banker, Thomas Hodgkin. Of greater importance were the connections, directorships, and insider knowledge that came with marriage. To those with financial and professional skills, who understood the market and the best investment opportunities, substantial sums of money were entrusted, which they were able to employ (perfectly legally) to further both their own and the wider family's interests.

The 'Family and kinship in the North East' theme is therefore an important key for tracing the evolution of the regional bourgeoisie, and helps to demonstrate the important role that the West Newcastle dynasties have played both in the post-war development of the region, and in the changes taking place in the wider economy. To plot this we need to consider in turn the main characteristics of change already described.

4.2 STATE INTERVENTION

While the 1930s had demonstrated that private capital needed the intervention of the State in the overall management of industry to ensure its profitability, the process of State interference had been taken a great deal further in war-time Britain. Central direction and planning of major industries to support the war effort was essential and greate at any other time. Unempl fell to virtually nil. To

Lord Armstrong (right) explaining plans for a residential development at his estate at Cragside originally purchased by the first Lord Armstrong. Picture: Newcastle Chronicle and Journal.

morale and the continued support of the masses, the Government became committed to introducing after the war a comprehensive reorganisation of national health, education and insurance services. The emphasis of post-war Britain was to be on social justice and a more equitable distribution of wealth and income.

Although much of the economic planning machinery was dismantled after 1945, it was clear that State involvement in many aspects of the economy would continue. Nationalisation of several industries such as coal, public utilities, steel and airways took place, but since many of them have subsequently operated at a loss, they have effectively provided a subsidised service to private industry. In the North-East the regional offices of the different Ministries were preparing plans for new towns at Newton Aycliffe and Peterlee in Co. Durham and working out the guidelines for industrial location policy generally. For the old regional bourgeoisie the setting up of regional development bodies like the Northern Industrial Group (see last section) and its successor the North-East Development Association (whose chairman was also Lord Ridley) provided major channels for influencing the form of the State's industrial policy in the region. As a Northern Industrial Group bulletin put it:

> "Decisions on the location of industry, which will have such far reaching effects on the whole future of the region, should not be taken by Government officials alone, but should be supplemented by the considerable knowledge of the area and its requirements possessed by bodies such as the Northern Industrial Group with its manifold sources of information, (and) the wide industrial experience of its members . . . Having regard to the close working arrangement reached with the Board of Trade it is evident that this point of view is shared in official circles."[4]

But these were not the only forums through which the old coalowners and industrialists were able to promote

R.A. Cookson (centre) as chairman of the northern region of the CBI promoting the entry of Britain to the EEC; 1972. Picture: Newcastle Chronicle and Journal.

particular policies. On nationalisation of the mines key positions on the National Coal Board were taken up by the former owners. Sir Walter Drummond, formerly managing director of Ashington Coal Company, was, by 1949, chairman of the North-West Division of the NCB, and became Deputy-Chairman of the NCB from 1951 to 1955.

And lower down in the management structure, exactly the same pattern was evident as a miner from Monkwearmouth Colliery recalled at a recent meeting in Newcastle:

> "When we nationalised in 1947, I can remember as a young man, standing at the pit head, with all the banners celebrating. My father and all the old men were there, thinking 'this is it, nationalisation, this is it'. But before too long they found they'd just swapped one boss for another. The first boss we got was a major from the Indian Army, followed six months later by a captain."

By the 1960s members of the West Newcastle dynasties held the chairmanship (or similar position) in a variety of State or state-financed agencies. J.M. Pumphrey (FT12) was Deputy-Chairman of the Northumberland and Durham Division of the NCB, and R.A. Cookson (FT7) was chairman of the Northern Regional Board for Industry, a statutory body set up shortly after the war to advise government departments. Composed of employer and trade union members in equal numbers, it was important *"because it was the finest form of joint consultation"*[5] that leading employers had ever had with the unions.

Although the Board was disbanded in 1965 when the Labour Government established the Economic Planning Council, Cookson has re-emerged as chairman of the Northern Industrial Development Board (NIDB), a body established by the Department of Industry under the 1972 Industry Act. It meets monthly to consider a list of all cases where the Department is intending to give selective financial assistance to companies under the Industry Act. In contrast to the earlier bodies which were seeking to incorporate the trade unions and where there was usually an equal split between management and union representatives, NIDB has only two trade unionists in a total membership of 12. The others are representatives of, or retired from mostly large companies such as Head Wrightson, Swan Hunter, Alcan (UK), ICI, Lead Industries and William Baird.

4.2A NEW TOWNS

The overall direction of the New Towns too has come under direct dynastic influence. The general planning concept that evolved for new industrial location was that of 'growth zones' where new industrial investment could be concentrated. To the first phase New Towns of Newton Aycliffe and Peterlee were added in the early 1960s a further two, Washington in Co. Durham and Cramlington in Northumberland; and it has been to these four towns, with their ready access to the motorway system and with a variety of subsidised factories and sites on offer, that a high proportion of mobile new industry has come, particularly in the 1960s and 1970s.[6] Throughout much of this period, H.H. Peile (FT12) from the Ashington and Priestman Collieries was the appointed chairman of both Peterlee Development Corporation (1957-1969) and Newton Aycliffe Development Corporation (1963-1969) while the chairmanship of Washington New Town was held by another major regional industrialist Sir James Steel who has a major interest in Acrow (Engineers) and is now chairman of the big Furness Withy shipping group.

Cramlington New Town has a rather different organizational structure from the other three, for it was set up not by central Government, but by Northumberland County Council as part of the Council's Development Plan. It is now managed by a joint sub-committee of county and district councillors, but responsibility for the development of industrial estates and the attraction of industry has always rested with Northumberland Council. Here again the 'West Newcastle' influence can be clearly seen, for a number of the families have played and continue to play a leading role in the ruling (Tory) Northumberland Voters Association; three men R.A. Barnett (FT3), G.H. Peile (FT12) and Lord Ridley (Chairman) are at present on the powerful Policy and Resources Committee, while Lord Ridley himself is also chairman of the Cramlington Sub-Committee and of the full Council — a position that he and his father, the third Viscount, have occupied for 20 out of the last 38 years.

4.2B RESEARCH AND THE UNIVERSITY

One of the three original objectives of the Northern Industrial Group had been *"to encourage commercial, technical and industrial research with a view to developing ancilliaries to the basic industries and to help to establish new industries"*. The main vehicles for developing this research have been the institutions of higher education, and in particular the University in Newcastle. The families' early involvement in the setting up of Armstrong College (the earlier name for Newcastle University) has again ensured their close and continuing connection — along with other representatives of industrial capital — as co-opted members of the university's council and court during its tremendous post-war growth period.[7]

The influence of individual committee members has some limits but the close ties with regional industrial and

The present Lord Ridley, chairman of Northumberland County Council since 1967.

WEST NEWCASTLE FAMILY MEMBERS ON NEWCASTLE UNIVERSITY COUNCIL* IN POST WAR PERIOD

1948	1963	1978
Visc. Ridley (Ch)	Visc. Ridley (Ch)	M.I.B. Straker (V-Ch)[1]
R.A. Cookson	C.I.C. Bosanquet (V-Chancellor)	R.A. Cookson[1]
R.J. Dickinson	R.A. Cookson	H.H. Peile
Sir F.R. Simpson	R.T. Pease	Sir L. Pumphrey[2]
	J.M. Pumphrey	Visc. Ridley[2]
	R.A. Barnett	

*Until 1963 it was part of Durham University and was known as Kings College.
1. Also member of Court
2. Member of Court only

Keeping ships on the move

SOLVING problems for industry is quite a common task for Newcastle University's Department of Marine Engineering which often uses computer power to predict the behaviour of machinery.

Latest research contract to come their way is a £184,000 study of how emulsified fuels would perform when used as fuel for marine diesel engines.

Awarded by the U.K. Atomic Energy Research Establishment and the Department of Industry, the research contract will take about two years to complete.

The programme involves trials on both slow-speed and medium-speed diesel engines and specialised tests on fuel systems.

Trials involving a medium-speed engine will be carried out initially on an engine in the University laboratories.

And the trials on a slow-speed engine involve Doxford Engines of Sunderland.

This programme of work which will help British marine engineers to produce a more efficient and economical product will culminate in trials at sea where the ideas worked out will be put to the real acid test.

Article on the University's links with industry. Journal, 18 May 1978.

First meeting of the Council of the University of Newcastle in 1963; Lord Ridley in the Chair, with the Vice-Chancellor, C.I.C. Bosanquet, on his right. Picture: Newcastle University, Dept. of Photography.

financial interests is clearly reflected in the technological orientation that the university has developed with applied science departments like those of Chemical Engineering, Metallurgy and Marine Technology being given a major boost. One key figure has been C.I.C. Bosanquet (FT12) — from a coalowning/banking dynasty — whose appointment as rector and then vice-chancellor, after earlier connections with insurance and investment trusts, covered a period of 16 formative years (1952-1968). For as Collison and Millen point out, the vice-chancellor has a place in every piece of the administrative machinery which has any consequence, and is able to direct the business of a university and shape its policy.[8]

Another important influence has been R.A. Cookson, the longest-standing member of Council and until recently chairman of Lead Industries Group (LIG). He has described the attitude of his company to providing extra financial support to the university as follows: *"Newcastle University is one of the best in the country from the point of view of links with industry and helping industry. Of all the universities we have contact with, we receive most help from Newcastle. It is the one university where the LIG Board consider it worthwhile to put all our money."*[9]

Nor is it just the obvious applied science departments that bring benefits to industry. In 1946 for instance a new Nuffield Chair of Industrial Health was established *"for the primary purpose of investigating the effect of occupation upon human health"*. One of the first reported research projects of the new professor suggests however far more of a work-study emphasis appropriate to the female-intensive light industry that has since moved into the region.[10]

"A completed investigation has been made into the nocturnal and diurnal variation in performance of girls doing a monotonous task. This has shown:

a) *that on the whole, performance at night was worse than during the day*

b) *that during the day, performance was irrespective of the amount of work which there was to do, but at night the more the work, the quicker it was done."*[11]

This kind of close association of the academic and business worlds is by no means unique to Tyneside as Thompson has shown in the case of Warwick University; he also picks up the point about how a small number of individuals on Council can have a disproportionate influence on major decisions:

M.I.B. Straker (right), another member of Council from an old coal-owning family, and himself chairman of the Newcastle Area Health Authority; he is seen here with Tory MP Geoffrey Rippon at a private garden party given by Viscount Lambton for Edward Heath MP. Picture: Dudley Muir.

"While all co-opted members are not regular attenders at Council, they have been present in force at crucial meetings where contested issues have arisen, and even a few of them, acting together with the Vice-Chancellor and officers and one or two academics, can be expected to dominate decisions. 'Industry' has therefore been able to influence the University at the level of its planning, financing and development, at a relatively low cost in terms of promotion and donations."[12]

Warwick University is a rather more extreme case than Newcastle in respect of the concentration of business interests (mostly engineering and motor manufacture) at the top of the power structure, but in terms of active promotion of scientific and economic research by industry it is probably not so different. Furthermore the direct input from Tyneside industry has been strengthened by the establishment in 1972 of the independent Newcastle University Development Trust for the purpose of developing *"a number of academic projects which would particularly benefit the Northern Region"*. Again there is a strong dynastic leavening for three of the ten trustees are from the old families — R.A. Cookson who is chairman, R.H. Dickinson (FT3) and Lord Ridley — while others include the chairman or a director of Tyne-Tees Television, Procter and Gamble, Jobling Purser, Hunting Gibson (crude oil and shipowning) and Northern Gas.

The trustees are quite explicitly *"appointed predominantly from outside the University"*, and its finances are administered separately from those of the University. By April 1978 £2.3 million had been raised mostly from large regional and national companies and financial institutions (many of which are mentioned in this report). Although a good deal of the money has been used to fund valuable developments in the medical field, and for general university facilities, it has also enabled the establishment of chairs and research posts in industrial related fields such as Marine Transport, Ocean Engineering, Energy Studies, International Business Machines and Regional Development. Moreover, the existence of an independent organisation with considerable amounts of uncommitted finance, gives those who control it an added leverage on other new developments within the University.

4.3 GROWTH OF THE MULTINATIONAL CORPORATIONS

It was not simply a case of Tyneside's old ruling class, through their influence on the new State or State-financed bodies being in a position to orchestrate the pattern of new industrial development in the region, and to argue for certain forms of State subsidy — such as motorways, industrial estates, factories and direct financial assistance. They were also able to benefit directly through their close involvement in many of the region's major industries.

We have already shown how in the inter-war years, family capital was being redeployed into the finance capital sector and away from the declining traditional sectors. In shipbuilding in particular in the post-war years many shipyards have disappeared either through a straight closure or following amalgamation; while in mining the compensation monies from nationalisation have provided a further boost for the move into finance capital.

In the case of some companies however — usually the larger ones that dominated a sector or had cornered a substantial share of the market — the response to concentration in the economy has been to follow suit via takeovers and diversification. In other words, the phenomenal growth of the multinational corporation in the post-war years has not come about simply by foreign-based companies buying out firms in the region (and in the country generally), but equally by companies that have originated in the region expanding outwards by takeovers and new investment in other countries.

Some idea of this growing concentration of economic power in the country generally can be seen in the decreasing number of companies that have produced 50 per cent of national output. From 1910 to 1935 the figure had dropped from 2000 companies to 800; by 1958 it had almost halved again to 420 companies, and by the 1970s it has reached, according to different estimates between 100 and 140 companies. The figures are dramatic, but it should not be forgotten that the extent of concentration is a relative question; W.G. Armstrong (later Vickers) was already far more than a Tyneside firm when it merged with Whitworths in 1897, and by the 1920s was diversifying into a £20 million scheme in Newfoundland. Those who comment on the penetration of multinational capital into the region, often emphasise the loss of local control over investment decisions. Undoubtedly this is correct in that local decision-making — in the sense that the board of directors regard Tyneside and the North-East as their principal centre of operations — has been replaced by corporate planning on a global scale. But this focus on the operations and characteristics of multinational corporations should not be allowed to obscure the continuing role of the old regional bourgeoisie.

The Cookson family interests in Lead Industries Group, large scale manufacturers of non-ferrous metals, chemicals and paints, are a good example of this process, and the way in which formerly region-based capital has become thoroughly integrated within the multinational economy. The original Cookson Lead interests became part of Goodlass Wall and Company in 1930. In the following years Clive Cookson was the architect of a deliberate policy of amalgamations designed to fight off foreign competition. By 1939 the company was one of the largest lead manufacturers in the world and had a direct controlling interest in 14 originally independent companies — including the Elswick Leadworks of Walkers Parker (now known as Associated Lead Manufacturers). It also had subsidiaries in Melbourne, Bombay, Calcutta and Buenos Aires.

With a turnover in 1977 of £287 million the company now has three separate plants on Tyneside — where there has been considerable investment in the post-war years — and has subsidiaries in many other parts of the country, in five European countries, and in Australia, New Zealand, South Africa and India. For more than 50 continuous years the chairman of the company has come from the same family, firstly Clive Cookson and then R.A. Cookson, from 1962 to 1973.[13]

Another major Tyneside company, Swan Hunter and Wigham Richardson, with which the Richardson family has been connected, has also undergone major changes. Already the largest shipbuilder in the North-East by the end of the war with an issued share capital of £2.5 million, the company with Smith's Dock Company has formed the main core of the present Swan Hunter Group. This was established in 1968 after the Geddes Report recommended that there should be greater government incentives to the industry and that the four main shipyards on the Tyne — Swan Hunter, Vickers Armstrong, Hawthorn Leslie and John Readhead — should amalgamate to create a larger unit that could become more competitive. Although the Richardsons' links ceased from this period, other family members have remained on the board, notably Lord Ridley and W.J. Straker-Smith (FT17) the present vice-chairman.

Like Lead Industries, Swan Hunter has developed its interests abroad, with subsidiary and associated companies and investments in Bahamas, Trinidad, South Africa and Singapore. Its activities too have diversified from shipbuilding alone to marine engineering, and civil engineering and building. A more complete transformation is however imminent, for the Government has now agreed to pay the company £15 million compensation for its nationalised shipbuilding interests, which have accounted in the past for about two-thirds of its total turnover.

George Angus provides a third example.

Oil Seal Division of G. Angus & Co on the Coast Road, adjacent to major motorway links; the policies promoted by the early regional bodies had paid off. Picture: G. Angus & Co. Below, G. Angus & Co at Cramlington New Town. Picture: Newcastle City Library.

The war-time years had been a period of rapid growth (see section 2) but by 1944 it was still relatively small with only one overseas subsidiary in South Africa. Post-war expansion however changed that, for Angus had diversified by 1962 into a major engineering company with five separate divisions covering fire armour, brake linings, oil seals, belting and gears. Overseas factories had been established in Canada, United States, France, Portugal and Italy, and marketing companies set up in South Africa, Rhodesia, Sweden and Finland. Expansion on Tyneside has been greatly facilitated by the policies of industrial location and infrastructure provision that the early regional bodies like the Northern Industrial Group advocated (see section 3). In 1956 a large new factory was built at Wallsend on the Coast Road for the Oil Seal Division, and other new plant have been established at Cramlington New Town and the Tyne Tunnel Trading Estates. Although a public company from the beginning of the century, control remained largely in the hands of the Angus family — with E.G. Angus (FT1) chairman, and D.D. Angus managing director of the Belting and Rubber Hose Division — until Angus was taken over in the mid 1960s by Dunlop Holdings. Trading under the old Angus name, it continues

Above: equipped by the Angus Fire Armour Group; one of the most profitable in the Dunlop Group. Below: The New Metro Bridge during construction; built by Cleveland Bridge Engineering, formerly a regional company, and now part of the multi-national Trafalgar House. Picture: Tyne & Wear Passenger Transport Executive.

compensation monies being used to buy a substantial (and eventually controlling) interest in one of the region's new light engineering companies. It was formed in 1954 to buy up an existing radiator manufacturer, H.G. Binder of Washington and had as major shareholders several people who were either directors or shareholders in the Ashington Coal Company, including J.L. Priestman (5,000 shares) and H.H. Peile (2,000 shares) from the Priestman dynasty, and R.H.C. Herron (3,500 shares with his wife) a Newcastle solicitor.

In 1964, most of the Binder family's controlling interest in the company[14] appears to have been transferred to Peile and Herron, who remained as two of the company's three directors until it was bought out in 1973 by Hawker Siddeley.

In the case of H.H. Peile this pattern of selling out to the big multinational corporations was repeated with at least two companies in which he was involved. The Newcastle tyre distributors A.F. Bell & Co — of which Peile was chairman — was formed in 1954 again with coal compensation monies (£40,000 from J.L. Priestman and his wife and £10,000 from Peile and his wife). Twenty years later it became part of Michelin Tyres, through its subsidiary Associated Tyre Specialists. Peile was also chairman and managing

A more recent example of selling out to the multi-nationals: I.C. Straker, Chief Executive of the Scottish firm of Glenlivet Distillers, who announced in January 1978 the purchase of his company by Seagram the giant Canadian distillers for £47 million. Picture: Glenlivet Distillers.

today as one of the most profitable sections within the Dunlop group.

There are many other companies in the region that have followed similar patterns. Two other firms represented on the 1946 Northern Industrial Group have become part of large multinational corporations; the Middlesborough-based Head Wrightson merged in 1977 with Davy International, a large steel engineering and construction group, while the Cleveland Bridge and Engineering Company is now part of Trafalgar House Investments.

Family involvement has not always continued, particularly where the company has become part of a much larger group, or where the interests or shareholding is relatively small. In these cases the former owners have merely facilitated the expansion of the larger group, and been content to relinquish control in return for the cash or shares offer from the acquiring company. A good example of this is the Hawker Siddeley Group which in the post-war years has taken over three companies in which the West Newcastle families have had interests — Airspeed Ltd (the Richardson family), Brush Electrical Engineering (Pease), and Washington Engineering (Priestman, Peile). Washington Engineering is one of the relatively few cases of coal director of the Weardale Lead Company which owned valuable lead and fluorspar mines in Co. Durham. In 1962, ICI bought a large shareholding in the company and now operate it as a wholly owned subsidiary.

There was one other company to be formed about this time which was probably financed by compensation monies. This was Stephenson and Wood (Pty), a South African company set up in 1949 by J.S. Stephenson (FT16) a solicitor and director of the Throckley Coal Company, together with A. Wood, a Hexham solicitor, and T.R. Cairns, a shipowner. In 1974 J.M. Pumphrey (FT12) formerly of Priestman Collieries joined the board. Its main business is as owners of mining royalties, but details of shares and profitability are not available.

An interesting diversification that has taken place more recently has involved G.H. Cookson (FT7) and a number of interlinked companies based at Thetford, Norfolk which have successfully developed vaporization techniques for the metallizing and coating of plastic films, laminates, and paper. The original company, Vacuum Research (Cambridge), renamed in 1978 Camvac, was formed in 1950 by two research scientists, but by 1973 it had become a subsidiary of High Vacuum Engineering in which Cookson and his wife had a large holding of 8,250 shares. In 1975 a new parent company, Camvac Holdings, was formed to take over these and other related subsidiaries. This time, however, it was on a bigger scale, for its initial capital was £610,000, of which Cookson and his wife put up £406,000.

4.4 MOVEMENT INTO FINANCE CAPITAL AND PROPERTY

While the links with manufacturing industry have been selectively maintained by a few members of the West Newcastle families — but without any commitment to the region as such — the movement into property and into the finance capital institutions and professions is more marked. The most important boost for this diver-

High hopes for the miners, but it was the coalowners who hit the rich seam. Picture: NCB.

sification came from the nationalisation of coal and public utilities in 1947.

In all £243 million was paid to the former royalty owners and coalowners by the State in compensation for the unworked coal and assets (plant, building, stock etc) that the National Coal Board took over.[15] A detailed breakdown of how this global figure was divided up between the different regions and companies is unobtainable, but from available sources it is possible to provide approximate figures for five of the main coal combines with which the families were involved (see list).

This coal compensation, payable in the main in Government Stock, was divided among a very small number of shareholders since most of the companies were effectively private family businesses. New investment over the years had been mostly financed out of profits and there had been little need to have recourse to the wider capital market. The Ashington Coal Company was probably the best example of this policy, although it was not very different from several of the others. As the chairman put it at the last annual general meeting in 1953: *"This is one of the few colliery companies which has never issued a debenture in its*

COMPENSATION PAID ON COAL NATIONALISATION

Name of Company	Approximate compensation*
Ashington Coal	£5m
Cookson Group (Mickley, Cowpen, Hazlerigg & Burradon, Wm. Benson)	£2m
Lambton, Hetton & Joicey	£12m
Pease and Partners	£9m
Strakers and Love	£1.2m

*Figures are based on details in the Register of Defunct Companies and in the Stock Exchange Year Books, interviews, and on archival sources. In some cases the monies paid out on liquidation may in part have represented liquid reserves already held by the company, rather than compensation.

history and it must be unique in that it has never called for any additional capital beyond that which was originally put into it on its formation" There was in addition to the coal payments a further £24 million paid in compensation for nationalisation of the public utility companies with which the dynasties had remained closely linked — North-East Electric Supply (£19 million), Newcastle and District Electric Lighting (£1.3 million), and Newcastle upon Tyne and Gateshead Gas (£4.4 million). Although the number of shareholders in these cases was far greater, there remained scope for the families' new finance professionals to expand their own professional interests by the redeployment of other people's money.

While the attitude of the coalowners remained publicly hostile to nationalisation, in private they appear to have been much more amenable — which is scarcely surprising given the run-down in the mines and the huge investment necessary for modernisation. At the last meeting of the Ashington Coal Company after a final figure of £5 million compensation had been agreed, the chairman had this to say:

"Whilst shareholders must regret seeing their assets taken over without their consent under the Nationalisation legislation, there must be some consolation to them to know that the amounts of compensation awarded to the company clearly show its pre-eminent position in the district and the country. The prosecution of the company's claim for compensation in the last few years whilst essentially not a happy one ... has in some part been alleviated by the satisfaction of knowing that all that could be done for the benefit of shareholders has been done and that settlements satisfactory to the shareholders have been made."[16]

The compensation terms not only enabled shareholders to diversify into more profitable new industries and sectors like property and banking, they also imposed a crippling burden on the new state-run coal industry and the miners. The National Coal Board was under no illusions about this from the outset: *"The Board's interest obligations have to be met in good years or bad irrespective of profits. This is in contrast to limited companies, which are largely capitalised by shares or stock and only pay dividends if there is a surplus to distribute."*[17] The annual interest charges — payable on the stock and cash that the coalowners received from the government — was likely, according to the 1947 annual report to be between £10 million and £12 million, which will not finally be paid off until 1997.[18]

To trace the West Newcastle dynasties' involvement in the new boom sectors after the war it is useful to consider firstly the regional manifestations and secondly the links with the wider financial world. At the outset however it needs to be stressed that the two levels — the regional apparatus on the one hand, and the wider national and international institutions on the other hand — are entirely and necessarily interdependent. While the distinction may be made for the sake of unravelling the families' changing interests it does not in any way imply the continuing existence of an autonomous regional bourgeoisie, whose general interests are in conflict with a wider ruling class.

4.4A REGIONAL FINANCIAL INSTITUTIONS

A feature of the post-war years has been the importance of house-building and construction in the wider economy. In 1972 for instance, the peak of the property boom, new fixed capital investment in dwellings and in buildings and works amounted to £1,303 million or 53 per cent of total fixed investment.[19]

Within the housing and property sector in particular, the financial institutions play an important role, for builders, developers, property companies and owner-occupiers all depend on the massive resources that only the banks, insurance companies and building societies can provide. With the mushrooming of owner-occupation — it now represents 53 per cent of all housing in the country by comparison with a figure of 29.5 per cent in 1950 — building societies in particular have grown in importance and size to the detriment of the clearing banks. With their preferential tax rates building societies have been able in the 15 years 1960-1975 to increase their deposits almost eightfold from £2,952 million to £22,696 million while the London clearing banks' deposits rose at less than half the rate for the same period — from £7,400 million to £26,102 million.[20]

In the Northern region owner-occupation is a smaller tenure group (45 per cent of all dwellings) than in any other part of the country except Scotland, but despite this its growth with the building of mass estates by firms such as William Leech, Bellway and Barratts has been a significant phenomenon.

To demonstrate one important connection between Tyneside's old ruling class and this new market, it is useful to look at the evolution of the Northern Rock Building Society, the biggest in the region and now the eighteenth largest in the country. From an early period the Dickinsons (FT3) were associated with the Rock Building Society because the original Robert Dickinson was its first solicitor in the nineteenth century. Until the Second World War most directors of building societies were relatively small property professionals (builders, estate agents, and landlords) small businessmen or shopkeepers. In this respect the Rock was little different from any of the others in the region. The one characteristic that distinguished it — and the slightly smaller Northern Counties Building Society — was that their assets (about £4 million each at the outbreak of war) were more than twice the size of any of their rivals.

Important changes, however, began in the war and in the decade following, when control of the Rock passed predominantly into the hands of the old coalowning families. In quick succession members of the West Newcastle dynasties (and others) were appointed onto the board of directors — R.J. Dickinson (1942), Lord Ridley, the third Viscount (1944), H.H. Peile (1954), and Lord Ravensworth (1947), from a former coal-owning family; while more recently over the last decade or so other younger members of the families have joined such as Lord Ridley (the fourth Viscount) and N.H.R. Speke (FT17) by 1966, and R.H. Dickinson (FT3) and J.S. Stephenson (FT16) in 1977. Accompanying this change in the composition of the board of directors, there has been a rapid growth in the society's assets which had increased to £435 million by 1977 from the pre-war figure of £4 million. The main method of achieving this has been via amalgamations, the most important being with the Northern Counties Building Society in 1965. In the post-war years 24 previously independent building societies in the region have been taken over in this manner to form the basis of the present Northern Rock — 10 of which occurred in the 1960s and eight in the 1970s.

The Northern Rock has become by far the biggest society in the North-East, its nearest rivals being the Newcastle upon Tyne Permanent with total assets of £61.8 million, and the Grainger with assets of £52.4 million (1977 figures); and of these the Grainger has a not dissimilar line-up of directors from the old coal-owning families — including R.H.C. Herron, the chairman (a former shareholder in Ashington Coal), Lord Ravensworth and C.J. Pumphrey (FT12), a stockbroker and again linked to Ashington Coal — while the Newcastle upon Tyne Permanent has as solicitors the Dickinsons' (FT3) firm of Dickinson Dees.

Since building societies are non-profit making organisations and the directors receive comparatively small fees, it is not the direct pecuniary advantage that the former coalowners have sought through their association with the movement. But it has given them control over the annual deployment of millions of pounds, and great influence over the building industry in the region, since firms like Bellway and William Leech rely upon a guaranteed supply of mortgages from Northern Rock and other building societies,

The 'new' and the old ruling class; R.J. Dickinson as chairman, with the Duke of Northumberland at the opening of the new offices of the Northern Rock Building Society, 1968. Picture: Dudley Muir.

both for their land acquisitions, and for would-be purchasers of their new houses.[21]

Building societies moreover are not simply lenders of money, but increasingly have provided a home for short-term institutional money because of the attractiveness of the interest rates offered. In this way and because of the sheer size of the building societies' funds, they have become major institutions within the finance capital sector — a status which gives key figures within the larger building societies like Northern Rock the means to obtain financial backing for other commercial and business activities of their own.

The way this operates can be seen by a case study of the Dickinson/Joicey property interests. A detailed examination of the evolution of various companies associated with this dynasty demonstrates three important features of the post-war years:

1. The use of coal capital for property development, and for the promotion of house building for owner-occupation.

2. The integral links between on the one hand property companies and on the other hand building societies and insurance companies as sources of finance.

3. The manner in which initially regional operations have become subsumed into wider property interests, whilst at the same time facilitating penetration of the region by large-scale companies through access to local knowledge and conditions.

4.4B DICKINSON/JOICEY CASE STUDY

The Dickinson family (FT3) by virtue of their marriage links both with the coalowning Joiceys and with the Newcastle banking family of Barnett have occupied an important though largely unrecognised position in the transformation of the region over the last forty years or so. For not only have they as solicitors funnelled considerable amounts of Joicey coal compensation monies into other sectors, but they have also acted, through their firm of solicitors (now known as Dickinson, Dees), for many more of Tyneside's big bourgeoisie — handling wills, settlements, and trusts and forming new companies etc. — for institutions like Northern Rock and Newcastle Permanent Building Societies, and for companies like William Leech and Bellway Holdings. Obtaining detailed information about this general role is difficult and haphazard, but it is possible from available sources to be a good deal more specific about the Dickinsons' and other related families' interests in land and property development.

One important area of involvement was in financing in the early 1960s a series of land deals during the initial development of Cramlington where, unlike the other New Towns in the region, most of the housing has been built for owner-occupation by two building companies William Leech and Bellway Holdings (formerly North British Properties).[22] In a study

The links between Leech and the Dickinson family have remained; I.J. Dickinson (left) with Leech (right) in 1976 at the Gosforth Races to watch the Leech Homes Handicap Steeplechase. Picture: Harrison Photography.

of the Cramlington project, Cousins has shown the intricate tangle of interlocking shareholdings and directorships that existed between Seaton Valley Properties — the company that speculatively bought a number of farms in the Cramlington area in 1963, and then rapidly sold them off — and the Grainger Trust, a property and investment company that provided much of the finance.[23]

In 1960 more than 40 per cent of the Grainger Trust's 35,000 shares were either owned or administered by the Dickinsons or their firm of solicitors. Cousins points out too the involvement of at least one national property company Metropolitan Railways Country Estates, both as an initial (50 per cent) shareholder in Seaton Valley Properties and as a provider of unsecured loans.

The Dickinson involvement in property and in the wider financial interests that fund the property sector can however be traced back a good deal further to the inter-war years. The most important member was Robert Joicey Dickinson, who became a solicitor in 1927 and inherited his father's position in the solicitors' firm of Dickinson, Miller and Turnbull. Only six years later he formed the Junior Property and Investment Company with a nominal capital of £15,000. The objects of the company were stated with a precision that is generally less common now: *"to buy lands, house property . . . acquire stocks, shares . . . and generally to carry out business as financiers . . . as an individual capitalist may lawfully undertake and carry out"*.

Already outside financial interests were involved for one of the other three directors was Henry John Enthoven, a member of the London Stock Exchange, who remained closely linked in to the Dickinsons' other property interests until his death in 1976. As early as 1935 the company had entered into an agreement to lend up to £7,000 on mortgage to William Leech for various developments he was undertaking, and in the following year agreed a further advance up to £4,000 at eight per cent for the purchase of the Bilborough Gardens area in Benwell — the latter being secured by Leech's collateral of some 7,000 building society shares (including 3,635 in Northern Counties and 692 in the Rock).

From the list of mortgages taken out by Junior Property it is clear however that the main activity was in building up a property portfolio, for between 1933 and 1937 there were 35 different charges recorded for a spread of properties in either Tyneside (Sandyford, Longbenton, Wallsend) or in London (Battersea, Fulham, Wandsworth), including one for £36,000 from the Rock Building Society. A stepping up of activity commenced in 1937, for in that year Junior Property became a public company with a nominal capital of £100,000, and Dickinson and Enthoven — joined this time by R.A. Barnett (FT2), Dickinson's brother-in-law and partner in Dickinson, Miller and Turnbull — bought out a London-based property company, Roe Green Garden Village. The break into the big-time league had now begun for over the next three years (1938-40), the Equitable Life Assurance Company was brought in to back Junior Property with total advances of £158,000 (in three separate mortgages) secured on all the properties and assets of the company.

Apart from an inter-regnum of the war years, expansion from then on was continuous. Roe Green's investments included a long list of properties at Roe Green, Middlesex, several farms in Northumberland and two cinemas in Haywards Heath, Sussex, but from 1950 onwards — when the farms had been sold — a policy of amalgamating the accounts with the parent company Junior Property resulted in Roe Green becoming mainly dormant. The rapid expansion of both companies up to this point (and Junior Property in the 1950s) was made possible by a continuous flow of loans from two main sources; the first was Equitable Life Assurance, which by 1955 had increased its total advances to the two companies to £406,000; the second was the Dickinson/Joicey dynasty itself. Between 1945 and 1954 the third Baron Joicey either on his own or jointly with R.J. Dickinson advanced £102,000 to these two companies alone — demonstrating clearly the use to which some of the Joiceys' £12 million coal compensation was being put. Properties purchased in the post-war years appear to have been almost exclusively in prestigous central London sites such as South Kensington, Piccadilly and the City. Marriott explains the reason. *"It was already apparent in 1953 to those in the business that the demand for offices in London was strong: it was on offices and in London that the majority of developers made their fortunes. There had not been a great need of office building between the wars and Victorian offices, many obsolete, were ripe for renewal."*[24]

By 1955 the company had an issued share capital of £237,000, total assets of £750,000 and two additional

SELECTED DIRECTORSHIPS OF ROBERT JOICEY DICKINSON 1937-1975*

Educ: Harrow
Dickinson, Miller & Turnbull, solicitors, Newcastle (now Dickinson, Dees)

1937:
Junior Property & Investment (Ch 1947)
Roe Green Garden Village
Grainger Trust (1938)
Gen. Accid. Fire & Life Assur. (local Board)

1947:
Lambton Hetton & Joicey Collieries
Metropolitan Estate & Property Cor (Ch 1966)
Tyneside Investment Trust (Ch 1967)
Brandling Laundry (Ch)
C.T. Making & Sons
Rock Building Society

1957:
Carliol Investment Trust
Industrial Plant Co
Langbourn Investment Trust

1967:
Alliance Insurance Co (Ch local Bd 1975)
Northern Rock B. Soc. (Ch 1971)
Owners of the Middlesborough Estate (Ch 1975)
Newabbey Investment Trust
Ozenford Properties
Sir Isaac Pitman & Sons

*Since the list is intended to show the development and spread of Dickinson's interests, it only shows a directorship at point of commencement, and not when it terminated. For the most part in fact the list is cumulative until the 1970s when Dickinson began to retire from a number of companies.

The first office block to be developed by MEPC in Newcastle in 1962.

wholly-owned subsidiaries, T.I. Properties and Sunholme Developments. It is quite clear that, although its main office was still at Cross House, Newcastle, the company had already transcended any particular regional identity and was operating like any other developer — looking for properties wherever they were located that could be redeveloped to give the greatest return on capital.

The longer-term direction in which Junior Property was heading can be seen however in Dickinson's other interests, for in the same year he is listed as a director of Metropolitan Estate and Property Corporation (and several of its subsidiaries), a much larger property empire with an issued capital of £3.3 million; and five years later in 1960, all but 3,000 of Junior Property's 448,000 shares were sold to MEPC (six directors retaining 500 each), with Dickinson himself becoming deputy-chairman and shortly afterwards chairman and managing director of MEPC. (See Table of selected directorships: R.J. Dickinson 1937-75.)

This expansion of Dickinson's interests away from the region in the early post-war years was greatly facilitated by the backing of Joicey coal capital; for not only was it used to finance particular purchases, but it also gave Junior Property the solidity and respectability for which a big insurance company like Equitable Life was looking. By the time it had been taken over by MEPC, however, the London property world was changing. With so many developers muscling in on the boom, supply was catching up with demand. The big companies now began casting their nets further afield to the large provincial centres where the fashion for new shopping precincts and city centre redevelopment was spreading.

MEPC was no exception and began buying property in several cities including Birmingham's Bull Ring and Manchester. In Newcastle the key figure was Dickinson, whose intimate knowledge of the local market, and connections with estate agents like Storey Sons and Parker, enabled MEPC to build up quietly a large portfolio of properties in the city. The first site to be redeveloped in 1962 was Percy House which was let to IBM and Barclays Bank local head office; another was Sandyford House, which has since been sold by MEPC to the Tyne and Wear Council. The collapse of the office boom in 1973 led to the company selling off a number of its properties in Grainger Street, Bigg Market and at the north end of Northumberland Street. But it was not a total withdrawal, for MEPC, now the third largest property company in the country with assets of £564 million, still has an interest in the IBM building and has retained two important undeveloped sites on the west and east sides of Pilgrim Street; the former comprising a block of land between Shakespeare Street and High Bridge, the latter being a rather larger area bounded by the Bank of England building, Carliol Square and the bus station.

While R.J. Dickinson retired from the board of MEPC and from the chairmanship of the Northern Rock Building Society in 1971, the interests of other members of the Dickinson family in the property sector have continued. R.J. Dickinson had been joined on the board of directors of the Grainger Trust — the property and investment company actively involved in the early stages of Cramlington — by his brother I.J. Dickinson in 1955, and then by his son R.H. Dickinson in 1963, both of whom were solicitors in Dickinson, Miller and Turnbull. The links with the wider property world were not however dropped for by 1965, three

Sandyford House, sold by MEPC to Tyne and Wear Council. Picture: Ian Harford.

new London-based directors had been appointed including H.J. Enthoven, Dickinson's original fellow-director in Junior Property, and R.H. Sheppard a director of MEPC; and from the last returns (1974) four of these men have remained as directors of the company.

A fuller picture of the more recent activities of the Dickinsons and the importance of links with the building societies can be gained from examining the Northumberland and Durham Trust, a wholly owned subsidiary of the Grainger Trust. Two members of the family — I.J. Dickinson and R.H. Dickinson — became the directors of the Northumberland and Durham in 1964 (when it appears to have had few if any assets) and were joined in 1975 by a third member, Stephen Dickinson.

In 1968, the turnover of the company was a modest £6,611 giving a £5,093 surplus before tax, and the value of its properties and investments was put at £40,660. Two years later the profit for the year had shown a small gain, but the directors recommended its retention *"in view of commitments to purchase freehold land and properties for about £900,000"*. In the following years there was a spate of buying for the 1973 report put the value of the company's properties at £618,000, and profits for the year at £92,600; and two years later net assets had almost doubled to £1,214,000 with profits at £117,000.

The origins of the funds for this expansion is interesting; in 1973 £286,000 had come from the Grainger Trust and its subsidiary Broadpool Property and Investment, and a further £260,000, lent on the security of properties that were purchased by the company, had come from three different sources. These were firstly the Agricultural Mortgage Corporation (£40,000) on 400 acres of Northumberland farmland, secondly the Leicester Permanent Building Society (more than £100,000) on a whole series of properties in Cumberland, and thirdly the Northern Rock Building Society (£120,000) — of which R.H. Dickinson was a director — on a block of 38 properties in Chiswick, London. The further expansion up to 1975 appears to have been financed by Lloyds Bank for in July of that year a floating charge was registered in their name on the whole company and all its properties and assets.[25]

While the second generation of Dickinson property interests are on a smaller scale than R.J. Dickinson's in the 1960s — reflecting the crisis that has affected the sector since the collapse of the market in 1973/1974 — the same characteristics reoccur — the search for profitable investment wherever it occurs, and the dependence on support from major financial institutions with which the directors are closely linked.

4.4C INVESTMENT AND INVESTMENT HOLDING COMPANIES

Building societies and property companies are not the only financial sectors in which the families have become involved. Another important area is in investment trusts and general investment companies, and here the familiar coal-owning names reappear.[26] The origins of three of these companies — Waste Heat, Tyneside Electrical Development and Industrial Plant — have already been discussed in the last section. The Tyneside had become transmuted into an investment trust by the 1930s, but Waste Heat did not formally change its name to Carliol Investment Trust until 1948. Although all three of the companies had links with some of the families from their early origins in waste heat generation, a substantial change in the profile of directors took place about 1950 with members from the three major coalowning dynasties — Joicey, Priestman and Pease — taking effective control. This can be seen quite clearly in each case (date of appointment as director is in brackets)-

Tyneside Investment Trust
R.J. Dickinson (1947):
C.I.C. Bosanquet (1950):
Sir R.A. Pease (1950).

Carliol Investment Trust
Sir R.A. Pease (1934):
C.I.C. Bosanquet (1948):
R.J. Dickinson (1950).

Industrial Plant
R.J. Dickinson (1952):
C.I.C. Bosanquet (1952):
Sir R.A. Pease (1952).

Family control of these companies — Industrial Plant is now a wholly-owned subsidiary of the other two — has remained unchanged to this day, the only difference being that R.H. Dickinson and D.A. Pease have taken their fathers' places, and C.J. Pumphrey was brought on to the boards of all three in 1974 to succeed his uncle C.I.C. Bosanquet, who has retired in 1978.

The most obvious explanation for this organised takeover was that the coal-owners immediately after nationalisation were looking for suitable vehicles for investing some of the coal compensation monies that they would soon be receiving. From the minutes of the Ashington Coal Company it is clear that the company was itself contemplating diversification into new industrial sectors,[27] but it came to nothing, and the compensation monies were distributed to shareholders. Assessment of the claims took some time, but the minutes give an approximate idea of the timetable. In December 1950, Ashington Coal had received £1.5 million partial satisfaction in Treasury stock and half of this had been sold realizing £770,000. Exactly three years later the chairman of the company (then in liquidation) was able to report a final settlement of £5,033,150 to the last meeting of shareholders. The other two companies followed a similar pattern. The Lambton Hetton and Joicey Collieries were liquidated voluntarily in October 1952 and Pease and Partners in December 1955.

The historical record of the Carliol Investment Trust and the Tyneside Investment Trust in the early post-war years shows a big increase in activities suggesting strongly an inflow of coal compensation. Immediately following nationalisation of the electricity supply industry Carliol appears to have received compensation, for its assets suddenly grew from £353,000 in 1948 to £691,000 in 1949 without any increase in its issued share capital. With Tyneside on the other hand, which had moved away from electricity supply by becoming an investment trust in 1929 (and therefore had no compensatable interests), there was no such increase. Five years later however when the compensation money was coming through, the position of the two investment trusts began to change substantially (see Table opp). In the four years 1953-1957, the net assets of Carliol grew from just over £750,000 to more than £2 million, and of Tyneside from £366,000 to £970,000. Although there is evidence that some of this growth was fuelled by insurance funds[28] as was the case with the property companies — it is also likely that a substantial amount is attributable to an inflow of coal compensation, given the close family and directorship links that the new directors had with the old coal companies; and this is

MIDDLESBOROUGH ESTATE

ANOTHER company that has been transformed over the years is The Owners of the Middlesbrough Estate ("Middlesborough Estate"). Formed in 1886 by the Peases (FT11) to buy estates at Middlesborough and Saltburn and various shares held by the family, it had an initial paid up capital of £420,000. The largest shareholders were Sir Joseph Whitwell Pease, MP and Arthur Pease. In 1952 a new memorandum of association was adopted with several new objects inserted. The intention was for the company to become an investment trust with powers to carry on a wide range of businesses, and financial activities. Several of the Peases have remained closely connected including Sir R.A. Pease, chairman in 1954 and Sir R.T. Pease who is at present on the board of directors.

Over the years new blood has been brought in, reflecting the widening range of interests. The new directors have included Lord Rupert Neville, a stockbroker and director of Sun Insurance (in 1953), James Fewster, the chairman of a Hexham-based company, Fewsters, and several of its plant-hire and agricultural services subsidiaries (in 1959), R.J. Dickinson (FT3) in 1964, and R.H. Dickinson (in 1968) who is the present chairman of the company.

Middlesbrough Estate has therefore remained largely in the hands of the old coal-owning families, and in the post-war years has been diversifying into some of the growth sectors in the region. By 1952 the company had a major shareholding in the Cleveland Car Company, a main distributor for Standard Triumph and 12 years later this became a wholly-owned subsidiary.

The motor division is now the largest side of the business with a turnover in 1976 of £2.6 million out of a total of £4 million. A second area of activity has been in timber merchanting and packing case manufacture, which in the same year had a turnover of £993,000.

The other principal activity — which explains the involvement of the Dickinsons — is in land and property owning and development, which has grown in importance recently. Partly this has resulted from the sale of land (£250,000 in 1976) but it is also attributable to the company expanding the development side. The 1965 annual report refers to progress continuing on "property development schemes, which mainly comprise construction of a number of purpose-built warehouses",[30] and two years later net rentals from property had grown from £26,000 to £40,000. The most recent report (1976) explained that Middlesborough Estate had attempted to acquire Cleveland Trust, an old-established company owning a substantial number of properties in the Teeside area, but since terms could not be agreed, its shareholding was for the present being restricted to 29 per cent, although it was intended in the future that an offer would be made for the remainder of Cleveland's share capital.

CARLIOL & TYNESIDE INVESTMENT TRUSTS: INCREASE IN SHARE CAPITAL AND ASSETS 1953-1957
(thousands)

	CARLIOL		TYNESIDE	
	Issued Loan & Share Capital	Assets	Issued Loan & Share Capital	Assets
1953	340	763	300	366
1954	590	1113	350	476
1955	688	1701	450	793
1956	1050	1897	550	886
1957	1125	2069	600	970

supported by the large shareholdings that R.H. Dickinson continues to hold to this day in the two companies — 27,000 in his own and family's name, and 304,000 as a trustee (presumably for the Joicey Trust).

As occurred in the 1930s with families like the Richardsons and Armstrongs, the new outlets for the two Trusts' investments shifted away from the North-East. As the Tyneside annual report for 1978 puts it: *"In the early days North-East industry was represented by 23 per cent of the portfolio, but just as a large part of local industry has now become national and international in its operations, so the Trust's interests have become diversified throughout the major stockmarkets of the world"*. In the case of both companies, the 1978 reports show that a little under half (48 per cent) of their £28 million worth of investments were in the UK, with the next largest USA (22 per cent) and Australia (seven per cent). Typically their largest holdings now are in big multinational corporations and in banking and insurance companies, including several in which there are personal or family interlocking directorships. Comparison for instance of the 42 largest holdings held by the two companies in 1977 and in 1978 shows some interesting features. During the year shares in British Petroleum have been increased from 36,000 to 58,000, in Inchcape and Company from 22,561 to 33,841, and 72,500 new shares have been acquired in Guardian Royal Exchange — all companies in which D.A. Pease's brother-in-law Lord Inchcape is a director; and in Trident Television, the parent company of Tyne Tees Television — of both of which R.H. Dickinson is a director — total shareholdings have been increased from 314,500 to 732,500.[29]

4.4D WIDER FINANCIAL WORLD

A discussion of the Carliol and Tyneside Investment Trusts naturally leads on to the wider financial institutions with which the family members have become involved — by comparison with which Carliol and Tyneside are very small. The career patterns of some of those who have become finance capital professionals are shown in the curricula vitae (opposite). The Pease family is one of the best examples. D.A. Pease, chairman of Carliol, is also chairman of National Mutual Life Assurance and St Georges Assurance, a director of Alexanders Discount (the fourth largest discount house with assets of £368 million) and managing director of the large merchant bank of Morgan Grenfell Holdings. D.A. Pease's brother is Sir R.T. Pease, chairman of The Owners of the Middlesborough Estate and vice-chairman of Barclays Bank and many of its subsidiaries (see appendix). Their brother-in-law, as we have seen, is Lord Inchcape chairman of both Inchcape & Co,[31] and Pensinsular and Oriental Steam Navigation and director of numerous other major companies.

R.H. Dickinson, the chairman of Tyneside Investment Trust, has an uncle R.L. Barnett whose whole career has been in insurance and who was until 1971 Chief General Manager and

---

CAREER PATTERNS OF FIVE CONTEMPORARY FINANCE CAPITAL PROFESSIONALS. Source: Who's Who in Finance.

BRACKENBURY, Mark Hereward.
Stockbroker; ptr (invest. dept) Sternberg, Flower and Co. from 1967.
   asst cont. (ops), Braintree R.D. Civ. Def. (until disbandment).
   b. 1931. marr., 1 s, 1 d. educ. Ampleforth Coll., New Coll. Oxf. mem. W. Mersea Yacht Cl., Cruising Assn, Little Ship Cl.,SE Sailing Assn, Arts Cl., Buckstone Cl.
   Sternberg, Flower and Co., Capel House, New Broad St, London EC2 (01-283 3155). Stubbards Croft, Great Bardfield, Essex (Gt Bardfield 418).

Clayton, John David, MA, AIB
Banker. Director (1972), Barclays Bank (London & International) Ltd, 54 Lombard St, London EC3P 3AH (01-626 1567). *And* dir (1973), Central & District Properties Ltd; hon. trsr, London Coun. of Social Service. *Past Appts:* 1954 joined Barclays Bank Ltd. b. 1929, m. *Educ:* Wellington Coll., Berks; Queen's Coll., Cambridge. *Clubs:* Turf Club.

NOBLE, Ian Andrew.
Merchant Banker; jt man. dir. Noble Grossart Ltd from 1969.
   chm. Pict Petroleum Ltd, Edinburgh (1971); dir. Noble Grossart Invests. Ltd (1969); dir. Century Aluminium Co. Ltd, Sanquhar, Dumfries (1969); dir. Chilton Bros Ltd, Girvan, Dumfries (1969); dir. Edinburgh Ch. Com. (1969). coun. Highland Fund Ltd, Glasgow; coun. Nat. Trust for Scot.
   1959-64 Matthews Wrightson and Co. Ltd; 1964-9 exec. Scot. Coun. (devel. and indus.) spec. in matters connected with Scot. econ.
   b. 1935. unmarr. educ. Oxf. Univ. (BA). pubs. (ed.) 'Sources of Finance'. mem. New Cl. (Edinburgh), Arts Cl. (Edinburgh).
   Noble Grossart Ltd, 48 Queen St, Edinburgh EH2 3NR (031-226 7011). 1 Albyn Place, Edinburgh 2.

Pease, Derrick Allix, BA, FCA
Managing Director (1964), Morgan Grenfell & Co. Ltd, 23 Great Winchester St, London EC2P 2AX (01-588 4545). *And* dep. chmn, National Mutual Life Assrnce Soc.; dir, Carliol Investment Trust Ltd. *Past Appts:* 1950-54 Price, Waterhouse, Newcastle-upon-Tyne; 1955-64 mng dir, John Govett & Co. Ltd; 1972-73 High Sheriff of London. b. 1927, m., 3s. 1d. *Educ:* Eton Coll., Trinity Coll., Cambridge. *Clubs:* Brooks'; City Univ. *Address:* 2 Britten St, London SW3.

Pease, Sir, Richard Thorn
Banker. Vice-Chairman (1970), Barclays Bank Ltd, 54 Lombard St, London EC3P 3AH (01-626 1567). *And* dir, Owners of the Middlesborough Estates Ltd. *Past Appts:* 1946 joined Barclays Bank Ltd, (1954) local dir, Windsor, (1957) local dir and chmn local bd, Newcastle-upon-Tyne, (1965) dir. b. 1922, m., 1s. 2d. *Educ:* Eton Coll. *Clubs:* Brooks's; N Cities Club, Newcastle-upon-Tyne; Pratts. *Address:* Hindley Hse, Stocksfield-upon-Tyne, Northumberland (Stocksfield 2361).

R.L. Barnett (right), formerly Deputy-Chairman of Sun Alliance at the opening in 1976 of the company's new offices on the old Town Hall site in Newcastle. Picture: Newcastle Chronicle & Journal.

Deputy Chairman of Sun Alliance and London Insurance, the most aristocratic of the large insurance companies. Similarly C.I.C. Bosanquet has a younger brother D.G. Bosanquet who is a solicitor with a large London firm, and a director of Provincial Life Assurance and Provincial Insurance (the fourteenth largest of the non-life companies).

It is beyond our scope here to do more than point to some of the ramifications of the dynasties' interests at the wider national level, for to do otherwise would involve research and discussion of a whole range of further companies. A more particular problem is that there is a major limitation in the data available, for it has only been possible to trace directorship and other details where these are made public. Even from these however it is clear that dynastic interests have spread and been transformed in parallel with more general changes taking place within the economy. Thus the present Lord Wardington from the Pendower Pease family (FT11) is a stockbroker and member of the Council of the Stock Exchange, while the insurance broking business of Sir G. Wigham Richardson (FT13) has now become part of Wigham Poland Holdings a major firm of Lloyds brokers[32] in which Jimmy Goldsmith's Paris-based company Generale Occidentale has a 66 per cent controlling interest.

Another interesting example is John David Clayton (FT6) whose great grand uncle was John Clayton, the financier and Town Clerk of Newcastle who saved Grainger from bankruptcy. After joining Barclays Bank at the age of 25 J.D. Clayton became in 1972 a director of Barclays Bank (London and International) where he sits on the board with Sir R.T. Pease (FT11) and W.J. Straker-Smith (FT13). The company is Barclay's main money market subsidiary, and is responsible for raising large-scale financing for multi-million pound projects and loans throughout the world. Clayton's subsequent involvement in two property companies, Towbar Properties and its wholly-owned subsidiary Central and District Properties — of both of which he became director in 1973 — is interesting not only for what it reveals about his own role, but also for the light it sheds on the close links between property and financial interests that developed in the office and property boom in the 1960s and its subsequent collapse in the early 1970s.

Central and District first came into prominence in the 1950s. Run by two men John Rubens and Barnett Shine, who became millionaires, the company was actively expanding into Canada as early as 1957 and in the 1960s received substantial backing from Norwich Union and Alliance Assurance. In 1972 the company, with assets valued at £61 million, was taken over by Keyser Ullman Holdings, a rapidly growing merchant bank, which was headed by Edward Du Cann the former chairman of the Tory Party; then only 15 months later in July 1973 it was announced that Keyser Ullman was selling the company to Town and City Properties and that Barclays Bank was to take a 25 per cent stake in the Town and City subsidiary, Towbar Properties that would control Central and District. The move took the City by surprise because it was the first substantial clearing bank equity stake in a property company, and because Keyser Ullman had made the original purchase as a long-term investment. Clayton was clearly representing the Bank on the boards of the two companies for the financing arrangements for the deal — organised by Barclays Bank (London and International) and the merchant bank N.M. Rothchild — involved 35 banks and three separate loans totalling £97 million. It was in the words of *The Times* "one of the largest ever syndicated sterling loans deals in the domestic market".[33]

Keyser Ullman's explanation at the time of the volte-face in its policy — that it had become necessary to redress the balance between the group's property and banking interests — can be seen with hindsight to have been far more accurate than probably they, and certainly Barclays dared to contemplate. For only a few months later in November, the first of the fringe banks, London and County Securities crashed, bringing a crisis to the whole banking system. Only the agreement of the Bank of England and the major clearing banks to launch a

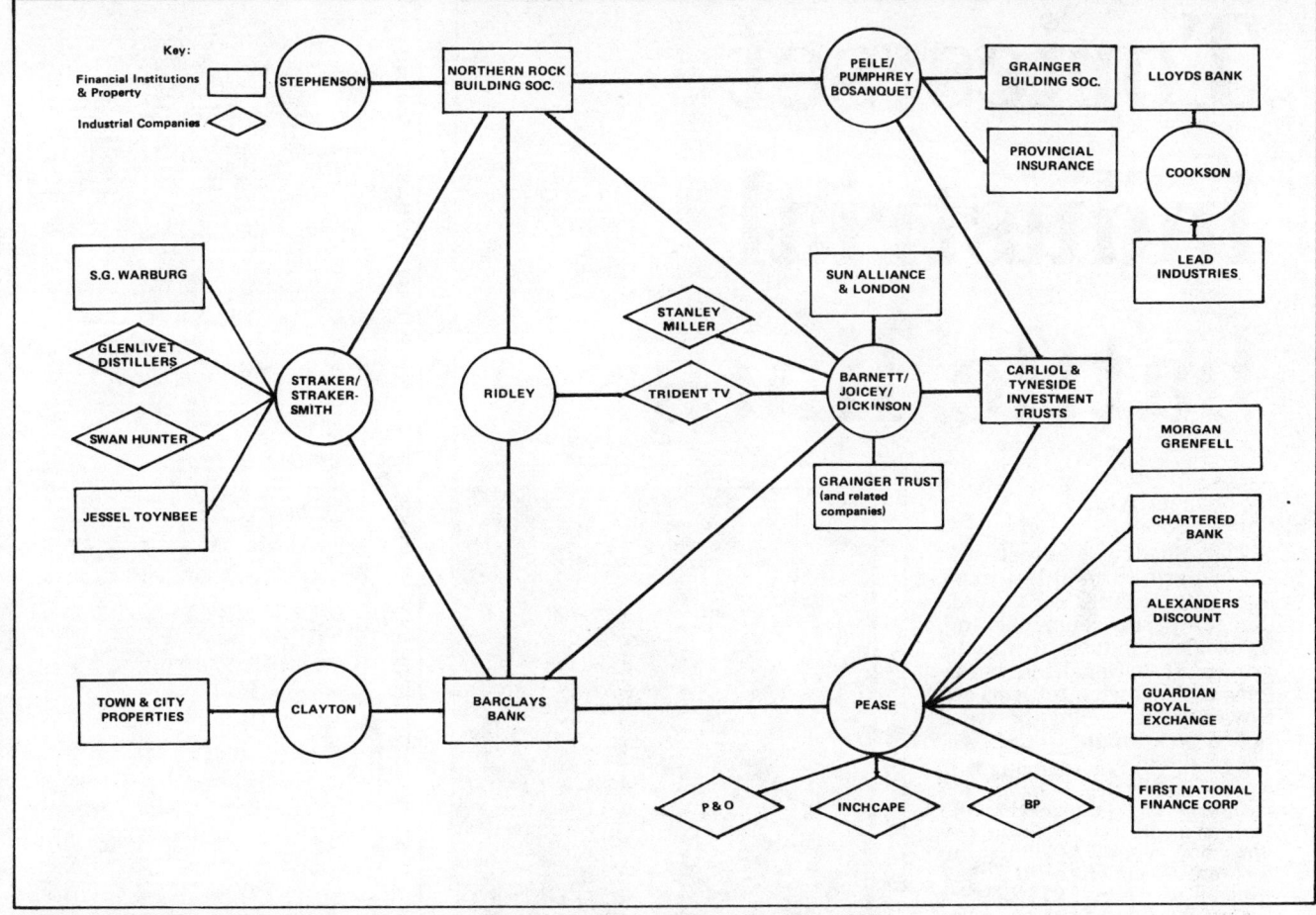

INTERLOCKING DIRECTORSHIPS OF WEST NEWCASTLE FAMILIES: 1978

"lifeboat" of £1200 million to 26 drowning secondary banks (of which Keyser Ullman, one of the worst affected, received £65 million) prevented a complete collapse.[34]

Although Keyser Ullman, to judge from its most recent report, is now largely disentangled from its property interests and out of the lifeboat — it showed a profit of £864,000 for 1977 — Barclays Bank and Clayton remain firmly entangled with Towbar and Central and District. Since purchased by Town and City in 1972 Central and District has continued to operate at a loss, although this had been reduced in 1977 to £71,000 (on a gross rental income of £34 million) from £323,000 in 1976. And just as in 1973 the banks could not pull out of the property companies without precipitating a crisis, so Barclays has to continue its backing for Town and City — a point that is underscored by the agreement earlier this year by Barclays to provide a £94 million loan for the long term financing of the company.

From this kind of evidence it becomes clear that over the years there has been a substantial movement of later generations of the families into key positions in many major financial institutions. This is not however to imply a growing divide between the industrial capital and finance capital sectors. Indeed the reverse can be seen for there has been a growing tendency for the big corporations and the major financial institutions to develop much closer working relationships (via inter-locking directorships, joint subsidiaries etc). Thus R.A. Cookson (FT7) a former chairman of Lead Industries Group is a director of Lloyds Bank, and Lord Inchcape (FT11) is a director of Standard Chartered Bank, the second largest British overseas bank.

The links with the merchant banks are also important; W.J. Straker-Smith (FT13), vice-chairman of the Swan Hunter Group is a director of S.G. Warburg, leading merchant bankers, who are at present advising Swan Hunter on the alternative policies open to the company following nationalization of its shipbuilding interests. The extent of this kind of interlock, and of the influence of the merchant banks in bringing about the growing concentration of the economy is emphasised even more clearly in the case of D.A. Pease, managing director of Morgan Grenfell since 1964. In the years 1971-1974 the bank was advising in acquisitions and mergers arranged in the UK involving 102 separate companies and total purchase prices of £1098 million. As one of the leaders in this field,[35] Morgan Grenfell was in 68 of the cases acting on behalf of the larger company that was carrying out the takeover.

Tories set industrial battle lines

By Michael White,
Political Staff

The Shadow Cabinet was thrown into turmoil last night over the leaking of a confidential party report listing, in order of industrial muscle, groups of nationalised industries with which a future Tory Government would be wise not to pick a fight.

As well as acknowledging that where industries "have the nation by the jugular vein the lonly feasible option is to pay up," the report, attributed to the radical and forceful Rightwing Tory MP, Mr Nicholas Ridley, considered the scope for widespread denationalisation in industries like coal, shipbuilding, docks, airports, car manufacture, buses and freight.

Picture: Colin Davey, Camera Press.

Nicholas Ridley MP; architect of the Tories' new hard-line industrial policy.

Ian Andrew Noble (FT10), nephew of a former President of the Board of Trade, Michael Noble, has been similarly at the centre of a network of financial and industrial interests, that have been closely associated with the North Sea oil boom. For in 1969 he launched with a young barrister Angus Grossart, the Edinburgh-based merchant bank Noble Grossart, backed by four major Scottish Investment Trusts — Scottish American, Scottish Northern, American and Ailsa. Noble Grossart was quick to enter the oil business and among the companies it helped to form or owned were Viking Resources an investment trust specialising in North Sea oil companies, Caber Oil, North Sea Assets, and Pict Petroleum, a consortium of 27 Scottish institutions backed by the Monsanto Deminex North Sea Exploration Group. Noble himself resigned from Noble Grossart in 1972 to concentrate on the development of Seaforth Maritime, another oil company based in Aberdeen which he founded in the same year and of which he remained chairman until 1976.[36]

4.5 RULING CLASS COHESION

Since the descendants of West Newcastle's old coalowning, industrial and banking families have become so thoroughly integrated within a wider ruling class, they can no longer be described as a locally-based hegemonic class. Many of the far-flung descendants of these 18 dynasties have probably never heard of each other. One example makes the point. The great grand uncle of J.D. Clayton (FT3) and the great-grandfather of R.J.L. Altham (FT18) both sat together on the same coal trade committee in the 1840s, but if their descendants met in the marbled halls of Barclays Lombard Street offices they would probably be unaware of the historical ties that bind their two families together. And the meeting might well take place since Clayton, as a director of Barclays main money market subsidiary, could quite conceivably be asked to arrange long-term financing by Altham, the deputy chairman of Rio Tinto Zinc Borax and a director of Rio Tinto Zinc, the tenth largest company in the UK. The common class interests remain therefore, but there is no necessary Tyneside or regional dimension that draws them together.

CAREERS OF SOME CONTEMPORARY MEMBERS OF THE PRIESTMAN DYNASTY. Source: Who's Who; Kelly's Handbook.

BOSANQUET, Charles Ion Carr, MA; DL; Vice-Chancellor of University of Newcastle upon Tyne, 1963-68 (Rector of King's College, Newcastle upon Tyne, 1952-63); *b* 19 April 1903; *s* of Robert Carr Bosanquet and Ellen S. Bosanquet; *m* 1931, Barbara, *d* of William Jay Schieffelin, New York; one *s* three *d*. *Educ:* Winchester; Trinity Coll., Cambridge (Scholar). Asst Gen. Manager, Friends Provident and Century Life Office, 1933-39; Principal Asst Sec., Ministry of Agriculture and Fisheries, 1941-45; Treasurer of Christ Church, Oxford, 1945-52. Fellow of Winchester Coll., 1951-73; Chm., Reorganisation Commission for Pigs and Bacon, 1955-56; Development Comr, 1956-70; Chm. Min. of Agric. Cttee of Enquiry into Demand for Agricultural Graduates. Hon DCL Durham; Hon LLD Cincinnati; Hon. DLitt Sierra Leone; Hon. DSc City. High Sheriff, 1948-49, DL 1971, Northumberland. Comdr, Order of St Olav. *Address:* Rock Moor, Alnwick, Northumberland. *T:* Charlton Mires 224. *Clubs:* Brooks's; Northern Counties (Newcastle).

HARDMAN, Sir Henry, KCB 1962 (CB 1956); Governor and Trustee, Reserve Bank of Rhodesia, since 1967; *b* 15 Dec. 1905; *s* of late Harry and late Bertha Hardman; *m* 1937, Helen Diana, *d* of late Robert Carr Bosanquet; one *s* two *d*. *Educ:* Manchester Central High Sch.; University of Manchester. Lecturer for Workers' Educational Association, 1929-34; Economics Tutor, University of Leeds, 1934-45; joined Ministry of Food, 1940; Deputy Head, British Food Mission to N America, 1946-48; Under-Sec., Ministry of Food, 1948-53; Minister, UK Permanent Delegation, Paris, 1953-54; Dep. Sec., Ministry of Agriculture, Fisheries and Food, 1955-60; Dep. Sec., Ministry of Aviation, 1960; Permanent Sec., 1961-63; Permanent Sec., Ministry of Defence, 1963-64; Permanent Under Sec. of State, Min. of Defence, 1964-66. Mem., Monopolies Commn, 1967-70 (Dep. Chm., 1967-68); Chm., Cttee of enquiry into the Post Office pay dispute, 1971; Consultant to CSD on dispersal of govt work from London, 1971-73 (report published, 1973). Chairman: Covent Garden Mkt Authority, 1967-75; Home-Grown Cereals Authority, 1968-77. Hon. LLD Manchester, 1965. *Address:* 33 Durand Gardens, SW9 0PS. *T:* 01-582 1757. *Club:* Reform.

PUMPHREY, Sir (John) Laurence, KCMG 1973 (CMG 1963); HM Diplomatic Service; Ambassador to Pakistan (formerly High Commissioner), 1971-76; *b* 22 July 1916; *s* of late Charles Ernest Pumphrey and Iris Mary (*née* Moberly-Bell); *m* 1945, Jean, *e d* of Sir Walter Buchanan Riddell, 12th Bt; four *s* one *d*. *Educ:* Winchester; New College, Oxford. Served War of 1939-45 in Army. Foreign Service from 1945. Head of Establishment and Organisation Department, Foreign Office, 1955-60; Counsellor, Staff of British Commissioner-General for SE Asia, Singapore, 1960-63; Counsellor, HM Embassy, Belgrade, 1963-65; Deputy High Commissioner, Nairobi, 1965-67; British High Comr, Zambia, 1967-71. Military Cross, 3rd Class (Greece), 1941. *Address:* Caistron, Thropton, Morpeth, Northumberland NE65 7LG.

Peile, George Howard, M.C. (1943) and bar (1944), yr. s. of Henry Peile, C.B.E. (d. 1935), of Broomshiel's Hall, Satley, co. Durham; b. 10 Sept. 1910; educ. Eton and Trinity Coll. Cambridge (B.A.); m. 1946, Rosemary Margherita Cecilia, dau. of maj. George Cecil Whitaker (d. 1959), of Britwell House, Watlington, Oxon; 1 s., 1 dau.; served in 1939-45 War with Surrey and Sussex Yeo., Q.M.R. 25th Field regt. R.A. (France, Italy and B.L.A.), ret. with rank of maj. T.A. Reserve; barr. Inner Temple 1932; formerly dir. The Priestman Collieries Ltd. and The Newcastle Brèweries Ltd. (asst man. dir. ret. 1956); J.P. (1959) Northumberland; Carlton and Northern Counties (Newcastle) clubs; Swallowship House, Hexham, Northumberland (Tel. 3591).

Peile, col. Henry Haswell, O.B.E. (1950), T.D. (1943), elder s. of Henry Peile, C.B.E. (d. 1935), of Broomshiel's Hall, Satley, co. Durham; b. 1903; educ. Harrow; m. 1933, Dorothy Weir, C.B.E. (1959), J.P. (1957) Northumberland, elder dau. of eng.-rear-admi. Hugh Sydney Garwood, C.B., O.B.E. (d. 1948); 1 s., 1 dau.; served 1923-31 with R.A. (T.A.) (France and Africa 1939-45), col. 1953; high sheriff Northumberland 1952; chm. Peterlee New Town Development Corp. 1957, and Newton Aycliffe Development Corp 1963; man dir A. F. Bell and Co Ltd; chm Washington Engineering Ltd; vice-chm Newcastle and Gateshead Water Co; dir Northern Rock Building Society; Army and Navy, International Sportsmen's, Northern Counties (Newcastle upon Tyne) and Union (Newcastle upon Tyne) clubs; Ogle Castle, Ponteland, Northumberland (Whalton 259).

The house and gardens of Clive Cookson at Netherwarden, Hexham; on his death in 1971 Cookson left his two gardeners (pictured) £500 each from his total estate of £399,000. Picture: Newcastle Chronicle & Journal.

The Northern Counties Club in Hood Street; few Tynesiders know it exists. Picture: Ian Harford.

NORTHERN COUNTIES CLUB: MEMBERS FROM THE WEST NEWCASTLE DYNASTIES, 1978.

E.G. Angus	Sir R.T. Pease*
R.A. Barnett	G.H. Peile
J.E. Benson*	H.H. Peile
C.I.C. Bosanquet	C.J. Pumphrey
R. Boys-Stones	Sir R.E. Renwick
M.J.B. Cookson	Lord Ridley
R.A. Cookson	Sir J.C.F. Simpson
I.J. Dickinson	N.H.R. Speke
R.H. Dickinson	J.S. Stephenson
R.J. Dickinson	M.I.B. Straker
Lord Joicey	

*Former member

Sources: Who's Who, Burke's Landed Gentry. Kelly's Titled Landed and Official Classes.

As family members have become absorbed into these wider industrial and financial networks, so others — though less frequently — have become significant political figures or taken up important positions within the civil and foreign service. The former role is illustrated by the part played in developing the Tory Government's industrial policy in the early 1970s firstly by Michael Noble (FT10) as President of the Board of Trade, and, secondly by Nicholas Ridley (FT14) as Under-Secretary of State with the Department of Trade and Industry. Ridley has made the news recently as the fiercely right wing author of a secret report commissioned by Sir Keith Joseph which outlines proposals for a new Tory Party industrial policy. Included in the report is an appendix which sets out a strategy for dealing with unions in the event of a major pay or redundancy struggle. This would involve the deployment of a large mobile squad of police and the use of "good non-union drivers" who would be willing to cross picket lines. Other proposals include denationalisation of various industries, and the cutting off of strike benefits to strikers.[37]

The Priestman/Pumphrey dynasty illustrates (see curricula vitae) the range of roles undertaken by members of the same family within both the regional and national state apparati,* for Sir Laurence Pumphrey has held senior positions in the Foreign and Diplomatic Service, and Sir Henry Hardman, formerly the Permanent Under-Secretary of State in the Ministry of Defence has been Deputy Chairman of the Monopolies Commission and Chairman of the Committee of enquiry into the Post Office workers ill-fated pay dispute in 1971.

Because of the small number of families involved, it is difficult at this wider level to do more than note these links between the economic and political spheres. At the regional level however as we have seen it is a different matter, for the old West Newcastle families have continued to play an important role in the economic and general development of the area; and in similar ways to the past they share common values and life-styles though their activities are more concealed than they were in the past, and their pronouncements more circumspect than those of their grandfathers.

* See also postscript p.121.

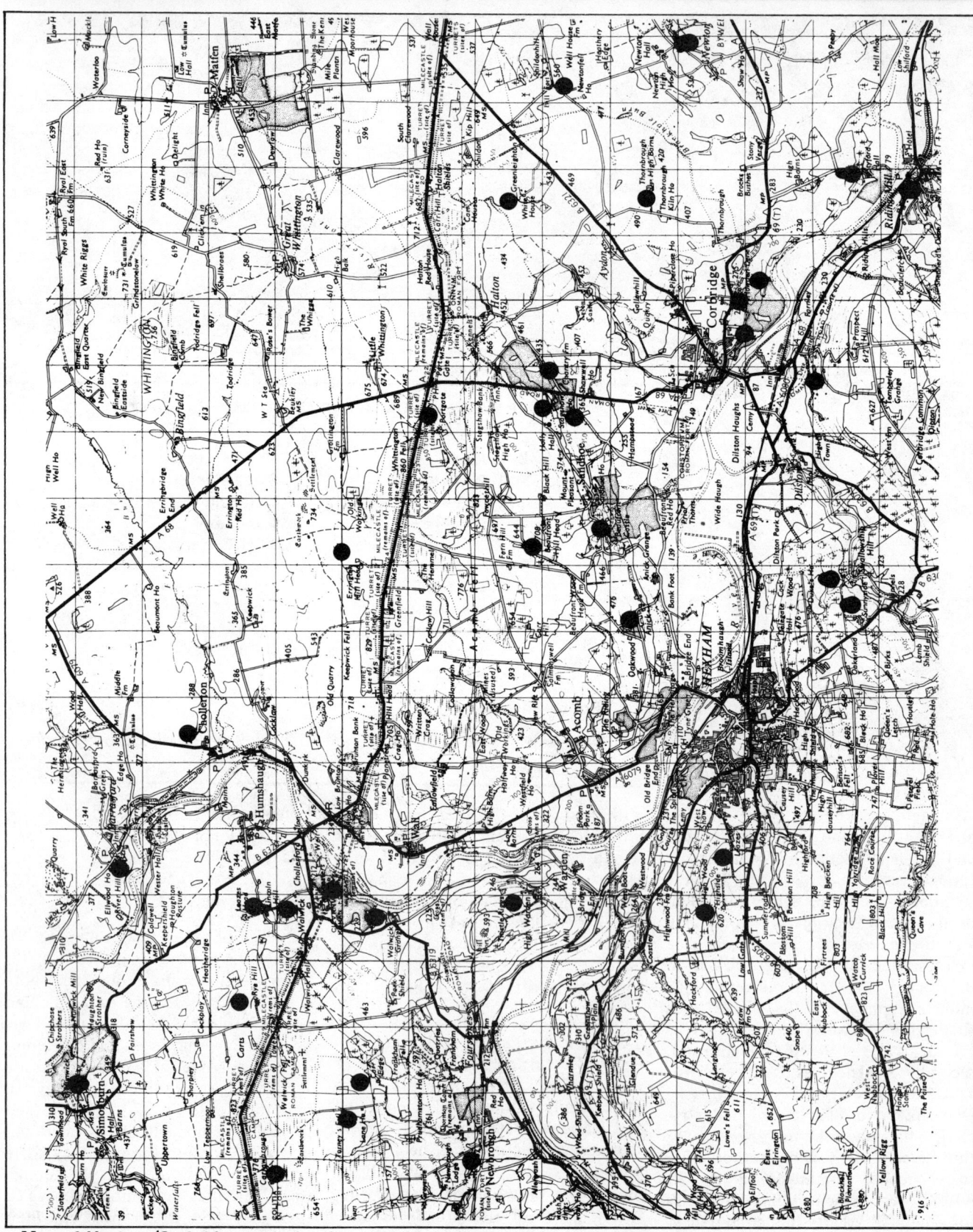

Map of Hexham/Corbridge areas showing residences of selected West Newcastle families (see list opposite). Map used by permission of the Ordinance Survey.

RESIDENCES AND ESTATES IN THE TYNE VALLEY OF SELECTED MEMBERS OF WEST END FAMILIES. 1978

Family Tree Number	Name	Address
1	ANGUS E.G.	Ravenstone, Corbridge
3	BARNETT R.G.	Chollerton House, Humshaugh
	BARNETT R.A.	Lincoln's Hill, Humshaugh
	JOICEY J.E.	*Blenkinsopp Hall, Haltwhistle
	DICKINSON R.J.	Howden Close, Corbridge
	DICKINSON R.H.	Styford Hall, Stocksfield
	DICKINSON I.J.	The Manor House, Riding Mill
	DICKINSON P.	Beech Close Farm, Newton
	DICKINSON S.	The Manor House, Barrasford
4	BENSON W.A.	Newbrough Hall, Fourstones
		Carr Edge Farm, Fourstones
		Carrowbrough Farm, Humshaugh
		Lane House Farm, Fourstones
	BENSON J.E.	The Chesters, Humshaugh
		Ryehill Farm, Humshaugh
		Walwick Farm, Humshaugh
		Walwick Grange Farm, Humshaugh
		Waterside Farm, Humshaugh
6	CLAYTON Mrs F.C.	Anick Old House, Hexham
	ALLGOOD L.G.	Nunwick Hall, Simonburn
7	COOKSON R.A.	Howden Dene
		Howden Dene Farm
		*High Edges Green Farm, Haltwhistle
	COOKSON G.H.	*Highfield Farm, Whittonstall
	CUTHBERT J.A.	Beaufront Castle, Hexham
		Beaufront Hill Head Farm, Hexham
11	PEASE Sir R.T.	*Hindley House, Stocksfield
12	PEILE G.H.	Swallowship House, Hexham
		Sunniside Farm, Hexham
	PUMPHREY J.M.	*Chesterwood Grange, Haydon Bridge
	PRIESTMAN Mrs J.L.	*Slaley Hall
		*Colpitts Grange Farm
15	BOYS-STONES R.	*Kyo Close, Wylam
	BOYS-STONES C.F.	Randle House, Corbridge
16	STEPHENSON J.S.	*West Mews, Wylam
17	STRAKER C.B.	Errington Hill Head Farm, Humshaugh
		The Leazes, Hexham
		Greenshaw House, Hexham
		Highside Farm, Hexham
	STRAKER Mrs J.J.	Stagshaw House, Corbridge
		Chantry Farm, Corbridge
	STRAKER Miss P.L.	Stagshaw Close House, Corbridge
		Portgate Farm, Hexham
	STRAKER M. I.B.	High Warden, Hexham
	SPEKE N.H.R.	Aydon White House, Corbridge
		Thornborough Kiln House, Corbridge
		Newton Fell House Farm, Stocksfield

*Denotes that property does not appear on the map opposite.

One important method of maintaining this sense of class cohesion has been the preservation of a separate form of education. The schedule of family trees shows how effectively this strategy has been implemented, for in almost all of the cases where the school is mentioned in records, it is one of the major four public schools — Eton, Harrow, Winchester or Rugby — to which the sons have been sent. Another unifying feature for those who have remained in the North-East is place of residence, for a large number of descendants of the old families have moved out to live within a six to seven mile radius of Hexham and Corbridge in the Tyne Valley (see map and list of names). Protected in this way from the mundane problems of city and suburban life, many of the male family members belong also to that most select and discreet of all clubs in the North-East, the Northern Counties Club in Newcastle's Hood Street, which intentionally has no sign on the outside to advertise its existence (see list of Club members). It is to these *"proper elite clubs"*, as Rex puts it, that local capitalist elites can *"retreat into and relax after the mayoral reception with its dropped aitches is over"*.[38]

The family members who have moved into the financial and industrial institutions based in the South, and several of those listed as members of the Northern Counties Club, have become members of the big London clubs. Of the nine most prestigous noted by Whitley,[39] the following have been joined by members of the 18 West Newcastle families — Brooks (six), The Turf (three), Pratts (two), Carlton (one).

Attending the same schools and patronising the same clubs cannot be taken, of course, as evidence per se of the cohesion or even existence of a ruling class, but when considered in the light of other family involvement in the region, they become much more significant. The domination of the regional economy by multinational companies and the growth of State intervention in the post-war years may have led to changes in the way that power is now exercised, but behind and within the new structures the families have clearly retained a major influence. It is the links outside the region however that locate this class power and family influence within a wider framework, and thus it is useful in the concluding section to discuss some of the more general questions that are raised by the Tyneside experience.

FOOTNOTES

1. See The Costs of Industrial Change. National CDP. 1977.
2. Guardian, 31 January 1977. "Is it time to break up the Giants?"

3. C. Kaysen. The Social Significance of the Modern Corporation. American Economic Review, May 1957. Quoted in P.A. Baran and P.M. Sweezy, Monopoly Capital, p.34. Penguin 1973.
4. Northern Industrial Group. Organisation and Methods. 1946.
5. R.A. Cookson. Interview with CDP. May 1978.
6. See for instance J. Northcott. Industry in the Development Areas: the experience of firms opening new factories. PEP 1977. In a survey of new factories opening in the Northern Region in 1973-76, 17 out of 32 were found to be concentrated in the New Towns of Washington, Peterlee and Cramlington, the remainder being scattered over the whole of Tyne and Wear, Cleveland, Durham, Northumberland and Cumbria.
7. In the period 1947-1977 the number of students more than doubled from 2,975 to 6,842 while the number of full-time academic staff increased at an even faster rate. The expansion has been made possible almost exclusively by State funding which is channelled through the University Grants Committee.
8. Collison P. and Miller J. University Chancellors, Vice-Chancellors and College Principals: A Social Profile. Sociology Vol.3, No.1, January 1969, p. 79.
9. CDP Interview May 1978. The informal contacts are as important as the formal positions on the various committees. Cookson gave two examples: the Professor of Chemical Engineering is a great friend of the local LIG managing director and Cookson himself, when he was chairman of the regional CBI was able to invite Henry Miller (the second vice-chancellor) to talk to a CBI meeting about his ideas for developing contacts between the university and industry.
10. English Industrial Estates Corporation's figures for 1977 show that in the Northumberland and Tyneside District, just over 50 per cent of all workers on EIEC estates were women. On some of the larger estates the percentage was even higher, e.g. West Chirton 55 per cent, South Shields 62 per cent.
11. Kings College. Rector's Report and Report on Research, 1949.
12. E.P. Thompson (Ed). Warwick University Ltd. p.30 Penguin Education 1970. See also F. and J. Wakeford. Universities and the study of elites, in P. Stanworth and A. Giddens, op.cit. for an interesting discussion of the links with industry in other universities.
13. R.A. Cookson remains today as a director and still has a large shareholding in the company bigger than any of the other directors. Its value at the current market price is in the region of £32,000.
14. State support for the company took the form of a £70,000 loan from Durham County Council in 1964, and a £100,000 debenture holding by the Board of Trade in 1967.
15. National Coal Board. Annual Report 1947. The royalty owners had received their compensation earlier under the Coal Act of 1938.
16. Minutes of the Ashington Coal Co. Northumberland County Record Office.
17. National Coal Board. Annual Report, p.92. 1947.
18. This process of the State bailing out the private sector is not restricted to the coal industry, for it happened again for example in the mid 1960s with re-nationalisation of the iron and steel industry. One company which did extremely well out of the deal was Tube Investments, now the second largest UK engineering holding company who used the £54 millions of compensation money to finance a major reinvestment and reorganisation programme. And now in the mid 1970s the story is being repeated with the depressed and technologically backward shipbuilding industry which became nationalised last year under the Aircraft and Shipbuilding Industries Act. Two Tyneside companies that will benefit from the compensation are Vickers in which W.G. Armstrong's Elswick and Scotswood Works were merged in 1926, and the Swan Hunter Group.
19. National Institute Economic Review. Table 10, p.65, 1975.
20. Bank of England Quarterly Bulletins.
21. It has also given the families added influence over Newcastle University. In the period 1972-1975, over £600,000 was advanced by Northern Rock to the University for the provision of student accommodation.
22. The local council, Seaton Valley UDC, has built some houses and in the period 1968-72 brought in the North-East Housing Association to build over 300 houses for rent. Formed in the 1930s, NEHA has or has had as directors mostly men from old coalowning and landowning families such as Lord Ridley (FT14) and R.A. Barnett (FT3).
23. J. Cousins, op.cit.
24. O. Marriott. The Property Boom, pps.15-16. Pan Books, 1967.
25. Links with the banks continue as with previous periods to be another important feature of the interlocking structure of regional financial organisation. Both the major banks historically associated with Tyneside have regional boards of directors, which in the case of Barclays has considerable executive power. The Barclays board includes Sir R.T. Pease (Ch) (FT11), Viscount Ridley (FT14), and R.H. Dickinson; the Lloyds Board includes R.A. Cookson (Ch) (FT7) and J.C. Blackett-Ord.
26. As well as the building societies, banks and investment trusts we might include here also a curious historical anachronism, the privately-controlled Newcastle and Gateshead Water Company, whose directors continue to be drawn from the West Newcastle dynasties. Of its £13.2 million issued stock £10.3 million (78 per cent) are held by 46 major insurance and financial interests. (1976 figures)
27. This did occur with the South Wales group, Powell Duffryn the second largest coal combine in the country. It is now a large multinational company with interests in engineering, shipping, fuel distribution and timber.
28. Cousins, for instance in his paper "The Cramlington New Town Company Structure", op.cit. – which points to the links between Carliol and the old coal companies – shows that in 1953-54 Carliol borrowed at least £300,000 from Commercial Union and that this figure had reached £1.3 million by 1965.
29. Playing the market in this way is of course greatly facilitated by the insider knowledge that comes from a seat on the board. Another aspect of this – playing the commodities market – can be seen from the accounts of Industrial Plant, whose assets included in 1972 £5,000 worth of whiskies' stock, and in 1976 £51,000 worth of copper wire bars.
30. For a discussion of the recent growth of warehousing on Tyneside, see Storing up Trouble, CDP Final Report Series No.1, 1978.
31. Inchcape is a general merchanting company with numerous interests particularly in the Far East. It is the thirty-second largest UK company with a turnover in 1977 of £1259 million and a profit of £94 million. Lord Inchcape himself holds either personally or through trusts just under six million shares in the company.
32. Wigham Poland was itself the subject of a major bid in April 1978 by the US firm of insurance brokers, Marsh and McLennan who have been trying to get a foothold in the lucrative Lloyds insurance market. The bid was turned down by the Committee of Lloyds.
33. Times, 11 August, 1973.
34. Sunday Times, 22 January 1978, p.63, "To the brink of ruin and back".
35. Crawford's Directory of City Connections 1977-78 provides a list of companies for which Morgan Grenfell act as merchant bankers. It includes some of the largest in the UK, such as BICC, Esso, General Electric, Imperial Group, Legal and General Insurance, Ranks Hovis McDougall, and Vickers.
36. Noble has recently become a member of the Scottish National Party and has been prominent in campaigning for the revival of Gaelic culture in Western Scotland. Tynesiders will be interested to see where next he redeploys the profits that his grandfather made from W.G. Armstrong's Elswick Works. Noble's original partner in the bank, Angus Grossart is at present (July 1978) in the news, found guilty with Sir Hugh Fraser and another director of Scottish and Universal Investments (SUITS) of failing to give a true view of the company's affairs to shareholders. A £4.2 million unsecured loan to Amalgamated Caledonian – a property investment company jointly owned by SUITS, House of Fraser and Noble Grossart – was wrongly described as "cash at bankers or in hand", and was never repaid.
37. See The Economist, 27 May 1978, p.21.
38. J. Rex, Capitalism Elites and the Ruling Class, p.217, in P. Stanworth and A. Giddens, op.cit.
39. R. Whitley, The City and Industry, p.71, in P. Stanworth and A. Giddens, op.cit.

5 Conclusion

Who are capitalists?

HAVING read the political correspondence over the last few weeks in these columns, I was struck by the heading "Only two classes" on W. Armstrong's letter.

I thought we were at last getting rid of the vote-catching element and down second place uses it to exploit his workers to increase his wealth without having to work himself.

Ten per cent. of 55,000,000 people in this country would make 5,500,000 of us capitalists. This must include every worker who "owns" a mortgaged house insurance companies and the pension funds of the employees of larger companies and nationalised undertakings. And their money largely comes from the insurance premiums and pension contributions of the workers.

So who are the capitalists?

Readers of the local press ask the question: Evening Chronicle, 18 Feb. 1977.

THE CONTEXT for this report has been the wider work undertaken by CDP in examining the nature of industrial and social change and its impact upon a working class community. From being an area that was at the end of the nineteenth century in the vanguard of the Industrial Revolution, West Newcastle has become the typical inner city area in decline; while the Northern region, which became known in the 1930s as a depressed area, and now is more politely described as a development area, still has one of the highest unemployment rates in the country. The emphasis of the study has been on the historical development of the area, but it differs from most histories in that it looks at those who have controlled the processes of industrial change taking place — the industrialists, coalowners and financiers — and what has happened to them once the ties with the area had been broken.

While the working class families of West Newcastle have consistently over the years experienced a pattern of poor housing and bad amenities, insecurity of work, high unemployment and low wages, the families studied in this report have undergone no such privations. Their fortunes have prospered, and their sphere of influence has extended far beyond the confines of Tyneside. While most people with the benefit of hindsight would accept that the families represented a ruling class on Tyneside at the turn of the century, the findings of the second half of the report on the present day position of these West Newcastle dynasties may cause more surprise. For contrary to those who have talked about the decomposition of the class structure in twentieth century Britain, this report shows that a capitalist class has continued to exist. Although the transformation that has taken place has made the class less visible, the positions of ownership and control still exercised by individual family members leaves them in a substantially similar structural position to that of the earlier generations.

It is true that the relatively independent regional economy at the turn of the century has become integrated within an economy that is now nationally and internationally organised, but the role of the old ruling class has been central to this transformation — through its active involvement in the State machinery that has encouraged the process, and through its direct participation in companies that have become major multinational corporations or significant parts of them. Furthermore, there is a clear pattern discernible of later generations becoming closely integrated within the finance capital sector, a pattern which has both regional and national manifestations. The control and influence now exercised over the main regional financial institutions by regionally-based members of this capitalist class is a reflection of this integration because local financial centres, which have a key role in the accumulation and circulation of capital, can now only conceivably operate by incorporation within a framework determined by a highly sophisticated central banking and finance system.

There are, of course, those that argue that demonstrating the existence of a group or class with economic power does not prove the existence of a ruling class. According to this view there has been in the present century a separation of those who wield economic power from those wielding political power or 'governing', and different interest groups or elites have thereby developed whose objectives and values are not necessarily the same. The evidence of the West Newcastle dynasties' much more limited involvement now as Members of Parliament in comparison with the pre-First World War years could be taken as superficial support for this view. But it begs the question about the nature of power that Parliament has, and the extent to which a government can act without the support of the major industrial and financial interests.

The emphasis of this report throughout has been on the economic level because we would argue that fundamentally power resides with those who have economic and financial control. As Aaronovitch puts it: *"Obviously the finance capitalists may truthfully be described as the ruling class if in fact the crucial political and economic decisions are taken by their representatives and in their interests."*[1]

It remains important, however, to isolate who it is that exercises economic power, for it is not uncommon to hear the argument that the growth of huge economic units has effectively muzzled the individual owner of capital. We would argue on the other hand that the significance of the growth of the giant corporation and large scale financial institutions is not that a ruling capitalist class has been superceded, but that in order to continue operating as a class it has had to become incorporated within the structure of these new institutions. As Baran and Sweezy put it:

"There is no implication in our description of the corporate paradigm that great wealth, or family connections, or large personal or family stockholdings are unimportant in the recruiting and promotion of management personnel — that, for example, the chances of a David Rockefeller's getting a job at the Chase Manhattan Bank and rising to the top position are the same as those of anyone else with similar personal and intellectual attributes. On the contrary, wealth and connections are of the utmost importance, and it may indeed be taken for granted that they are normally decisive. What we are implying is something quite different: that stock ownership, wealth, connections, etc, do not as a rule enable a man to control or exercise great influence on a giant corporation from the outside. They are rather tickets of admission to the inside, where real corporate power is wielded."[2]

A persistently critical attack on this position is to be found in a good deal of modern sociological writing, which Giddens has summarised:

"Most hold that the 'ruling class' which Marx (correctly) identified in nineteenth century capitalism, has today disappeared or become radically changed; and most are in accord that it is the expansion of the joint-stock company, with its attendant progressive separation of capital 'ownership' from managerial 'control', which is at least one primary factor which has undercut the position of the old ruling class."[3]

It is correct, of course, to point out that the sheer size of the large corporation with its separate (and often totally unrelated) divisions and subsidiaries stretched across the world has resulted in a separation of overall control from day-to-day management. But this does not imply that objective power and control has been pushed further down to the managers and technocrats who oversee the production at plant level. The reverse in fact is more likely to be the case as Whitley has argued in a study of the directorship links between the City and Industry:

"Although it is arguable that directors of very large industrial companies may not wield much power in terms of day-to-day administration, the increasing sophistication of financial control techniques and importance of major financial decisions which traditionally are the preserve of the Board of Directors, make it more rather than less likely that directors exercise substantial control."[4]

In the case of chairman of major companies, particularly where they have long standing connections with the business, this personal power is likely to be even further entrenched as can be seen with two examples from the West Newcastle dynasties — R.A. Cookson, chairman until 1971 of Lead Industries Group, and Lord Inchcape,[5] chairman of both Inchcape & Co, and P&O Steam Navigation, respectively the thirty-second and forty-fourth largest companies in the UK (*Times 1000* 1977/78).

Nor is the powerful influence of single families particularly unusual as Barratt-Brown has shown, for he estimated that in 1966 almost a third (38) of the 120 largest UK countries were tycoon or family controlled.[6]

A further point needs to be made here about the background and training of the men who hold the key positions in the big financial institutions. It is not uncommon to hear the argument that the boards of directors of the banks and insurance companies are purely window dressing; that they are full of titled members of no particular importance, and that effective power lies with the cadre of highly skilled and trained professionals who have worked their way up to the top through the ranks. Thus Anthony Sampson quotes the cartoon in an old Insurance Guild Journal showing a decrepit old man staggering through the office: *"No, that's not an accident claim, Clogg"*, said one clerk to another, *"that's a director"*. While this view seriously underestimates the importance and significance of the interlocking directorships between the finance capital and industrial capital sectors, it is also fundamentally misleading about the class background of the key executives in banking and insurance. The men from the West Newcastle dynasties who have held or now hold some of these key positions are "professionals"[7] in that they are career accountants, bankers or insurance managers, but there is no doubt about their social and class origins; and other evidence collected by Whitley suggests this is not atypical. In a study[8] of 27 large financial institutions — the largest clearing banks, merchant banks, discount houses and insurance companies and the Bank of England — he found that out of a total of 341 directors for whom educational data was available, 269 (79 per cent) were educated at public schools and 115 (34 per cent) went to Eton alone.

Unfortunately Whitley's work suffers from being a "snapshot" at one point in time only. The strength of this present study lies in its historical detail. Although it is frequently claimed that the class structure has fundamentally changed over the last 70 years, we have not, in undertaking this research on two centuries of capital development on Tyneside, come across any other historically-based empirical work that has attempted to look at what has happened to a capitalist ruling class. The gap is a major one, for there is nothing to compare with the Tyneside experience. We do not know in detail what happened to the big industrial capital of, say, nineteenth century Manchester or Birmingham.[9] In general there is no reason, however, to doubt that a similar process of adaptation has taken place as it has on Tyneside, and that the descendants of this earlier ruling class have moved on to key positions similar to those occupied by the West Newcastle dynasties. The need to undertake further research to substantiate the argument of this report is clear, but until this is carried out the more complete picture will remain imprecise.

FOOTNOTES

1. S. Aaronovitch, The Ruling Class. Lawrence and Wishart, 1961.
2. P.A. Baran and P.M. Sweezy, Monopoly Capital, p.29. Pelican, 1973.
3. A. Giddens, Elites in the British Class Structure, p.3. in Elites and Power in British Society, op.cit.
4. R. Whitley, The City and Industry, p.66 in P. Stanworth and A. Giddens, op.cit.
5. Lord Inchcape married into the Pease family. His grandfather, the 1st Earl, was chairman and managing director of P & O and was employed after the First World War to dispose of surplus government and enemy ships — the sale of which raised £56 million. His son, Viscount Glenapp is listed in Who's Who as having a "business career; c/o National Westminster Bank" which suggests that he is working his way to the top via a banking career.
6. M. Barratt Brown, The Controllers of British Industry in K. Coates (Ed.) Can the Workers Run Industry? Sphere Books, 1968. See also S. Lindstrom and S. Nordin, Vem Ager Storforetagen? Tidens Forlag, 1977. *This is a study of 20 "finance families" in Sweden, who control a large number of multinational companies and financial institutions.*
7. *In this respect they are not unlike other key finance capitalists. Of the present chairmen of 20 major financial institutions (the four biggest banks, the eight biggest merchant banks, and the eight biggest life insurance companies), about whom early career information is readily available, eight are bankers, three lawyers, three insurance managers, and two civil servants.*
8. R. Whitley, op.cit.
9. *Although there is evidence from unpublished work done by Graham Ive that a good deal of Liverpool's shipping and merchant capital has now become transformed into more general financial interests — see for instance two originally Liverpool-based companies, the insurance brokers C.T. Bowring, and the merchant bank Brown Shipley — or into major multinational shipping and trading companies such as Ocean Transport and Trading, P & O, and Ellerman Lines.*

Appendix 1
Family Trees

Slaley Hall, the home of J.L. Priestman in the 1930s; it is still occupied by the family (see FT12). Picture: Newcastle City Library.

1. Angus/Spencer
2. Armstrong/Potter/Cochrane
3. Barnett/Joicey/Dickinson
4. Benson
5. Buddle/Browne/Brackenbury
6. Clayton
7. Cookson/Cuthbert
8. Cruddas/Renwick
9. Lamb
10. Noble
11. Pease/Inchcape
12. Priestman/Pumphrey/Peile/ Hodgkin/Bosanquet
13. Richardson/Spence Watson/Merz
14. Ridley
15. Simpson
16. Stephenson
17. Straker/Straker-Smith/Speke
18. Surtees/Altham.

1. Angus/Spencer

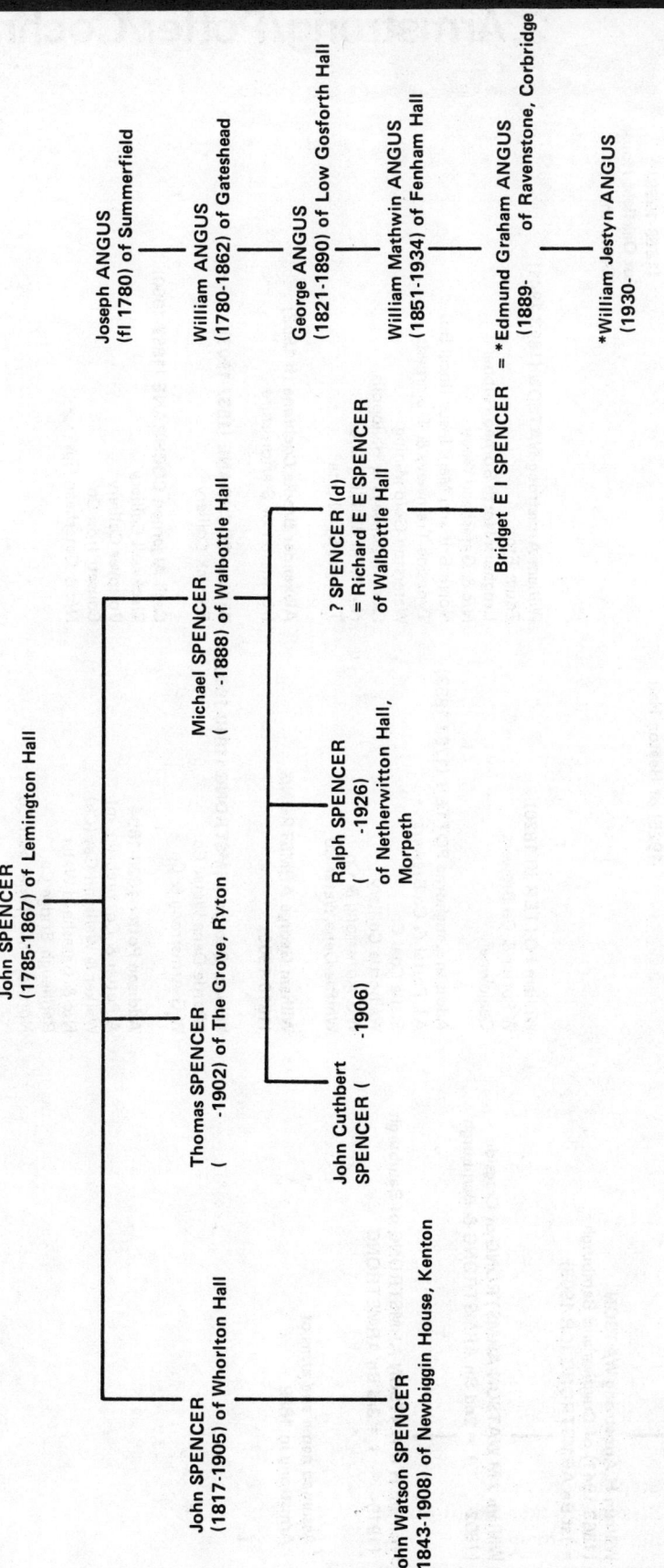

Joseph ANGUS (fl 1780)
J. Angus & Son, Leather works, Close

George ANGUS (1821-1890)
G. Angus & Co., leather and rubber

William Mathwin ANGUS (1851-1934)
G. Angus & Co (Ch)
N/c and Dist Elec Lighting
N/c Perm Building Soc

*Edmund Graham ANGUS (1889-)
G Angus & Co (Ch)
N/c and Gateshead Water
Moor Line
Tyne Tees Television
N/c Perm Building Soc (Pres)
Royal Insurance (Ch local Bd)
Lloyds Bank (Local Bd)

John SPENCER (1785-1867)
J Spencer & Sons,
Newburn Steel Works

John SPENCER (1817-1905)
J Spencer & Sons, Newburn
John Abbot & Co
Healeyfield Mining Co
Throckley Coal Co

Thomas SPENCER (-1902)
Consett Iron Co
Consett Spanish Ore
Throckley Coal Co
Tyne Coal Co (Ch)

John Watson SPENCER (1843-1908)
J Spencer & Sons, Newburn
John Abott & Co

Ralph SPENCER (-1926)
J Spencer & Sons, Newburn (Ch)

NB*Asterisk by name on all family trees indicates that the person is still alive.

2. Armstrong/Potter/Cochrane

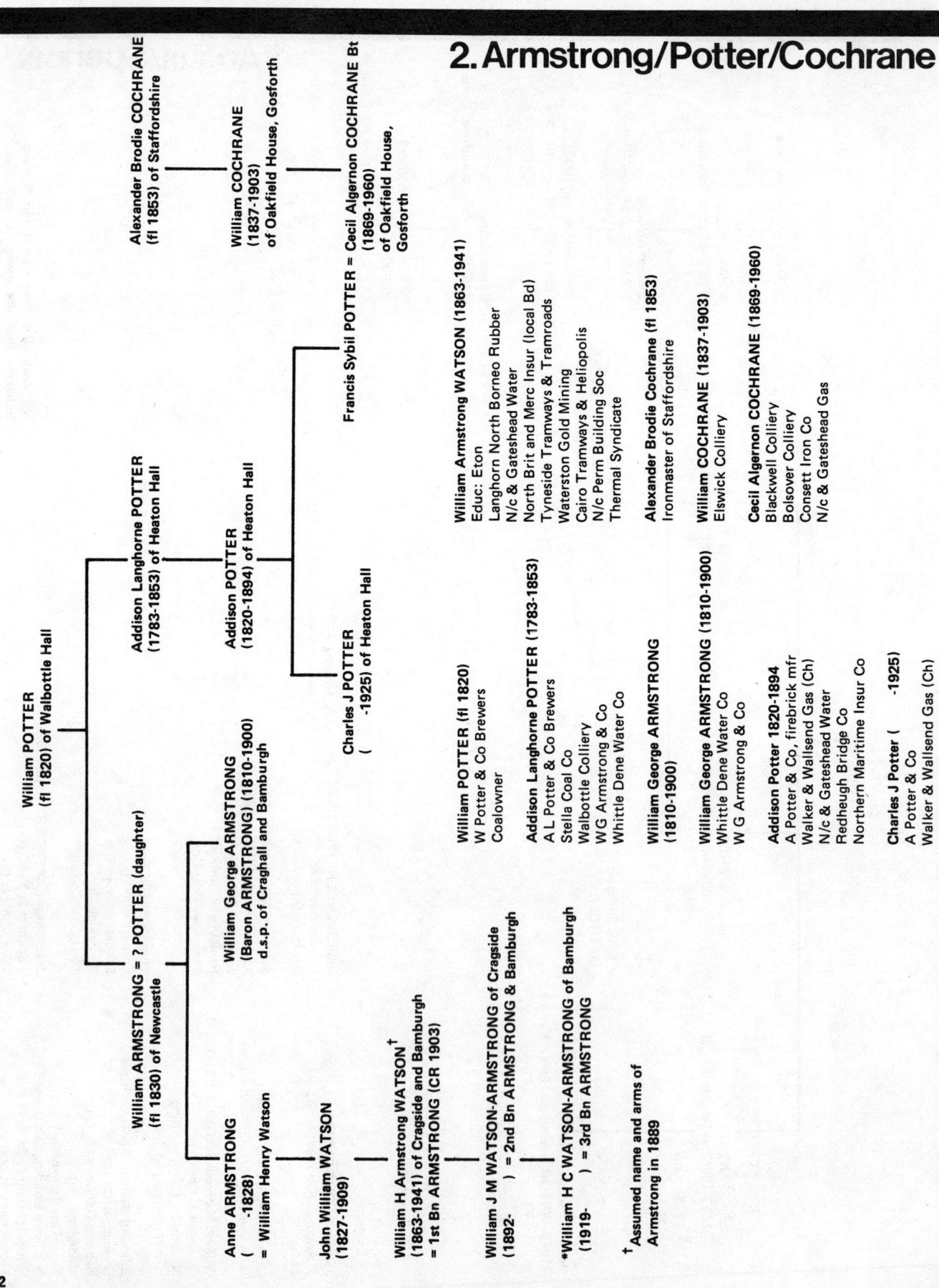

William POTTER (fl 1820) of Walbottle Hall
- W Potter & Co Brewers
- Coalowner

Addison Langhorne POTTER (1783-1853)
- A L Potter & Co Brewers
- Stella Coal Co
- Walbottle Colliery
- W G Armstrong & Co
- Whittle Dene Water Co

William George ARMSTRONG (1810-1900)
- Whittle Dene Water Co
- W G Armstrong & Co

Addison Potter 1820-1894
- A Potter & Co, firebrick mfr
- Walker & Wallsend Gas (Ch)
- N/c & Gateshead Water
- Redheugh Bridge Co
- Northern Maritime Insur Co

Charles J Potter (-1925)
- A Potter & Co
- Walker & Wallsend Gas (Ch)

William Armstrong WATSON (1863-1941)
- Educ: Eton
- Langhorn North Borneo Rubber
- N/c & Gateshead Water
- North Brit and Merc Insur (local Bd)
- Tyneside Tramways & Tramroads
- Waterston Gold Mining
- Cairo Tramways & Heliopolis
- N/c Perm Building Soc
- Thermal Syndicate

Alexander Brodie Cochrane (fl 1853)
- Ironmaster of Staffordshire

William COCHRANE (1837-1903)
- Elswick Colliery

Cecil Algernon COCHRANE (1869-1960)
- Blackwell Colliery
- Bolsover Colliery
- Consett Iron Co
- N/c & Gateshead Gas

† Assumed name and arms of Armstrong in 1889

3. Joicey/Barnett/Dickinson

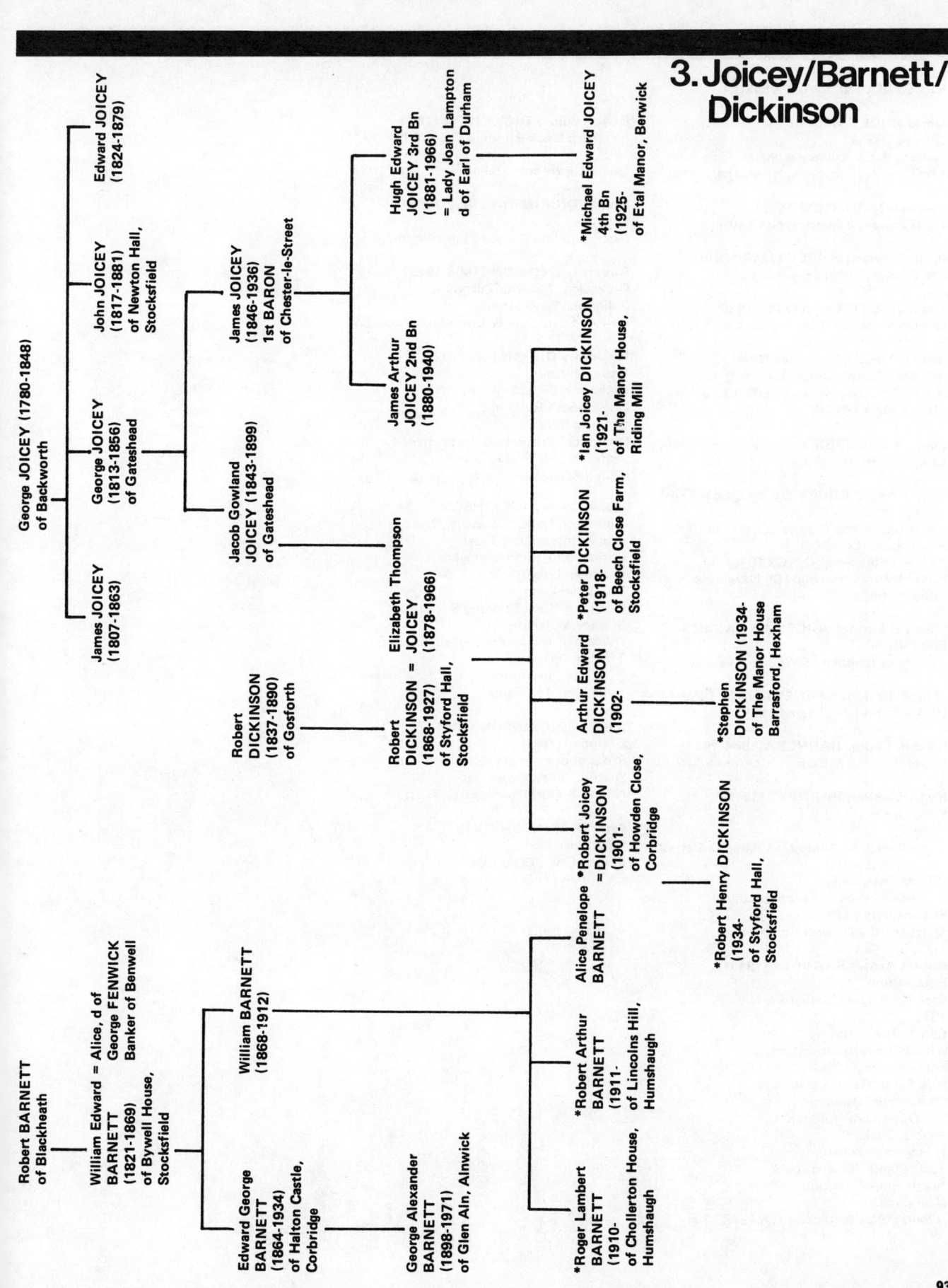

JOICEY/BARNETT/DICKINSON

James JOICEY (1807-1863)
Colliery viewer
J Joicey & Co, colliery owners
J & G Joicey, Engineers, Newcastle

George JOICEY (1813-1856)
J & G Joicey, Engineers, Newcastle

Jacob Gowland JOICEY (1843-1899)
J & G Joicey, Engineers (Mng Ch)

James JOICEY 1st Bn (1846-1936)
Lambton, Hetton & Joicey Collieries (Ch)
North Eastern Railway
Mining Assoc, of GB (Pres 1904)
N/c Chamber of Commerce (Pres)
N/c Daily Leader (owner 1885-1903)
Liberal MP 1885-1906

James Arthur JOICEY 2nd Bn (1880-1940)
Lambton, Hetton & Joicey Collieries

Hugh Edward JOICEY 3rd Bn (1881-1966)
Educ: Harrow
Lambton Hetton & Joicey Collieries (Ch)
Albyn Line (Ch 1940)
Tanfield Steamship Co (Ch 1940)
Royal Insurance Group (Ch Newcastle
  Board 1940)

*****Michael Edward JOICEY 4th Bn (1925-**
Educ: Eton
Very large landowner, Wooler area

William Edward BARNETT (1821-1869)
Hodgkin, Barnett, Pease Bank, N/c

Edward George BARNETT (1864-1934)
Hoyle, Robson & Barnett, Colour makers

*****Roger Lambert BARNETT (1910-**
Educ: Eton
1976:
Sun Alliance & London Ins (Mngr & Dep Ch)
Alliance Assurance
London Assurance
Sun Alliance and London Assurance
Sun Insurance Office
Master of the Drapers Company

*****Robert Arthur BARNETT (1911-**
Educ: Eton
Dickinson, Dees, Solicitors, N/c
1975:
Carr-Ellison Estates
William Leech Foundation
William Leech Charity
Roe Green Garden Village
Cross House Buildings
Lee Dagenham Holdings
Smiths Docks Co
W Harriman & Co
East N'land Housing Assoc
North Housing Group
N'land cllr
N'land Police Authority (Ch 1969-73)

*****Robert Joicey DICKINSON (1901-**
Northern Rock Building Society (Ch 1971)
  etc
(see separate comprehensive list for 1937-75,
                                   page 76)

Robert DICKINSON (1837-1890)
Solicitor
Rock Building Society. 1st solicitor

Robert DICKINSON (1868-1927)
Dickinson, Miller & Turnbull,
Solicitors, Newcastle
Gen Accident Fire & Life Assur (local bd)

*****Ian Joicey DICKINSON (1921-**
Educ: Harrow
Dickinson Dees, Solicitors, N/c
Cross House Buildings
Grainger Trust
Broadpool Property & Investment Co
Seaton Valley Properties
N'land & Durham Property Trust

*****Robert Henry DICKINSON (1934-**
Dickinson Dees, Solicitors, N/c
Carliol Investment Trust
Carliol Unit Fund Managers
Grainger Trust
Industrial Plant
Northern Rock Building Society
Stanley Miller Holdings
Owners of the Middlesborough Estate
Trident Television
Tyneside Investment Trust
Tyne Tees Television

*****Stephen DICKINSON (1934-**
Grainger Trust
Broadpool Property & Investment
Seaton Valley Properties
N'land & Durham Property Trust

*****Peter DICKINSON (1918-**
Educ: Harrow
Smiths Gore, Corbridge,
Ch Surveyors & Land Agents

4. Benson

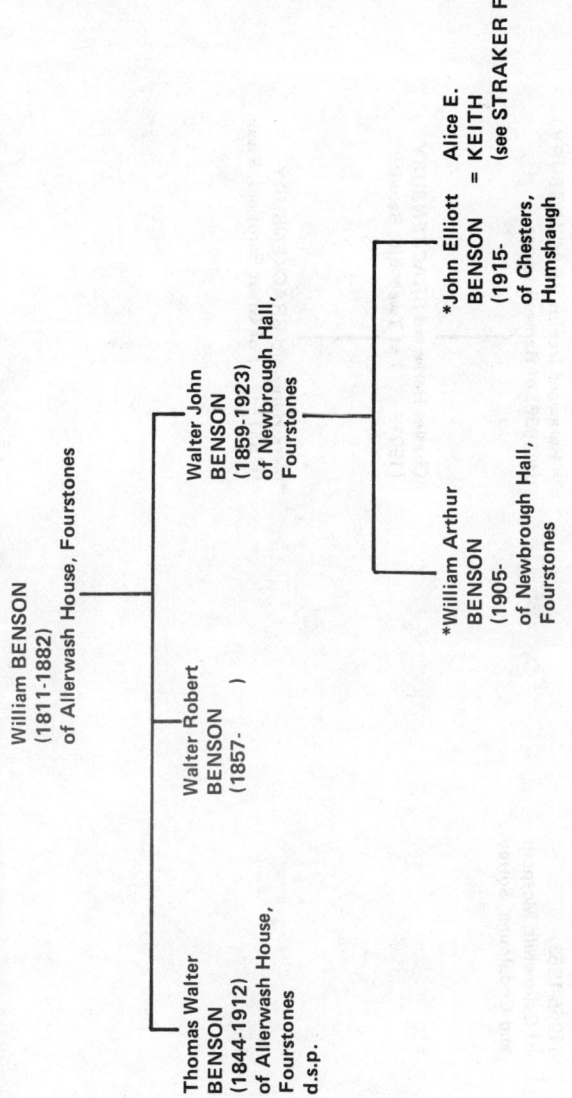

William BENSON (1811-1882)
of Allerwash House, Fourstones

Thomas Walter BENSON (1844-1912) of Allerwash House, Fourstones d.s.p.

Walter Robert BENSON (1857-)

Walter John BENSON (1859-1923) of Newbrough Hall, Fourstones

*William Arthur BENSON (1905-) of Newbrough Hall, Fourstones

*John Elliott BENSON (1915-) of Chesters, Humshaugh = Alice E. KEITH (see STRAKER FT)

William BENSON (1811-1882)
W Benson & Sons (Founding owner)
— mining and quarrying Co, Fourstones
Montague Colliery, Scotswood (1st lease 1857)
Steam ship owner (1871)

Thomas Walter BENSON (1844-1912)
T W Benson & Co, Firebricks, Bells Close (1873)
W Benson & Sons (owners of collieries and limeworks)
N'land Coalowners Assoc (mem)
N E Inst of Mining (Pres 1904-06)

Walter John BENSON (1859-1923)
W Benson & Sons (Mng Dr 1920)
N'land Coalowners Assoc (mem)
High Sheriff, N'land 1916

*William Arthur BENSON (1905-)
Educ: Eton
W Benson & Son (Main shldr 1925)
High Gosforth Park Co
Large landowner — Fourstones area
High Sheriff N'land 1951

*John Elliott BENSON (1915-)
Educ: Eton
Large landowner — Humshaugh area
High Sheriff, N'land

5. Buddle/Browne/Brackenbury

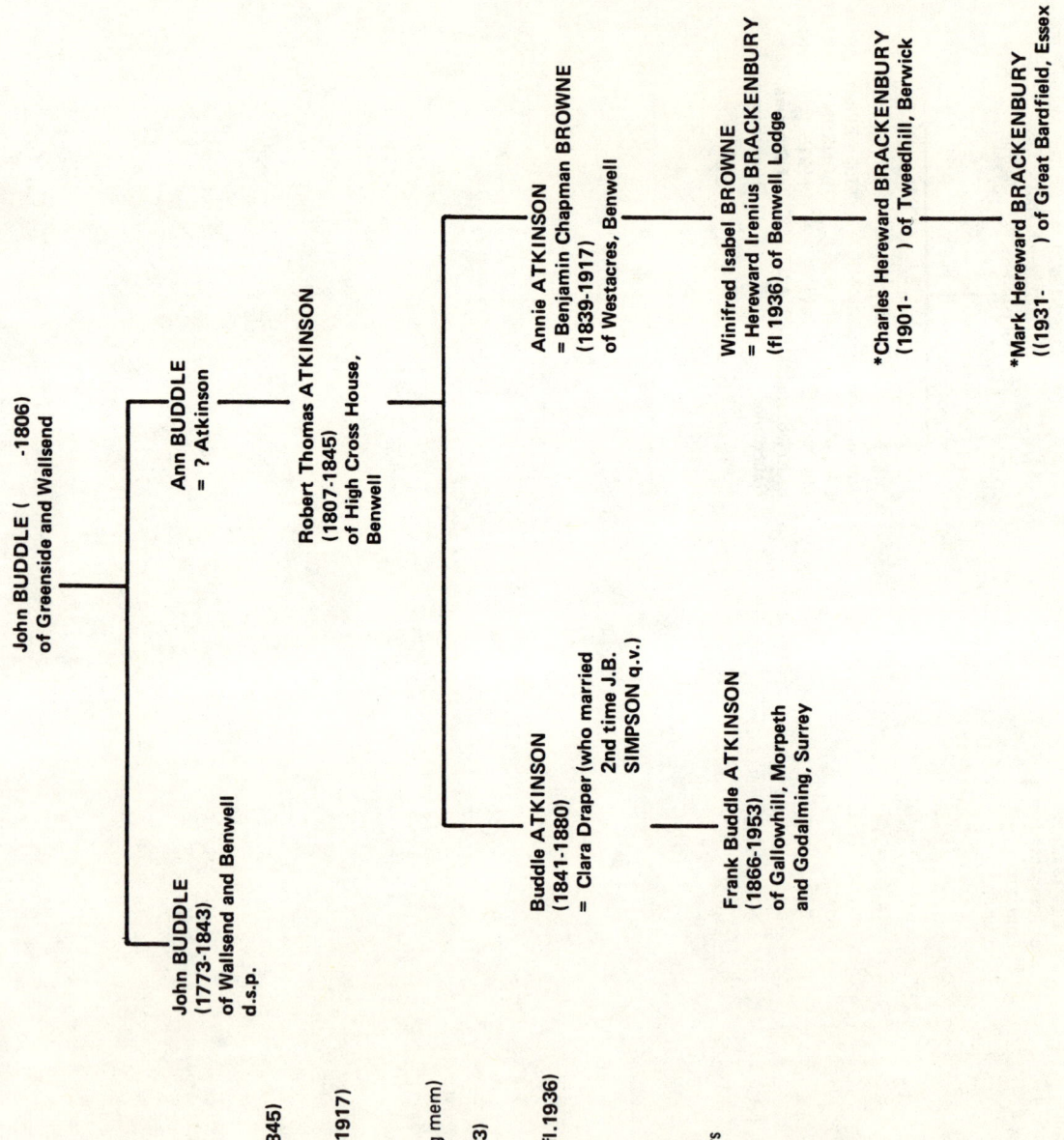

John BUDDLE (-1806)
Viewer of Wallsend Colliery

John BUDDLE (1773-1843)
Viewer Wallsend Colliery
Benwell Colliery
Stella Colliery
Coal Owners' Committee (Sec)
Owner of S Benwell Estate

Robert Thomas ATKINSON (-1845)
Stella Coal

Benjamin Chapman BROWNE (1839-1917)
R & W Hawthorn Leslie (Ch)
N/c and District Elec Lighting
N Brit & Mercantile Insur (local bd)
Engineering Employers Fedn (founding mem)

Frank Buddle ATKINSON (1866-1953)
Stella Coal (Ch)

Hereward Irenius BRACKENBURY (fl.1936)
N/c & Dist Elec Lighting
R & W Hawthorn, Leslie
British Automatic Refrigerators

*Charles Hereward BRACKENBURY
(1901-
CH Brackenbury & Partners, Engineers
R & W Hawthorn, Leslie

*Mark Hereward BRACKENBURY
(1931-
Sternberg, Flower & Co Stockbrokers

6. Clayton

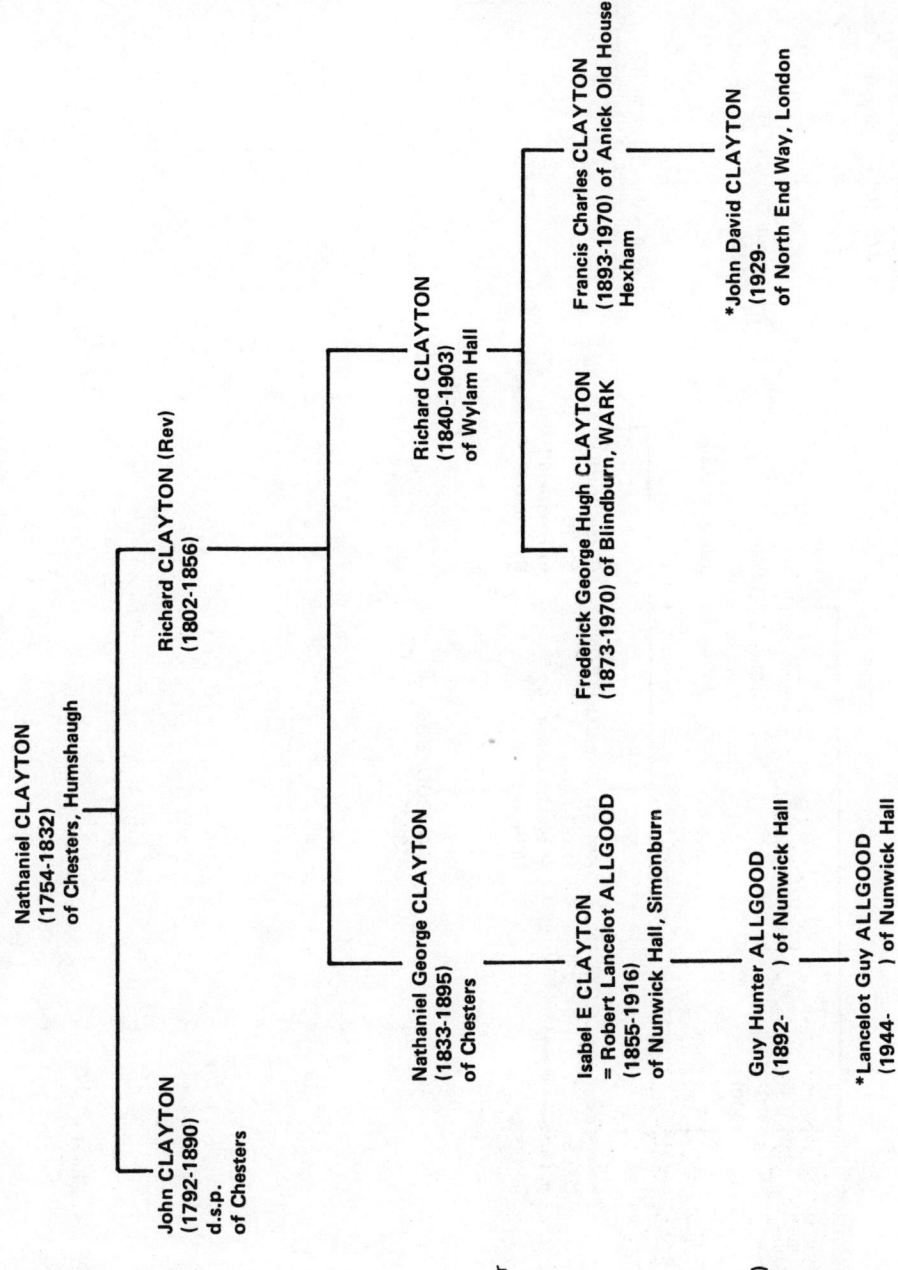

Nathaniel CLAYTON (1754-1832)
Solicitor, Town Clerk of N/c 1789-1822
Owned Chesters estate

John CLAYTON (1792-1890)
Solicitor of Clayton & Gibson
Town Clerk of N/c 1822-1867
Legal adviser and financial backer to Richard Grainger, N/c city centre developer
Stella royalty owner (lease from Bishop of Durham 1830)
Heddon royalty owner 1860 (with brother Matthew)
North Brit & Merc Insur Co
Large landowner — 11,000 acres

Rev Richard CLAYTON (1802-1856)
Master of St Mary Magdalene Hospital (under patronage)
"Head of religious and philanthropic movements" in Newcastle

Nathaniel George CLAYTON (1833-1895)
Educ: Harrow
Solicitor of Clayton & Gibson
N/c Daily Journal (Ch 1867-1895)
North British & Merc Ins Co
High Sheriff 1895
MP for Hexham

Richard CLAYTON (1840-1903)
Woods & Co, Bankers, Newcastle
Barclays Bank

Frederick George Hugh CLAYTON (1873-1946)
Barclays Bank (-1946)

Francis Charles CLAYTON (1893-1970)
Educ: Harrow
Barclays Bank (local bd - Ch 1963)

*John David CLAYTON (1929-)
Educ: Wellington
Barclays Bank (London & International)
Central and District Properties
Towbar Properties

7. Cookson/Cuthbert

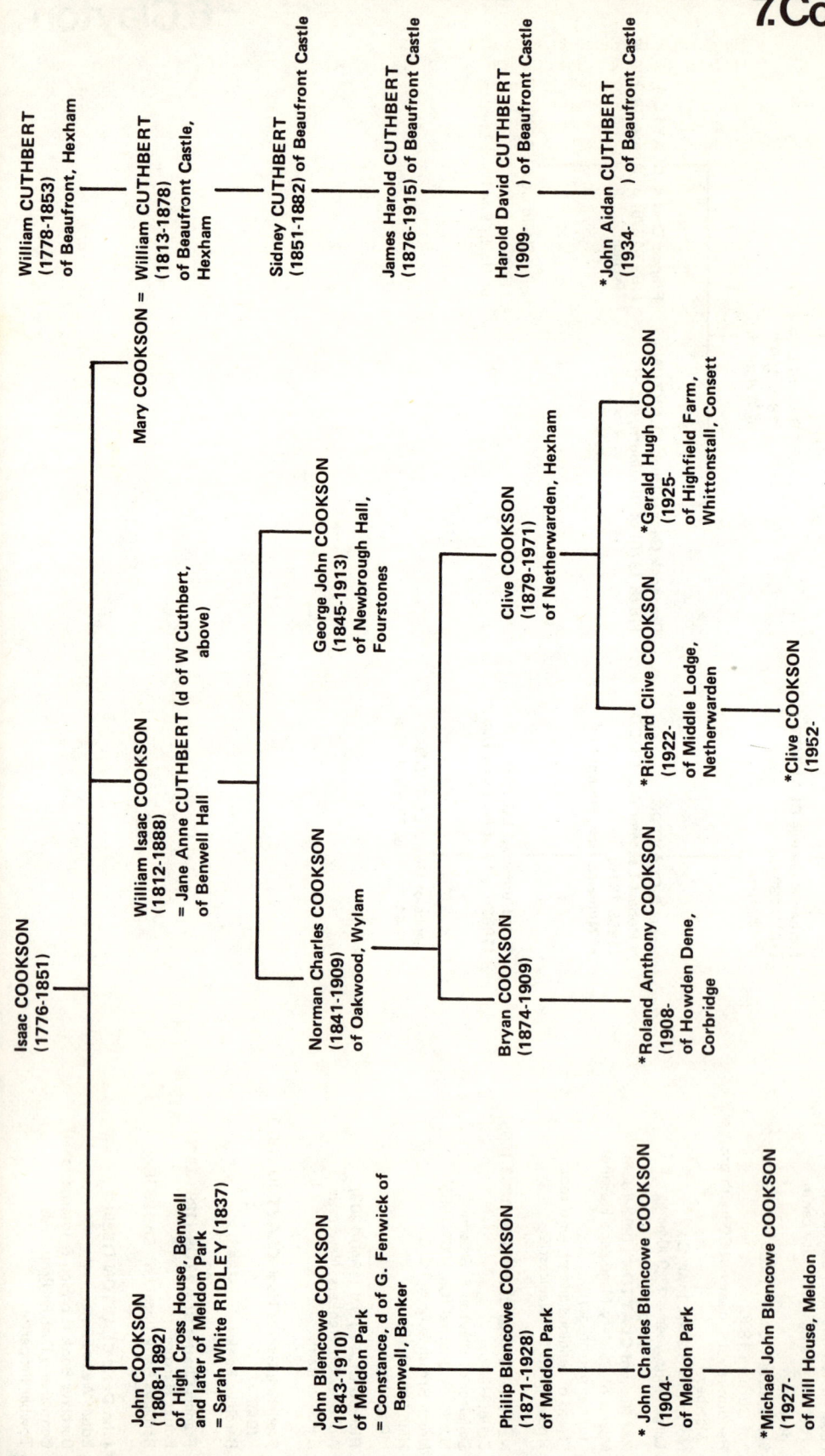

COOKSON/CUTHBERT

Isaac COOKSON (1776-1851)
Banker and Industrialist
Steel and Brass Foundry. (Close) 1778
Glass Warehouse (Close)
North Elswick & Montagu Collieries
  (lessee)

John COOKSON (1808-1892)
W.I. Cookson & Co (lead mfrs)
Mickley Coal Company

William Isaac COOKSON (1812-1888)
William Cookson & Co (Forth Banks) 1845
W I Cookson & Co (Forth Banks, Gateshead
  and Willington Quay)

John Blencowe COOKSON (1843-
High Gosforth Park Company (V Ch)

John Charles Blencowe COOKSON (1904-
Educ: Eton
Acomb Coal Co
Wm Benson & Son (Scotswood Colliery)
Cowpen Coal Co
Hazlerigg and Burradon Coal Co
Mickley Coal Company

*****Michael John Blencowe COOKSON (1927-**
Educ: Eton
High Sheriff, N'land 1977

William CUTHBERT (1778-1853)
Montagu Colliery (lessee)

William CUTHBERT (1813-1878)
Mickley and Prudhoe Colliery Co
Cookson, Cuthbert & Co

James Harold CUTHBERT (1876-1915)
Educ: Eton
High Sheriff, N'land 1911

Norman Charles COOKSON (1842-1909)
Cookson & Co (lead mfrs)
Wallsend and Hebburn Coal Co
Parsons Marine Steam Turbine Co
W C Gibson & Co (Ch 1895-1903)
  (Later Adamsez)

George John COOKSON (1845-1913)
Educ: Charterhouse
Cookson and Company

Clive COOKSON (1879-1971)
Educ: Harrow
Federation of British Industries (V-Pres)
Cookson and Co (Ch)
Associated Lead Mfg (Ch)
Cowpen Coal Co (Ch)
Mickley Coal Co (Ch)
Erredosa Tin Mines
Acomb Coal Co (Ch)
British & Foreign Metal & Chemical (Ch)
Consett Iron Co (Ch)
Consett Spanish Ore Co
Cookson Lead & Antimony Co (Ch & Man.
  Dir)
Cookson Produce & Chem Co (Ch)
Goodlass Wall & Lead Industries (Ch)
Hazelrigg & Burradon Coal Co (Ch)
Howdon Barge & Transp Co (Ch)
Northern Development & Finance (Ch)
North Brit & Merc Ins
Redheugh Trust Limited (Ch)
Republic Mining & Metal Co (Ch)
Wm Benson & Son (Ch)
New Jarrow Steel Company
Orconera Steel Company

*****Roland Anthony COOKSON (1908-**
Educ: Harrow
1936
Cookson & Co
1947
Acomb Coal Co
Cowpen Coal Co
Mickley Coal Co
Hazelrigg & Burradon Coal Co
Wm Benson & Son
N E Electric Supply Co
Walkers, Parker & Co
1957
Goodlass Wall & Lead Industries (Ch)
Consett Iron Co (Ch 1967)
Greenside Mines
Martins Bank (N E Board)
1967
Lead Industries Group (Ch)
Lloyds Bank (Ch N Reg Bd)
North Reg Board for Industry (V Ch)
North Econ Planning Council
Tyneside Chamber of Commerce (Pres)
CBI (Ch N Reg)
1978
Lead Industries Group
Lloyds Bank
North Indust Devpt Bd (Ch)

*****Gerald Hugh COOKSON (1925-**
Camvac Holdings
High Vacuum Engineering
Athene Yachts

8. Cruddas/Renwick

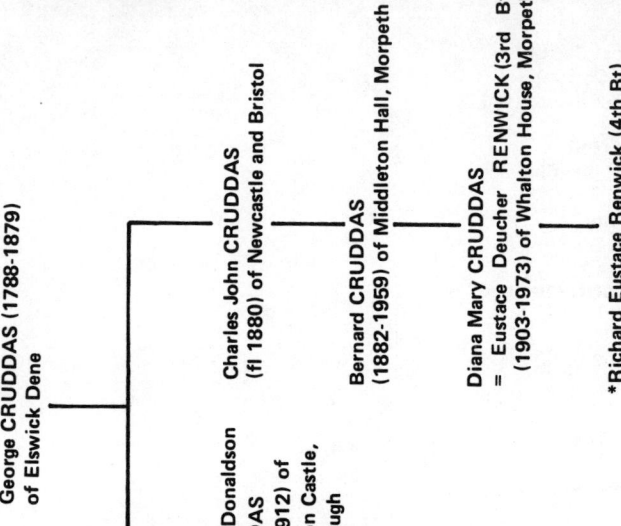

George CRUDDAS (1788-1879)
of Elswick Dene

Charles John CRUDDAS (fl 1880) of Newcastle and Bristol

William Donaldson CRUDDAS (1831-1912) of Haughton Castle, Humshaugh

Bernard CRUDDAS (1882-1959) of Middleton Hall, Morpeth

Diana Mary CRUDDAS = Eustace Deucher RENWICK (3rd Bt) (1903-1973) of Whalton House, Morpeth

*Richard Eustace Renwick (4th Bt) (1938-) of Whalton House, Morpeth

George CRUDDAS (1788-1879)
Linen draper & ship owner
N/c and N Shields Rwy
W G Armstrong & Co

William Donaldson CRUDDAS (1831-1912)
W G Armstrong & Co
N/c Daily Journal (Ch 1895-1912)
Tory MP, Newcastle (1895-1900)
High Sheriff, N'land 1903

Charles John CRUDDAS (fl 1880)
Land speculator in Benwell

Bernard CRUDDAS (1882-1959)
N/c & Gateshead Water Co
MP for Wansbeck

Eustace Deuchar Renwick 3rd Bt (1903-1973)
Educ: Uppingham
Stephens, Sutton
Whalton Shipping Co

9. Lamb

Joseph LAMB (1732-1800) of Ryton Hall

Humble LAMB (1773-1844) of Ryton Hall

Joseph LAMB (1781-1859) of Lemington Hall, West Denton

Joseph Chatto LAMB (1803-1884) of Ryton Hall

Richard Westbrook LAMB (1826-1895) of West Denton and London

Robert Ormston LAMB (1836-1912) of Hayton House, How Mill, Carlisle

Stephen Eaton LAMB (1860-1928)

Edmund George LAMB (1863-1925)

Everard Joseph LAMB (1885-1914)

Richard Anthony LAMB (1911-) of Hayton House, How Mill

Stephen Eaton LAMB (1860-1928)
Cramlington Coal Co

Edmund George LAMB (1863-1925)
Seaton Delaval Colliery
Liberal MP, N Herefordshire

Richard Anthony LAMB (1911-)
Cramlington Estates
Hartley Main Collieries

Joseph LAMB (1732-1800)
Linen draper and soap maker
Northumberland Glass Works
Heddon & Percy Main Collieries
Tyne Bank (founding ptnr)

Joseph LAMB (1781-1859)
Lemington Glass Works
Cramlington Coal Co
Elswick & Walbottle Collieries
Northern Coalowners' Assoc (Ch)

Joseph Chatto LAMB (1803-1884)
Stella, South Hetton and Ryhope Collieries

Richard Westbrook LAMB (1826-1895)
Seaton Delaval Colliery

Robert Ormston LAMB (1836-1912)
Cramlington Coal Co (Ch)
Seaton Delaval Collieries (Ch)
N'land Coalowners (Ch)

10. Noble

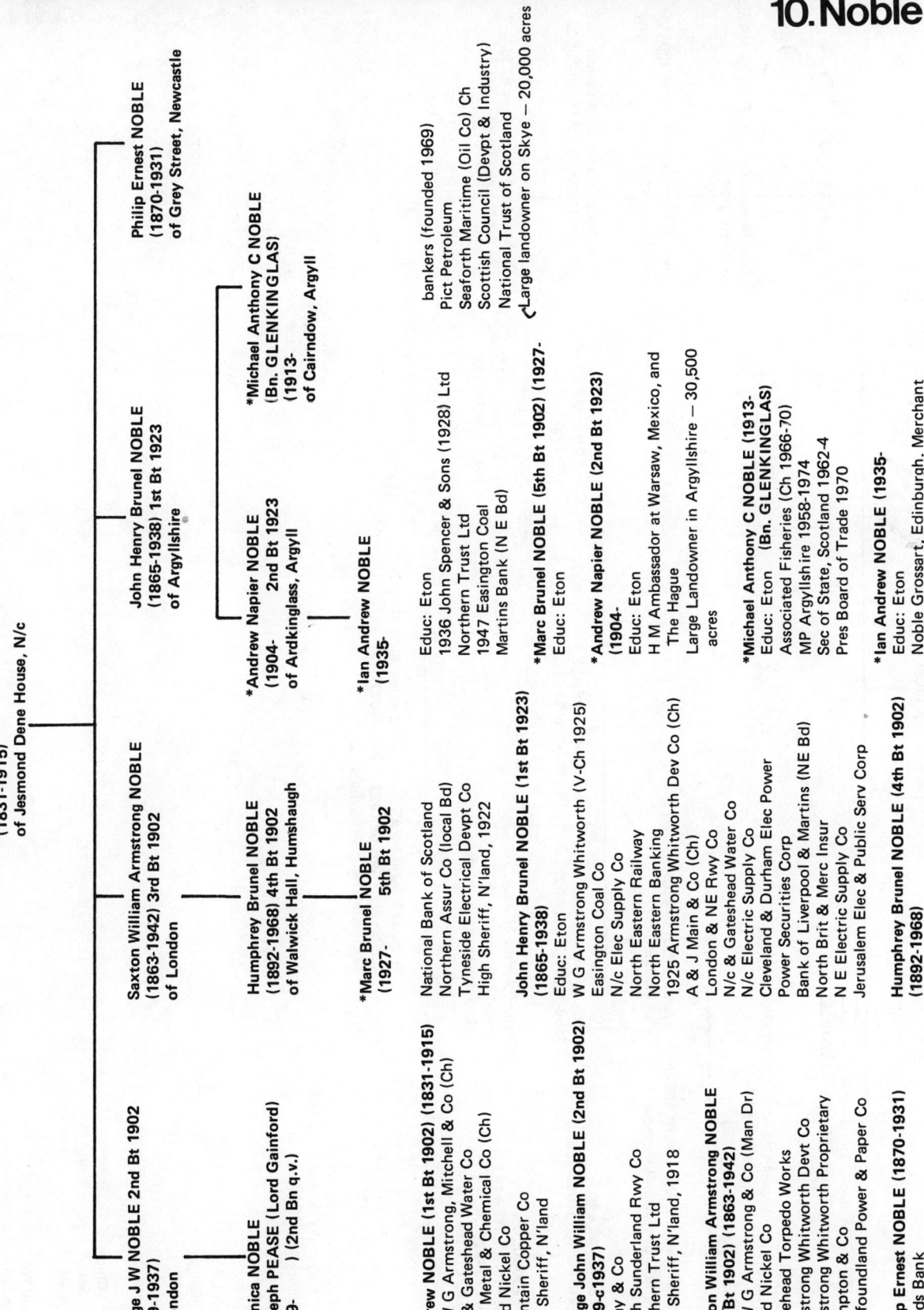

11. Pease

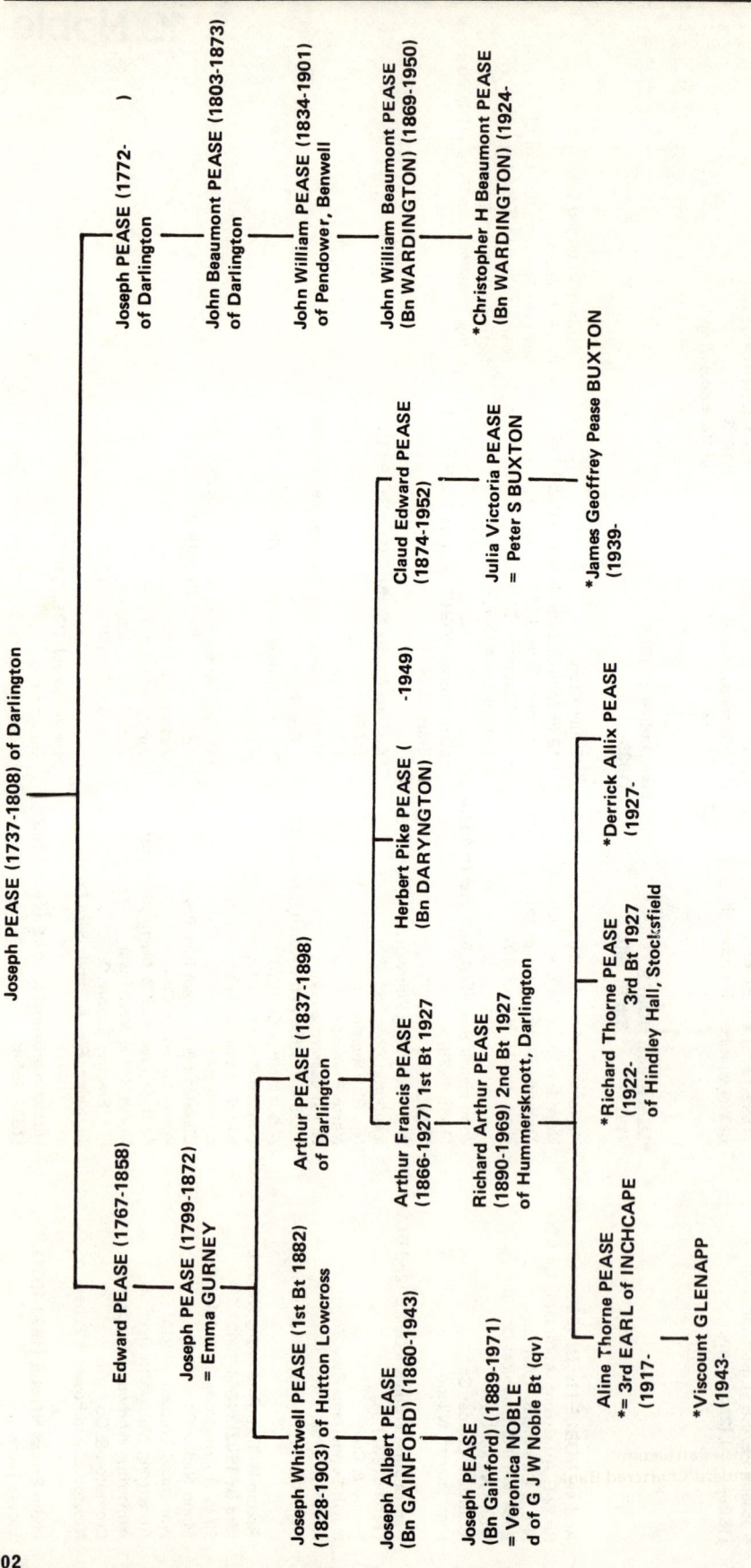

Joseph PEASE (1772-   )
Woollen merchant and banker
Stockton & Darlington Railway

John William PEASE (1836-1901)
Hodgkin, Barnett, Pease & Spence
  Bank, Newcastle (founding partner)
  (Bank taken over by Lloyds Bank 1903)
North Eastern Railway Co

Howard PEASE (1863-   )
Hodgkin, Barnett, Pease & Spence
  (Partner)

John W B PEASE. 1st Bn WARDINGTON (1869-1950)
Educ: Marlborough
Hodgkin, Barnett, Pease & Spence (Partner)
Cannop Coal Co 1910
Cornhill Steamship Co 1910
N'land Public House Trust Co 1910
Lloyds Bank (Ch 1922-1945)
Lloyds and Nat Prov Foreign Bank (Ch)
Bank of London and S America (Ch)
British Italian Banking Corp (Ch)
National Bank of Scotland (1925-)
Corp of Foreign Bondholders (Council
  member)
Alliance Assurance Co 1936
Fed of British Industry (member of Council
  1925-)

Christopher B PEASE. 2nd Bn WARDINGTON (1924-
Educ: Eton
Hoare & Co, Stockbrokers, London
Stock Exchange (member of Council)

Edward PEASE (1767-1858)
Woollen merchant and banker
Stockton & Darlington Railway
R Stephenson & Co, Forth Banks
  (princ shareholder)

Joseph PEASE (1799-1872)
MP for S Durham (1832-41)
Wife = co-heir to discount banker J Gurney

Joseph Whitwell PEASE (1st Bt 1882) (1828-1903)
R Stephenson & Co (V Ch)
Owners of the Middlesborough Estate
MP for S Durham (1865-85) and
Barnard Castle (1885-1903)

Joseph Albert PEASE (Lord GAINFORD) (1860-1943)
Fedn of British Industries (Pres 1927)
Nat Confed of Employers Assocs (Pres 1932)
Radio Manufacturers Assoc (Pres 1935)
BBC (Ch 1922-6)
MP for Tyneside Div, N'land; N Essex;
  Rotherham
Pres Board of Educ; Postmaster-General

Arthur Francis PEASE (1st Bt 1927) (1866-1927)
Pease & Partners (Coal and Iron Co) Ch
Furness Withy & Co
Broomhill Collieries
Horden Collieries
W Whitwell & Co
N E Rwy Co
Forth Bridge Rwy Co
Lloyds Bank
Owners of the Middlesborough Estate (Ch)
N E Improved Dwellings Co

Claud Edward PEASE (1874-1952)
Educ: Harrow
Barclays Bank
Cleveland Bridge & Engineering
Cleveland Trust (Ch)
Horden Collieries (Ch)
Owners of the Middlesborough Est (Ch)
N E Improved Dwellings (Ch)

James G. Pease BUXTON (1939-
Educ: Eton
Barclays Bank (local Dr)

Richard Arthur PEASE (2nd Bt 1927) (1890-1969)
Educ: Eton
East Hetton Collieries
Pease and Partners
National Benzole
Cleveland Bridge & Engineering
Cleveland Trust
Carliol Investment Trust
Tyneside Investment Trust
Industrial Plant
Owners of the Middlesborough Estate
Tyne Tees Television

Richard Thorn PEASE (3rd Bt 1927) (1922-
Educ: Eton
Barclays Bank (V-Ch); also on N/c local
  Board
Barclays Bank Trust
Barclays Bank UK Manag (V-Ch)
Barclays Export & Finance Co
Barclays Life Assur Co
Barclays Bank (London & Intnl)
Barclays Unicorn
First Nat Finance Corp
Owners of the Middlesborough Est

Derrick Allix PEASE (1927-
Morgan, Grenfell Holdings
Alexanders Discount Co
Nat Mutual Life Assur (Ch)
St George Assur (Ch)
Sphere Investment Trust
Industrial Plant Co
Tyneside Investment Trust
Carliol Investment Trust (Ch)
Carliol Unit Fund Managers

Earl of INCHCAPE (1917-
Educ: Eton
Inchcape & Co (Ch)
P&O Steam Navigation (Ch)
Guardian Royal Exchange
British Petroleum
Standard Chartered Bank
Bain Dawes Group

12. Priestman/Pumphrey/Peile/Bosanquet/Hodgkin

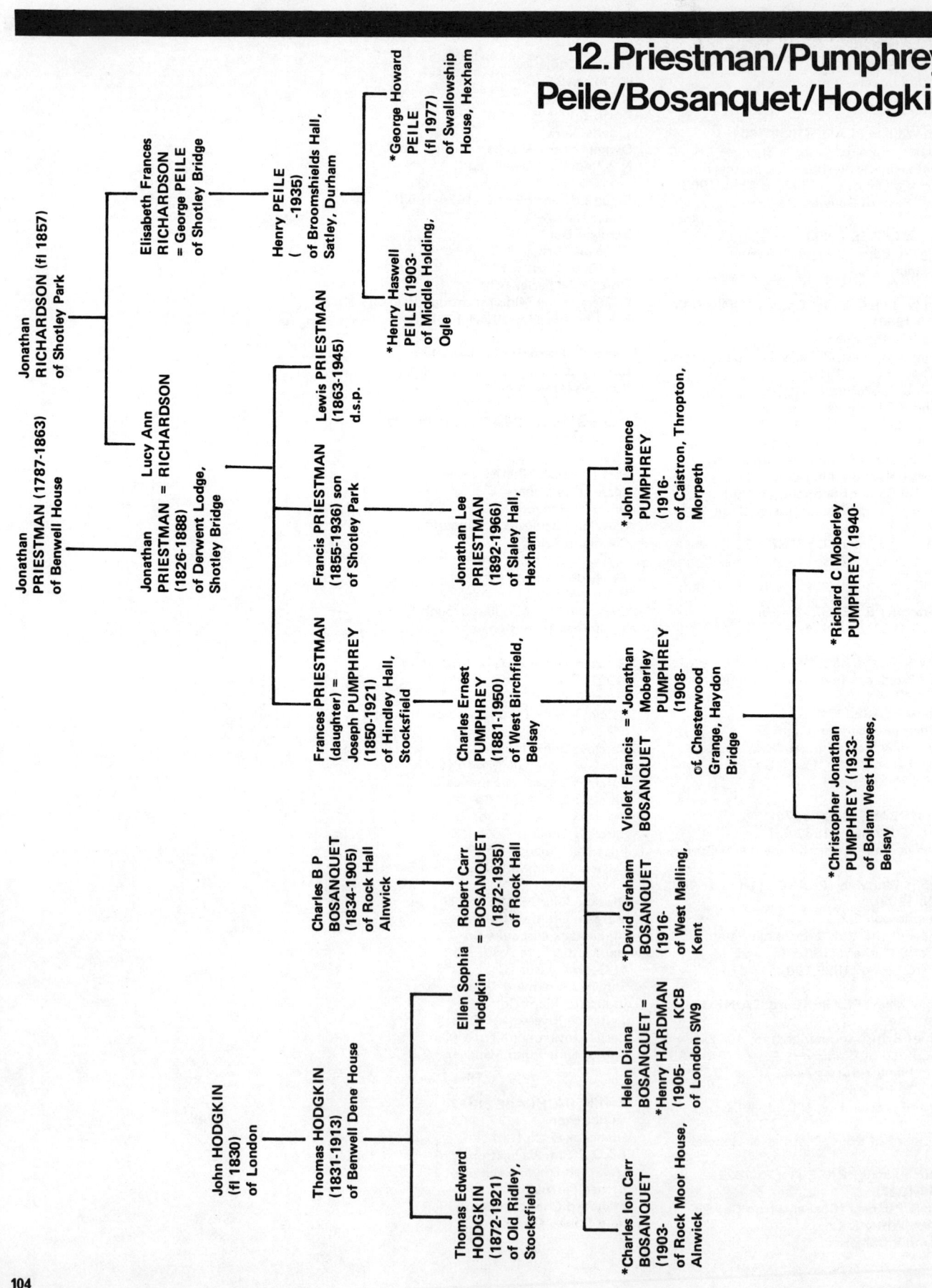

Thomas HODGKIN (1831-1913)
Hodgkin, Barnett & Pease, N/c Bankers

Thomas Edward HODGKIN (1872-1921)
Lloyds Bank (Mng N/c Branch)

Jonathan PRIESTMAN (1787-1863)
Tannery, Newgate St, N/c 1811
Glue Works, Low Friar St 1841
Glue Works/Tannery Benwell 1843
Durham & N'land Dist Bank (Shrhldr)
Derwent & Consett Iron Co 1857

Jonathan RICHARDSON (fl 1857)
Derwent & Consett Iron Co (Fndr)
Durham & N'land Dist. Bank — Mng Dir

Jonathan PRIESTMAN (1826-1888)
Derwent & Consett Iron Co — Mng Dir
Consett Iron Co — Mng Dir 1864
Ashington Coal Co — Mng Ptnr 1869
Victoria Garesfield Colliery

Francis PRIESTMAN (1855-1936)
Educ: Rugby
Priestman Collieries (Ch 1906-36)
Ashington Coal Co (Ch 1908-36)
Priestman Whitehaven Colls (Ch 1935)
Priestman Power Co (Ch 1906)
Waste Heat & Gas EGS (later Carliol Investment Trust)
Tyneside Electrical Dev Co (1922-36) (later Tyneside Investment Trust)
Bank of Liverpool & Martins (Ch N E District)
Newcastle & Gateshead Gas Co
Newcastle Benzol Co
N British & Merc Ins Co (Local Bd)

Lewis PRIESTMAN (1863-1945)
Educ: Rugby
Priestman Collieries
Ashington Coal Co

Joseph PUMPHREY (1850-1921)
Coalowner
Waste Heat & Gas EGS

Henry PEILE (-1935)
Priestman Collieries (Jt Mang Dir)
Priestman Whitehaven Collieries
Northern Coke Research Centre (Ch)

Jonathan Lee PRIESTMAN (1892-1966)
Educ: Rugby
Ashington Coal Co (Ch 1946)
Priestman Collieries (Ch 1945)
Priestman Whitehaven Collieries
Newcastle & Gateshead Gas Co
N Brit & Merc Ins (local bd)
A F Bell & Co

*Charles Ion Carr BOSANQUET (1903-
Educ: Winchester
North East Electric Supply
Carliol Investment Trust (Ch 1977)
Carliol Unit Fund Managers
Industrial Plant Co
Tyneside Investment Trust
Kings College, N/c — Rector (1952-63)
Newcastle University — 1st Vice-Chancellor (1963-68)

*David Graham BOSANQUET (1916-
Currey & Co, London, Solicitors
Fitzwilliam Peterborough Properties
Provincial Insurance Co
Provincial Life Assurance Co

*Henry Haswell PEILE (1903-
Priestman Collieries (jt Mng Dr 1945)
Priestman Whitehaven Collieries (1935)
A F Bell & Co (Mng Dr 1954)
Owners of Settlingstones Mines
Weardale Lead Co (Mng Dir 1962)
Washington Engineering (Ch 1963)
N/c & Gateshead Water Co (V Ch 1972-)
Northern Rock Building Soc (1954-
Peterleee New Town Dev Corp (Ch)
Newton Aycliffe Dev Corp (Ch)
Northern Gas Board (Member 1962)

*George Howard PEILE (fl 1977)
Priestman Collieries
Priestman Whitehaven Collieries
N'land County Cllr (1977)

Charles Ernest PUMPHREY (1881-1950)
Ashington Coal Co
Priestman Collieries

*Jonathan Moberley PUMPHREY (1908-
Educ: Winchester
Priestman Collieries (1945)
National Coal Board (Dep Ch N'land & Durham 1965)
Stephenson and Wood Pty (S African Co)

*Christopher Jonathan PUMPHREY (1933-
Educ: Winchester
Wise, Speke & Co, Stockbrokers, N/c
Carliol Investment Trust
Carliol Unit Fund Managers
Carliol Investment Management Ltd
Tyneside Investment Trust Ltd
Simonside Investment Trust Ltd
Industrial Plant Co
Grainger Building Soc

*Richard Charles M PUMPHREY (1940-
Educ: Winchester
Stewarts & Lloyds of Ireland Ltd (Man Dir)

*John Laurence PUMPHREY (KCMG) (1916-
Educ: Winchester
H M Ambassador, Pakistan (1971-76)
N/c University, member of Court

*Henry Hardman (KCB) (1905-
Perm Under Sec of State, Min of Defence (1964-1966)
Monopolies Commission (Dep Ch 1967-68)
Reserve Bank of Rhodesia (Gov & Trustee 1967-

13. Richardson/Merz/Watson

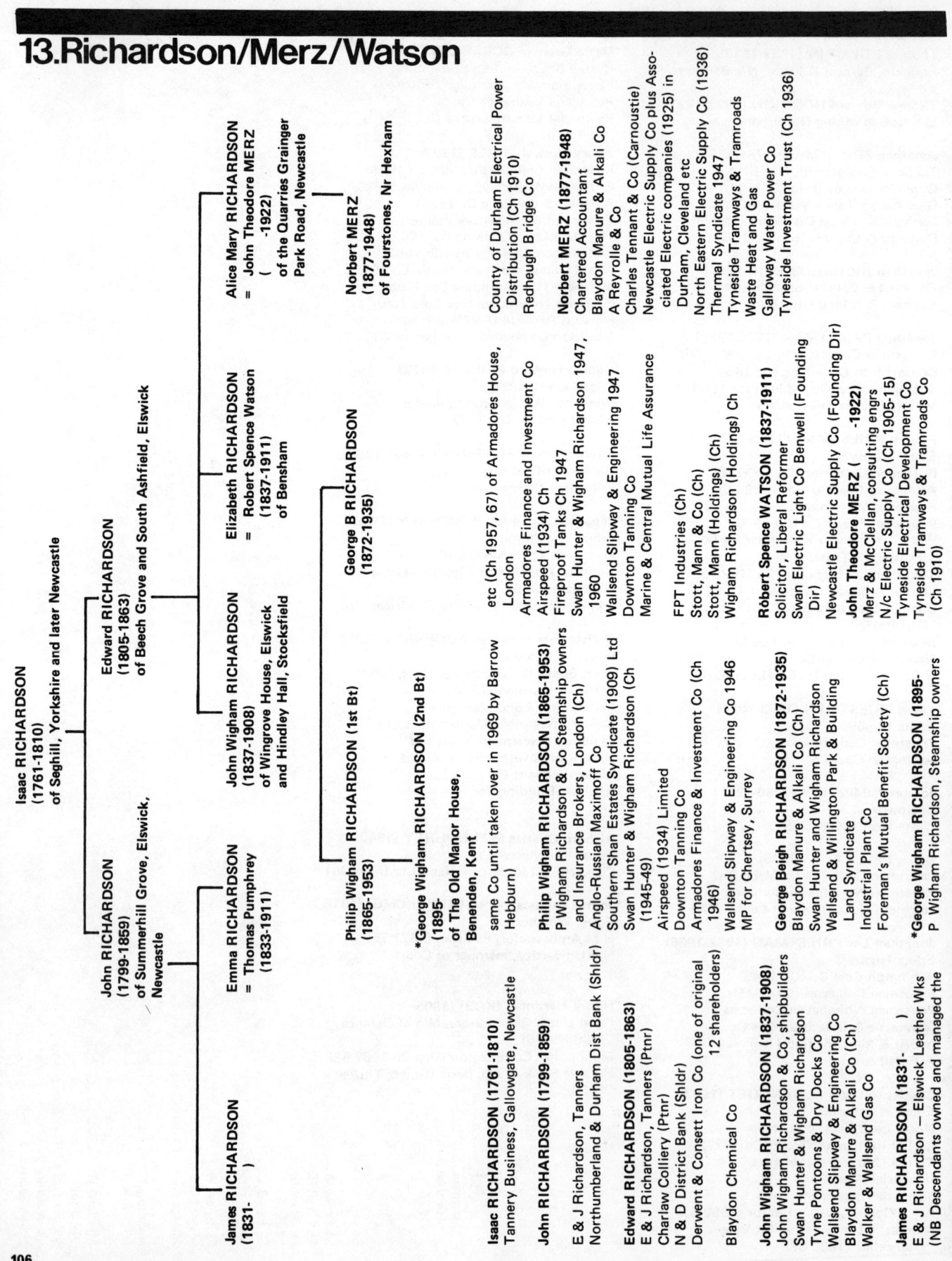

14. Ridley

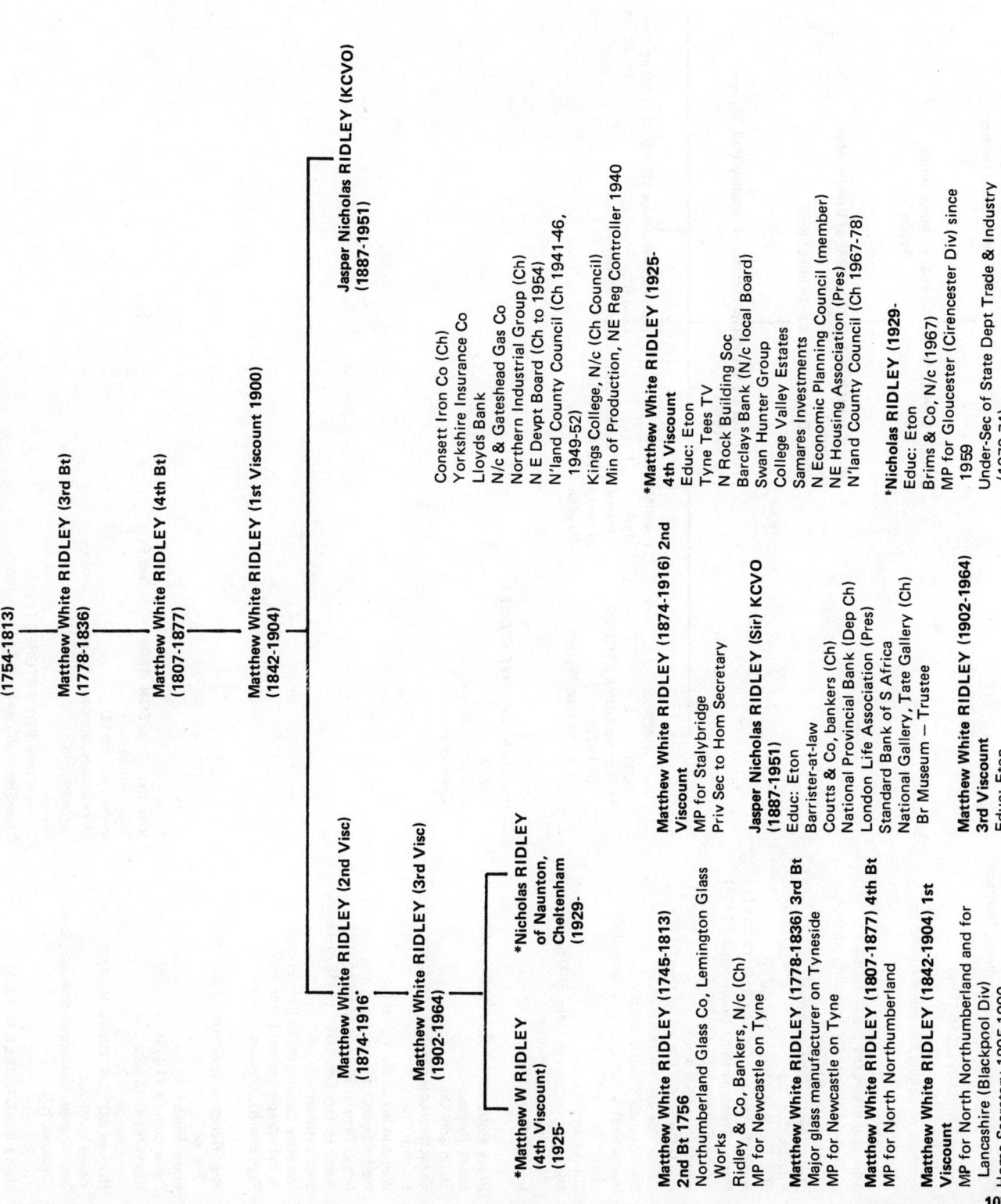

15. Simpson

Family Tree

John SIMPSON (1790-1857) of Gate Cote, Butterknowle Hamsterley, Durham
│
├─ **Robert SIMPSON (1814-1894)** of Moor House, Ryton
│
└─ **John Bell SIMPSON (1837-1926)** of Bradley Hall, Wylam
   (m 2ndly) = Clara Buddle Atkinson (widow) qv
   │
   ├─ **Frank Robert SIMPSON (1st Bt)** of Bradley Hall, Wylam (1864-1949)
   │ │
   │ ├─ **Vera SIMPSON (1893-)**
   │ │ *= Richard BOYS-STONES (fl 1978) of Kyo Close, Wylam
   │ │ │
   │ │ └─ *Claude Frank BOYS-STONES (1920-) of Randle House, Corbridge
   │ │
   │ └─ **Iris SIMPSON (1896-)**
   │   = Henry E B DANIELL of Hedgefield House, Blaydon
   │
   ├─ **Basil Robert James SIMPSON (2nd Bt) (1898-1968)**
   │ │
   │ └─ *John Cyril SIMPSON (1899-) 3rd Bt
   │   Educ: Rugby
   │   Stella Coal (1945)
   │   Boys-Stones, Simpson & Spencer, Stock-brokers, N/c
   │   │
   │   └─ *Claude Frank BOYS-STONES (1920—)
   │   Boys-Stones, Simpson & Spencer, Stock-broker, N/c
   │
   └─ ***John Cyril Finucane SIMPSON (3rd Bt)** of Bradley Hall (1899-)

John SIMPSON (1790-1857)
Owner of coal mines at Hamsterley, Durham

Robert SIMPSON (1814-1894)
Stella Coal Co
Institute of Mining Engineers (founding member)

John Bell SIMPSON (1837-1926)
of Throckley Coal Co (founding partner, 1867; mang dir 1906)
Stella Coal Co (Mang partner)
Elswick Coal Co
Wallsend & Hebburn Coal Co
Walter Scott Ltd (Colliery Steel Co) 1911
Marine Steam Turbine (founding dir 1889) (later Parsons MST Co 1897)
Hawthorn Leslie & Co
N/c & District Electric Lighting Co (Ch)
Cambridge Electric Supply Co
Scarborough Electric Supply Co
Waste Heat & Gas EGS (founding dir) (later Carliol I Trust)
Sunderland Gas Co
Mining consultant to Duke of N'land and Sir Matthew White Ridley
Inst of Mining engineers (Pres)

Frank Robert SIMPSON (1864-1949) 1st Bt
Educ: Rugby
Stella Coal Co
Throckley Coal Co
Elswick Coal Co
Wallsend & Hebburn Coal Co
Walter Scott Ltd
N/c & District Electric Lighting (Ch)
Waste Heat & Gas EGS Ltd (1921-1949)
Battle Hill Estates Co
Northern Assurance Co (N/c Board)
R Tyne Improvement Commission
High Sheriff, Durham (1935)

Basil Robert J SIMPSON (1898-1968) 2nd Bt
Educ: Rugby
Stella Coal Co (1935)
High Sheriff 1955

***Richard BOYS-STONES (fl 1976)**
Elswick Coal Co
Boys-Stones, Simpson & Spencer, Stock-brokers, N/c

Henry E B DANIELL (fl 1936)
Stella Coal Co

16. Stephenson

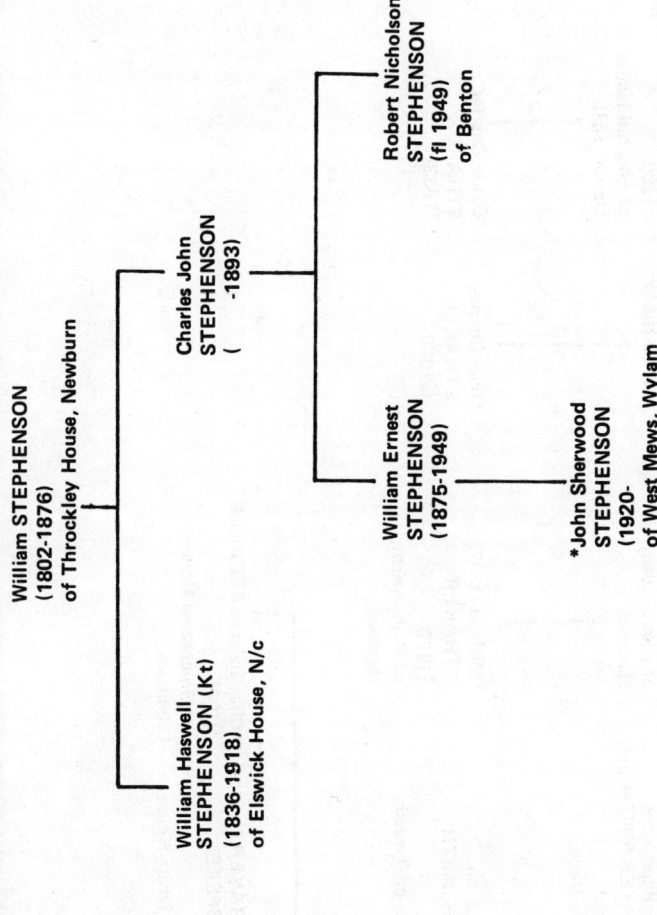

```
                    William STEPHENSON
                         (1802-1876)
                of Throckley House, Newburn
                              |
         ┌────────────────────┴────────────────────┐
   William Haswell                          Charles John
    STEPHENSON (Kt)                          STEPHENSON
     (1836-1918)                              ( -1893)
  of Elswick House, N/c                           |
                                    ┌─────────────┴─────────────┐
                              William Ernest            Robert Nicholson
                               STEPHENSON                  STEPHENSON
                               (1875-1949)                  (fl 1949)
                                    |                       of Benton
                             *John Sherwood
                               STEPHENSON
                                (1920-    )
                             of West Mews, Wylam
```

William STEPHENSON (1802-1876)
W Stephenson & Sons, firebricks

Sir William Haswell STEPHENSON (1836-1918)
W Stephenson & Sons (Chr)
Throckley Coal Co (fndr & Ch)
Walter Scott Ltd (Ch)
John Spencer & Sons, Newburn Steel Wks
Scotswood, Newburn & Wylam Rwy Co
Tyne Steam Shipping
Tyne Tees Steam Shipping (Ch)
N/c Grain Warehouse Co
Cairn Line of Steamships
Free Trade Wharf Co (Ch)
Leeds Phosphate Co (Ch)
Cerebos Co (Ch)
National Peat Co (Ch)
North Eastern Banking
North Accident Insurance
Royal Insurance Co (Ch local Bd)
N/c & Gateshead Water Co
N/c & Gateshead Gas Co (Ch)
N/c Commercial Exchange (Ch)
R Tyne Commission (Ch 1901-18)

Charles John STEPHENSON (fl 1894)
Throckley Coal Co (fndg partner)

William Ernest STEPHENSON (1875-1949)
Educ: Leys School
Throckley Coal Co (Mng Dr)
N'land Coalowners' Mutual Protection Assoc
N/c & Gateshead Water Co

Robert Nicholson STEPHENSON (fl 1949)
Land agent
Throckley Coal Co

*John Sherwood STEPHENSON (1920-)
Solicitor, of Ingledew, Mark Pybus, Newcastle
Throckley Coal Co 1950
N/c & Gateshead Water Co (1961-
Stephenson & Wood (Pty) S Africa (1949-
Northern Rock Building Society (1977-
Law Society (N/c Pres 1977)

17. Straker

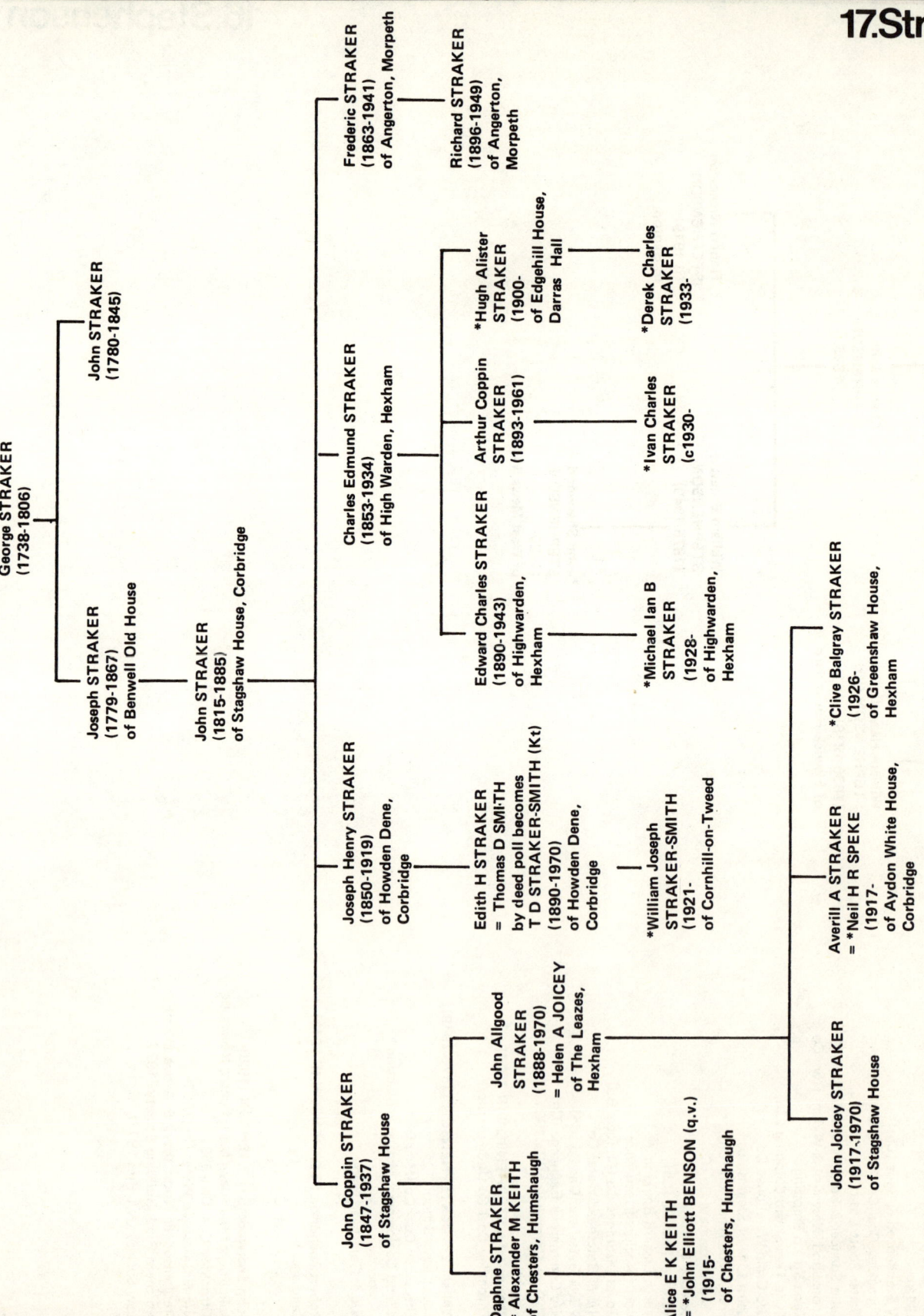

Joseph STRAKER (1784-1867)
Strakers and Love, founder
Collieries at Willington, Brancepeth

John STRAKER (1815-1885)
Strakers & Love (Ch)
Cowpen & North Seaton Coal Co
N Eastern Railway Co
Large landowner in Durham and in North-
 umberland (over 12,000 acres)

John Coppin STRAKER (1847-1937)
Woods & Co (N/c bankers)
High Gosforth Park 1890
North Brit & Merc Ins (local Bd) 1890
Strakers & Love (Ch & Mng 1936)
Wallsend & Hebburn Coal Co 1910
Cowpen Coal Co 1925
Battle Hill Estate Co 1936
High Sheriff N'land 1907

Joseph Henry STRAKER (1850-1919)
large N'land landowner
High Sheriff N'land

Frederic STRAKER (1863-1941)
Educ: Harrow
Woods & Co (N/c bankers) 1880
Barclays Bank (local board) 1910
Strakers & Love
Baghill Coal Co
High Gosforth Park Co
North Caucasian Oil Fields 1925

Charles Edmund STRAKER (1852-1934)
R & W Hawthorn Leslie (Mng Dir & Ch)
Mold Collieries
Wallsend & Hebburn Coal Co

John Allgood STRAKER (1888-1970)
Educ: Eton
1925 High Gosforth Park Co (Ch 1959)
1936 Strakers & Love
Cowpen Coal Co
Brancepeth Gas & Coke (Strakers & Love)
 (Ch)
1947 Newcastle & Gateshead Water Co
North British & Mercantile Insurance
Standard Pulverised Fuel Co
1957 Hexham Racecourse

Thomas Dalrymple STRAKER-SMITH (1890-1970)
Smiths Dock Co

Richard STRAKER (1896-1949)
Barclays Bank (Ch local Bd)
Strakers & Love
Brancepeth Gas & Coke (Strakers & Love)
High Gosforth Park

Edward Charles STRAKER (1890-1943)
Educ: Repton
R & W Hawthorn Leslie (Ch)
Robert Stephenson & Hawthorns, loco
 builders (Ch)
Strakers & Love
Strakers (N/c) Motor dealers

***Hugh Alister STRAKER (1900-**
Educ: Harrow
Strakers (N/c) (Ch and Mng) 1955

John Joicey STRAKER (1917-1970)
Educ: Eton
Gosforth Park Co
Hexham Racecourse (Ch)

***Clive Balgray STRAKER (1926-**
Educ: Haileybury
Large landowner in Hexham area

***Neil Hanning Reed SPEKE (1917-**
Educ: Eton
Wise, Speke & Co, Stockbrokers, N/c
Northern Rock B Soc
High Sheriff, N'land (1959)

***William Joseph STRAKER SMITH (1921-**
Associated Shipbuilders (Dep Ch)
Smiths Docks Co
John Gardner (London)
S G Warburg & Co
Jessel Toynbee & Co
Swan Hunter Group (V Ch)
Barclays Bank (London & International)

***Michael Ian B STRAKER (1928-**
Educ: Eton
Newcastle Area Health Authority (Ch)
Newcastle & Gateshead Water Co
Landowner
N'land County Cllr

***Ivan Charles STRAKER (c1930-**
Glenlivet Distillers (Ch Exec)
Glen Grant Whisky
Hill, Thomson & Co

***Derek Charles STRAKER (1933-**
Strakers (Newcastle) 1955

18. Surtees/Altham/Eldon

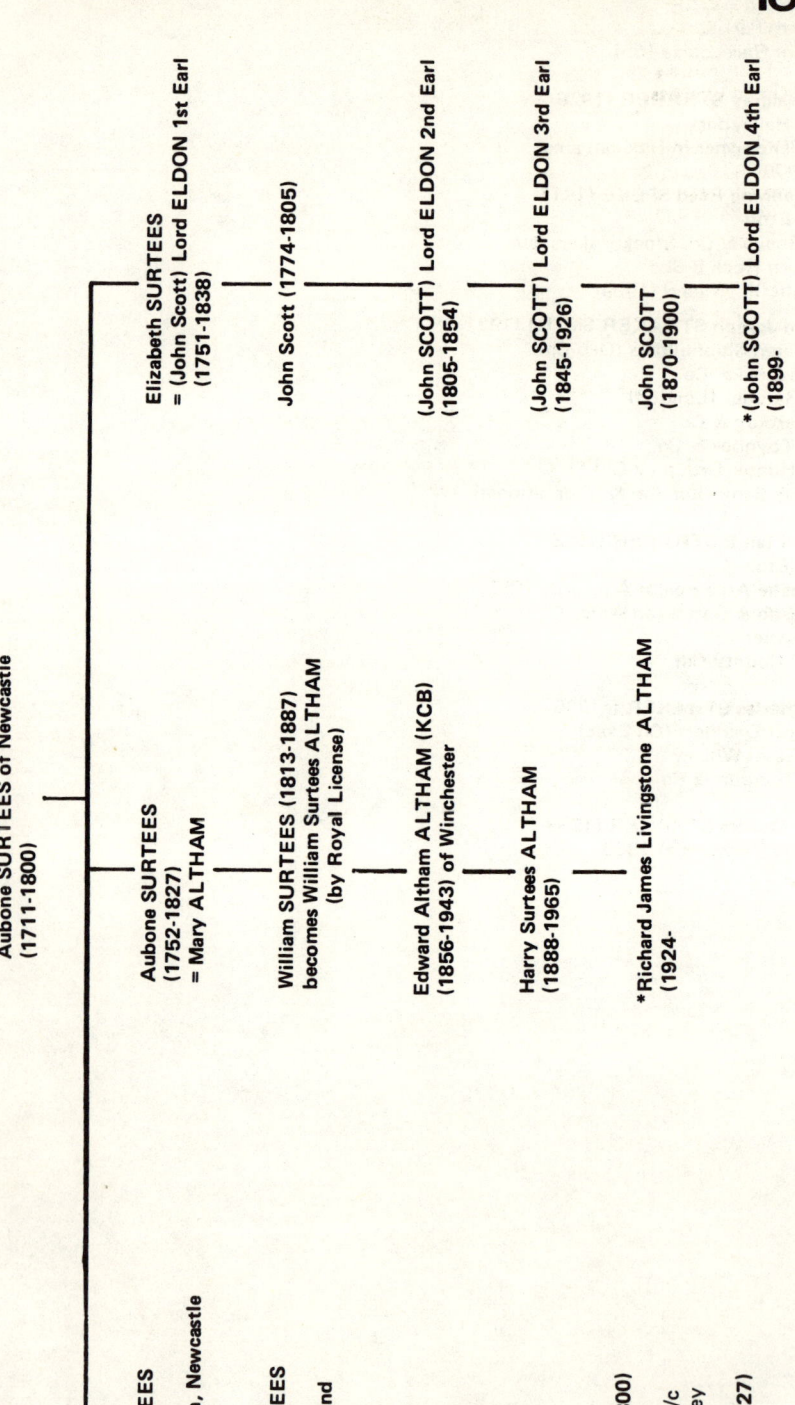

Aubone SURTEES of Newcastle (1711-1800)

William SURTEES (1750-1832) of Seaton Burn, Newcastle

Aubone SURTEES (1777-) of Pigdon, N'land

Aubone SURTEES (1711-1800) Wine and timber merchant Surtees and Burdon Bank, N/c Estates at Woodhead & Hedley

Aubone SURTEES (1752-1827) Lead mining Co, Derwent Benwell Colliery

Aubone SURTEES (1777-) Benwell Colliery

1st Earl of ELDON (1751-1838) Lord High Chancellor (1801-1827)

Edward Altham ALTHAM KCB (1856-1943)
Educ: Winchester
Lt Gen: QMG in India (1917-1919)

*Richard James L ALTHAM (1924-)
Educ: Marlborough
Rio Tinto Zinc
Rio Tinto Zinc Borax (Dep Ch)

*4th Earl of ELDON (1899-)
Educ: Ampleforth
Lord-in-Waiting to King George VI and Queen Elizabeth II

Appendix 2
Sample of Estates

Seventeen Families originally involved in Nineteenth Century Industrial Development in West Newcastle

NAME and FAMILY TREE	Date of Death	Estate Value
1.		
John SPENCER	1905	£370,000
John Cuthbert SPENCER	1906	£135,000
Seymour SPENCER	1907	£139,000
John Watson SPENCER	1908	£149,000
Ralph SPENCER	1926	£160,000
2.		
William ARMSTRONG	1901	£1,400,000
William Watson ARMSTRONG	1941	£217,000
Addison POTTER	1894	£30,000
William COCHRANE	1903	£127,000
Cecil Algernon COCHRANE	1960	£410,000
3.		
William Edward BARNETT	1869	£35,000
Edward George BARNETT	1934	£15,000
George Alex BARNETT	1971	£111,000
James JOICEY	1863	£100,000
Jacob JOICEY	1899	£32,000
James JOICEY	1936	£1,520,000
James Arthur JOICEY	1940	£784,000
Hugh Edward JOICEY	1966	£747,000
Robert DICKINSON	1890	£10,000
Robert DICKINSON	1927	£109,000
Elisabeth Thompson DICKINSON	1966	£66,000
4.		
William BENSON	1882	£37,000
Walter John BENSON	1923	£483,000
Thomas Walter BENSON	1912	£321,000
5.		
John BUDDLE	1843	£150,000
Benjamin Chapman BROWNE	1917	£77,000
Frank Buddle ATKINSON	1953	£760,000
6.		
John CLAYTON	1890	£713,000
Nathaniel George CLAYTON	1895	£525,000
Richard CLAYTON	1903	£115,000
Frederick George Hugh CLAYTON	1946	£109,000
Francis Charles CLAYTON	1970	£76,000
7.		
William CUTHBERT	1878	£250,000
William Isaac COOKSON	1888	£592,000
John COOKSON	1892	£92,000
Norman Charles COOKSON	1909	£201,000
George John COOKSON	1913	£103,000
James Harold CUTHBERT	1915	£92,000
Philip Blencowe COOKSON	1928	£83,000
Clive COOKSON	1971	£399,000
8.		
George CRUDDAS	1879	£400,000
Rev George CRUDDAS	1895	£142,000
William Donaldson CRUDDAS	1912	£1,042,000
Bernard CRUDDAS	1959	£121,000
Eustace Deuchar RENWICK	1973	£301,000

NAME AND FAMILY TREE	Date of Death	Estate Value
9.		
Joseph LAMB	1859	£60,000
Joseph Chatto LAMB	1884	£37,000
Richard Westbrook LAMB	1895	£87,000
Robert Ormstom LAMB	1912	£211,000
Everard Joseph LAMB	1914	£175,000
Stephen Eaton LAMB	1928	£167,000
10.		
Andrew NOBLE	1915	£734,000
Saxton Wm A NOBLE	1942	£372,000
John Henry Brunel NOBLE	1938	£639,000
Humphrey Brunel NOBLE	1968	£320,000
11.		
Joseph PEASE	1872	£350,000
John William PEASE	1901	£278,000
Joseph Whitwell PEASE	1903	£2,800
Arthur PEASE	1898	£409,000
Arthur Francis PEASE	1927	£114,000
John W B PEASE	1950	£83,000
Richard Arthur PEASE	1969	£71,000
12.		
Jonathan PRIESTMAN	1863	£3,000
Jonathan PRIESTMAN	1888	£103,000
Francis PRIESTMAN	1936	£220,000
Lewis PRIESTMAN	1945	£291,000
Jonathan Lee PRIESTMAN	1966	£33,000
Joseph PUMPHREY	1921	£89,000
Charles Ernest PUMPHREY	1950	£64,000
Henry PEILE	1935	£64,000
Thomas HODGKIN	1913	£150,000
Thomas Edward HODGKIN	1921	£108,000
Robert Carr BOSANQUET	1935	£62,000
13.		
Edward RICHARDSON	1863	£45,000
John Wigham RICHARDSON	1908	£92,000
Robert Spence WATSON	1911	£36,000
John Theodore MERZ	1922	£19,000
Philip Wigham RICHARDSON	1953	£100,000
George B RICHARDSON	1935	£78,000
Norbert MERZ	1948	£82,000
14.		
Matthew White RIDLEY (4th Bt)	1877	£140,000
Matthew White RIDLEY (1st Visc)	1904	£535,000
Matthew White RIDLEY (2nd Visc)	1916	£439,000
Jasper Nicholas RIDLEY	1951	£48,000
Matthew White RIDLEY (3rd Visc)	1964	£898,000
15.		
Robert SIMPSON	1894	£34,000
Frank Robert SIMPSON	1949	£34,000
16.		
William STEPHENSON	1876	£12,000
William Haswell STEPHENSON	1918	£86,000
William Ernest STEPHENSON	1949	£17,000

NAME and FAMILY TREE	Date of Death	Estate Value	
17.			
Joseph STRAKER	1867	£300,000	
John STRAKER	1885	£919,000	
Joseph Henry STRAKER	1919	£982,000	
Charles Edmund STRAKER	1934	£77,000	
Edward Charles STRAKER	1943	£218,000	
John Coppin STRAKER	1937	£560,000	
Helen Audrey STRAKER	1969	£109,000	Source: Probate Registry
John Allgood STRAKER	1970	£290,000	Note: Until 1882, the exact figure was not given, but rounded up to the nearest large number e.g. W E Barnett "under £35,000".
John Joicey STRAKER	1970	£208,000	

Appendix 3
Schedule of Industrial Development

COAL-MINING

AREA	NAME OF PIT	OWNERS/PARTNERS	SOCIAL BACKGROUND	OTHER DETAILS	YEAR
1. Elswick	Gallowgate or North Elswick	Isaac COOKSON (7)	Merchant Banker and industrialist Great grandfather had come to Newcastle c1700 and founded glass and alum works at South Shields		1770-c1840s
	Elswick	Joseph LAMB & Co (9)	Son of Newcastle linen draper & soap manufacturer, with coal and glass interests	Rateable value of mine = £600 pa	1843
	Elswick	Alexander Brodie COCHRANE (2)	Ironmaster from Staffs		1853
		+ son William COCHRANE	Founder of huge Cochrane Iron Co at Middlesborough in 1854	Son came North in 1857 to develop collieries at New Brancepeth & Elswick	
	Elswick and North Elswick Collieries	Elswick Coal Co Partners include: Robert SIMPSON (15) and son John Bell SIMPSON	mining engineer & Coalowner		1881
		William Cochrane Carr			
	[North Elswick Pit closed 1941]				
2. Benwell	Charlotte, Delaval and Beaumont	William Surtees (18)	Son of Aubone Surtees, Newcastle merchant and banker (see Tyne Iron Works)		1805
	Charlotte, Delaval, Aubone, Edward and Paradise	Aubone & William Surtees in conjunction with landowner			
		John BUDDLE (5)	Wallsend viewer. Son of Durham schoolteacher turned viewer		1826-1848
	Charlotte, (Brockwell seam) Drift mine near near Elswick Station	William Cochrane CARR	Born at Blaydon, of humble family. Married daughter of market gardener.	(see Benwell brick factory) After starting brick works, gradually reopened pits	c1852
	[Pit closed in 1939 after being sold in 1931 to Elswick Coal Co]				
	Delaval	John Oliver Scott (1819-90)	Son of Longbenton labourer	Owned adjoining brickworks Coal agent on Quayside in 1850	1863
3. Fenham		William ORD (landowner)	Old Northumberland landed gentry		c1800
		John BUDDLE	(see Benwell Colliery)		
		John Straker (17)	Son of merchant & Coalowner		c1830

AREA	NAME OF PIT	OWNERS/PARTNERS	SOCIAL BACKGROUND	OTHER DETAILS	YEAR
4. Scotswood	Montague (Denton Main)	Edward Montagu (Lord Rokeby)	Old landed family		1765-1807
	Montague (Denton Main)	Cookson, Cuthbert & Co Wm Cuthbert	same Isaac Cookson as Elswick Pit (q.v.) from established Tyneside family; grandfather had come to Newcastle c1700		1807-1812
	Montague (Denton Main)	Messrs CARR & RIDLEY			
		Messrs W BENSON & Sons)))	Gentry stock; ancestors included rector, farmer, and agent to Bowes family at Bradley Hall	Hexham-based, started business with limited capital. By 1880s had several colliery, quarry and brickwork interests	1857-c1930
		R HAWTHORN (initial, non-executive partner)))		of R & W Hawthorn engineering works (qv)	
		MICKLEY COAL Co		Controlled by Cooksons (7)	c1930-1948
	[Pit closed November 1959 by NCB]				
5. Walbottle	Walbottle	Duke of Northumberland (landowner)	Old landed family	Ended involvement by 1799	c1790
		Addison Potter & Co (2)	Newcastle brewer	Colliery included associated brickworks	1844
		Joseph LAMB & Co (9)	(see Elswick Colliery)	incl associated brickworks (Potter probably still involved as listed as joint owner of Staiths for Walbottle Coals at Lemington	1850
		Messrs STEPHENSON & Ptn (THROCKLEY Coal Co)(16)	Methodist background. Family were hostmen and merchants in Newcastle in eighteenth century	Owned neighbouring Throckley Colliery (qv)	1877
		Lemington Colliery Co		Acquired interest	1928
	Working of colliery halted pre-WW1 Recommenced 1918 with new electrical installations East and North Walbottle Pits closed by NCB in 1966 and 1968				
6. Throckley	Isabella	Messrs STEPHENSON & PTNS. (see above) (Throckley Coal Co) Partners of which were 1. WH & CJ Stephenson 2. SPENCER Brothers 3. John Bell SIMPSON	Owners of John Spencer & Sons, Newburn Steel Works (see Elswick Colliery)	Pit previously dormant 1902 Company purchases Heddon colliery	1867
	Four pits — Maria, Isabella, Coronation & Blucher closed by NCB 1953-1956				
7. Stella	Emma, Stargate and Addison	John Buddle (5) Addison L. Potter (2) Humble Lamb (9) R.T. Atkinson (5) T.Y. Hall	see Benwell Colliery see Wallbottle Colliery	By 1894 J.B. Simpson (15) had become managing partner	1837
	[1947: Taken over by NCB]				

115

IRON WORKS, FOUNDRIES, LEAD WORKS & GLASS FACTORIES

AREA	TYPE OF ACTIVITY NAME	OWNERS/PARTNERS	SOCIAL BACKGROUND	OTHER DETAILS	YEAR
1. Elswick	Lead-works	Samuel WALKER (1715-82)	Son of Rotherham nailer	Nonconformist. Large Rotherham ironfounder. Provided most of initial capital	1778
		Richard Fishwick Archer WARD	merchant from Hull merchant from Hull	(Partnership ended in 1799. Set up Tyne Iron Works in 1800 [qv])	
	Walkers, Parker & Walker	Sons of Samuel Walker & nephew Samuel Walker Parker			1802
		Samuel Parker (son of SWP) = Chairman		Founding partner in Woods & Co Newcastle bankers	1841
		Boardroom dispute — reconstituted Co			1889
	1978 – Part of Lead Industries Group (Associated Lead Co)				
2. Close Gate	Iron Foundry and brass foundry	Isaac Cookson & Co (7)	M Banker and industrialist. Great grandfather had come to Newcastle c1700 and founded glass and alum works at S Shields		1778
	Cookson Foundry continued on Close and Forth Banks until about 1860s				
3. Skinnerburn	Iron Foundry	SURTEES & Co (18)	Newcastle merchant and banker	Founding partner in Tyne Iron Works (qv)	1778
4. Lemington	Northumberland Crown Glass works	Sir M W RIDLEY & others (14)	Ridley = established Tyneside family with coal and glass interests		1787
		Joseph LAMB & Co (9)			1833
		George SOWERBY & Sons			1898
		General Electric Co		Purchased old Co outright	1906
	1978 – Glass Tubes & Components (owned 50:50 by GEC and Thorn Electrical Co)				
5. West Denton (Bell's Close)	Tyne Iron Works	George Gibsons (father and son)	London architects. Father married daughter of Hull merchant	Initial capital of £100,000 but Co collapsed in 1803 with bankruptcy of Surtees' bank	1797
		Richard Fishwick	Merchant from Hull		
		Aubone and John Surtees	Newcastle merchant in corn, and wine. Coalowner and banker		
		Peter John BULMER			
		Peter John Bulmer and later Charles Bulmer		Continue reconstituted Co	1828
	[1869 Company taken over by John Spencer and Sons, and closed in 1876]				
6. Orchard St & South Street	Iron Foundry	John & Isaac BURRELL		Originally provided castings for R Stephenson & Co	1815
	Eventually taken over by R Stephenson & Co 1863				
7. Newburn	File manufactory Newburn Steel Works	John Spencer & Sons (1)	Apprentice file-cutter in Sheffield	Started business in 1810 in Bigg Market, Newcastle	1822
				Company wound up owing to depression	1926
		John Spencer (1928) Ltd		New Co formed, manufacturing steel springs	1928
	[1960 – Purchased by Jonas Woodhead Group and becomes TOLEDO WOODHEAD] [1978 – TOLEDO WOODHEAD continues]				

AREA	TYPE OF ACTIVITY SITE	OWNERS/PARTNERS	SOCIAL BACKGROUND	OTHER DETAILS	YEAR
8. Forth Banks & Close	Glass and bottle factory	Isaac Cookson & Son (7)	see above	Had owned warehouse in The Close since 1778	1838
9. Close & Quayside	Lead manufacture + refining of antinomy [1978 Is part of Lead Industries Group]	W I Cookson & Co (7) W I Cookson John Cookson	sons of Isaac Cookson	Already had works at Gateshead and East Howden. In 1856 Co took over Willington Quay land works	1855

ENGINEERING

AREA	TYPE OF ACTIVITY NAME	OWNERS/PARTNERS	SOCIAL BACKGROUND	OTHER DETAILS	YEAR
1. Forth Banks	R & W Hawthorn Engineering Works — marine, stationary & locomotive engines 1937 Loco works fused with Robert STEPHENSON & Co (see below) 1978 Hawthorn Leslie continues at St Peters Works, Walker	Robert HAWTHORN William HAWTHORN Benjamin Chapman BROWNE (5) John STRAKER (17) Frances Carr MARSHALL	Sons of engineer at Walbottle Colliery Born Gloucester; son of army colonel From old merchant family; wealthy coalowner & shipowner	Started business with 4 workers Bought out Hawthorns; company valued at £63,000 All marine engine work to Walker leaving locos at Forth Banks Amalgamation with A Leslie to become HAWTHORN-LESLIE Acquired part of adjoining Stephenson site (see below)	1817 1869 1882 1883 1900
2. Forth	Robert STEPHENSON & Co 1900 Co expands to greenfield site in Darlington, and in 1937 fuses with Hawthorn Leslie 1960 Forth Banks loco works finally closed down	George STEPHENSON & son Robert STEPHENSON Michael Longridge Edward PEASE	Son of fireman at Wylam Pit Quaker woollen merchant and banker from Darlington	Built Stockton & Darlington Railway Owned Bedlington Iron Works Provided over half of initial capital of £4000	1823
3. Low ELSWICK	W G ARMSTRONG & Co Engine factory Amalgamations with Mitchells (1882) Whitworths (1897) and Vickers (1927) 1978 Vickers continues with works at Elswick, Scotswood and Michell Bearings	William G Armstrong (2) Armorer Donkin Addison L Potter (2) George Cruddas (8) Richard Lambert	Son of N/c corn merchant Son of South Shields timber merchant Brewer and Coalowner Linen draper and shipowner from North Shields ?Son of R L, principal agent to Lord Ravensworth & coalfitter	Solicitor. Later = Lord A Solicitor & Coalowner Large shareholder in N/c and N Shields Railway Co, Coalowner Solicitor	1847
4. Forth Banks/ Pottery Lane	J & G JOICEY Engineering and loco works 1926 Appears to have closed down	James and George JOICEY (3)	Sons of Backworth Colliery supervisor	James opened first pit at Tanfield, Co Durham in 1837 George = Man Dir of loco works	1849
5. Low ELSWICK	Foundry/ Engineering	John Waterston		1880 Last reference in Directory to the company	1850

AREA	TYPE OF ACTIVITY SITE	OWNERS/PARTNERS	SOCIAL BACKGROUND	OTHER DETAILS	YEAR
6. Low ELSWICK	Ironfounders and engineers	T Clark			1853
7. Scotswood	Shipbuilding/ engineering SCOTSWOOD SHIPBUILDING	Campbell, Mackintosh & Bowstead			1883
	1899 Bought out by W Armstrong & Co, and land developed for New Brass Foundry (Now = Vickers Scotswood Works)				

GENERAL INDUSTRIES

AREA	TYPE OF ACTIVITY SITE	OWNERS/PARTNERS	SOCIAL BACKGROUND	OTHER DETAILS	YEAR
1. The Close	Leather Works (= GEORGE ANGUS & Co)	Joseph ANGUS (1)	from long line of skinners and glovers	Moved to larger premises in Grainger Street	1788
	By 1920s, offices in Liverpool and America. Expansion to Walker (1930s) and Coast Road, Wallsend (1956) 1968 Taken over by DUNLOP Group, as wholly owned subsidiaries				
2. Benwell (Paradise)	Colour factory	John GIBSON	One of 3 sons of London architect. All family moved to Newcastle c1800	(see Tyne Iron Works)	c1800
		Richard HOYLE (1779-1889)	A chemist from Ripponden, Yorks Came to N/c about 1800		1818
		William ROBSON	Married grand-niece of John Buddle (qv)		
		Edward George BARNETT & Frederick Pierie Barnett (3)	Sons of N/c banker	Bought out previous owners	1886
	By 1876 Co had extended to Bill Quay, Gateshead and by 1888 had closed down the Benwell Works In 1930 Co amalgamated with J Dampney & Co which continues in 1977 to trade as subsidiary of British Paints Ltd				
3. Forth Banks	Brewery	William Potter (2)			1811
		Addison Langhorne POTTER	Founding partner in W G Armstrong & Co		1828
	1918 Company merged with Newcastle Breweries Ltd which later became Scottish & Newcastle Breweries				
4. Scotswood	Lampblack and coal tar manufactory	John HAIR (1774-1845)			1821
		Hair brothers			1844
5. Low Elswick	Copperas Works	Bilton & Co			1821
		J Stanton & Co			1833
		John & F W Ridley & Co			1850
	c1850s land purchased for expanding Armstrong's Works				
6. Scotswood (East Denton)	Copperas Works	Scotswood Copperas Co			1821
		C Hunter & Co		By 1855 had other works at Low Walker	1844
		William Benson & Co (4)		Owners of Montagu Colliery (qv)	1879

AREA	TYPE OF ACTIVITY NAME	OWNERS/PARTNERS	SOCIAL BACKGROUND	OTHER DETAILS	YEAR
7. Scotswood	Northumberland Paper Mill	Nathaniel Grace (1778-1865)	Newcastle solicitor		1821
	By 1907 Co appears to have moved to Swalwell under name of W Grace & Co				
8. Scotswood (East Denton)	Scotswood Paper Mill	Thomas Ramsay Fletcher, Falconar & Co Thomas Simpson & Fletcher F & Co			1828 1850 1871
	1907 Co appears to have closed down or moved away from area				
9. Elswick	Glue factory	Jonathan PRIESTMAN (12)	Quaker from Yorkshire. Started Co originally in centre of N/c (Low Friar St) before moving to Elswick. Son became major coalowner		1843
		Joseph Arundale	Daughter married Richard Grainger (see below)		
	Business closed down some time after family had moved into coal trade in 1857				
10. Elswick	Stone Quarries (Elswick Rd)	Richard GRAINGER (1796-1861)	Methodist, son of Quayside porter Major developer of Newcastle city centre	Purchased 700 acre Elswick estate in 1839 as speculative investment	1843
11. Lemington	Brewery	Harrison, Colbeck & Co			1844
12. Forth Banks	Colour Works	William Cookson & Co (7)	Son of old-established N/c banker, industrialist & merchant		1845
13. Elswick	Leather works and glue works	Edward & John RICHARDSON (13)	Sons of Quaker, Isaac R, who started business in centre of N/c in 1785, after moving from Yorks	Both major shareholders in District Bank	1862
	Company run by descendants of family until taken over in 1969 by Barrow Hepburn and closed down in 1971				

BRICK AND CRUCIBLE FACTORIES

AREA	TYPE OF ACTIVITY SITE	OWNERS/PARTNERS	SOCIAL BACKGROUND	OTHER DETAILS	YEAR
1. Scotswood	Brick Factory	John Sowler			1811
2. Bell's Close	Brick Yard	William Fothergill			1821
3. Scotswood	Firebricks, Tiles Lamps	Thomas CARR			1828

119

AREA	TYPE OF ACTIVITY NAME	OWNERS/PARTNERS	SOCIAL BACKGROUND	OTHER DETAILS	YEAR
4. Scotswood Elswick & Benwell	Firebrick, Crucible, Chimney Top, Ornamental Vases	Robert Lister & Son			1841
Benwell	Brick factory (with associated colliery)	William Cochrane Carr (1815-1889)	Born at Blaydon of humble family. Married daughter of market gardener	Firebrick business started at Blaydon in 1848. Took over Lister's site. Shortly after re-opened Benwell colliery	1851
Elswick	Crucible factory	John Carr	Probably son of Thomas Carr (above)	Owned firebrick works at Scotswood (above) and coke works at Jarrow & Wallsend. Colliery interests at Felling and Member of Coal Trade Committee	1850
5. Low Elswick	Brick Yard	John FINDLEY (FINLAY?)		Owned other site at Shieldfield	1850
6. West Denton	Firebrick Factory	William HARRIMAN (1821-1878)	Grocer	Moved/Expanded to Blaydon in 1844	1843
	1978 Co still trading under same name				
7. Walbottle	Fire Brick factory (with associated colliery)	Addison POTTER (2)	Brewer at Forth Banks (qv)		1844
	Fire Brick factory (with associated colliery)	Joseph LAMB & Co (see under Elswick Colliery)			1850
8. Throckley	Fireclay, gas retort and blast furnace lining factory	William Stephenson & Sons (16)	Old Methodist family (selling site in central Newcastle to John Wesley in 1740)	Owned associated collieries at Throckley and Wallbottle (qv)	1856
9. Delaral	Brickworks (with associated colliery)	J O Scott (1819-1890)	Son of Longbenton Labourer	(site of present Mitchell Bearings)	1863
	c1900 taken over for development of Vickers Scotswood Works				
10. Scotswood (Bells Close)	Brickworks	T W BENSON & Sons (4)	Son of W Benson, owner of Montagu colliery (Scotswood)	Quarrying, lead and coal	
11. Scotswood	Brick factory	Walter SCOTT	of humble origins Journeyman mason from Cumberland	By death was national building contractor with extensive coal steel and chemical interests c1890s? Moved/Expanded from Forth Lane site	1900
12. Scotswood	Brick and firebrick factory	William Colville GIBSON & Co		On site of works previously owned by Listers. Co reconstructed in 1895 under chairmanship of industrialist and coalowner N C Cookson (7)	1873
	ADAMSEZ Manufacturers of TOILETS AND BASINS	Moses T Adams Samuel H Adams	Quakers from YORK	Owned Leeds Co desiging and assembling cisterns. Bought out W C Gibson for £35,000	1903
	1975 Factory closed down after Adams family bought out in 1972				

Appendix 4
Sources & Methods

AN ESSENTIAL requirement for research of this nature is access to standard reference books, which can be found in the central library of a large town or city, or in a university or polytechnic library. The most useful for biographical details are *Who's Who, Who Was Who,* Burke's *Peerage,* Burke's *Landed Gentry,* Kelly's *Titled, Landed and Official Classes, Who's Who in Finance* and *Who's Who in Building Societies*. The standard sources covering companies are the *Stock Exchange Yearbook, Register of Defunct Companies, Who Owns Whom, Kompass Register U.K., Times 1000 Leading Companies, Extel Cards* and the *Directory of Directors*. Many libraries keep the earlier editions, so it is often possible for instance to get information about the early history of a company from back copies of the Stock Exchange Year book, or biographical details of an earlier family member from a contemporary edition of *Who's Who* or Burke's *Landed Gentry*. Unfortunately some libraries regard the *Directory of Directors* (first published in 1880) as ephemera and not worth keeping more than a few years. This makes the tracing of interlocking directorships more difficult. Copies are available at some of the bigger university and public libraries, and it is always possible through the inter-library loans service to have these sent to a library of your choice for perusal.

For more detailed information about a company, there is no substitute for a search of the file at Companies House in London. This will (or should) include the date of formation, original objects and directors, lists of all mortgages taken out, and of all shareholders, and annual returns on turnover, profit and changing activities. Recently it has been decided to transfer the files themselves to a new Companies House in Cardiff, so gradually the London service is being reduced to that of providing a set of microfilmed "fiches" of what are regarded as relevant details. While this has the advantage that fiches can be read at leisure in a library that has a microfilm reader, it means that the information on the early history of the company rarely appears.

Another good source for contemporary information is the company's own annual report, which — if the company is a public one — can usually be obtained (free of charge) if a letter is sent to the Company Secretary. Some libraries will also keep regular newspaper cuttings on some of the larger local firms, so it is worth checking through these.

For the local historical material however, upon which this report is based, these general sources cannot provide sufficient detail. For this a good local history collection, such as the one at Newcastle Central Library, is invaluable. This will contain pamphlets, lectures and books written often by the big industrialists themselves on nineteenth century industrialisation; a complete run of local directories (*Kelly's, Ward's* and others) from the late eighteenth century, listing companies, their owners and places of residence; and biographical and company indexes referring to contemporary newspaper and other articles. It should also have back copies of local industrial magazines, such as those published by the local chamber of commerce, or by particular industries like shipbuilding and engineering; of Council proceedings which until recently in Newcastle were published verbatim; and of the annual reports of other bodies like Planning Councils, Development Boards and the local university.

Since this report has been based on the study of a number of families, a good deal of time has been spent on establishing genealogical links. Where a daughter marries, the family name disappears but often reappears in the next generation (e.g. Robert Joicey Dickinson). It is more than likely that several more names of significance could be added to the family trees if a comprehensive history of each family was known. Where the family or individual is not involved in one of the standard biographical sources, details can be obtained from a variety of other places — birth announcements in national and local papers, from gravestones, from checking the birth certificate at Somerset House — and these can be cross-checked with the date of birth appearing beside a director's name in the company file. The sources that have been used are numerous, and it has not been possible to mention all of them either here or in the text. Anyone interested in discussing this further or engaged in similar work elsewhere, can contact Ian Harford c/o Benwell Project, 85 Adelaide Terrace, Newcastle upon Tyne 4, for further information.

Postscript

SINCE the first draft of this report was written we have sumbled on a further significant ramification of the Priestman/Pumphrey dynasty's connections via marriage (see p.83). Sir Laurence Pumphrey's borther-in-law and neighbour is Sir John Riddell of Hepple, Morepeth, who in turn is married to the daughter of Gordon Richardson, formerly deputy-chairman of Legal and General Assurance and chairman of the merchant bank Schroders, and, since 1973 Governor of the Bank of England — a handy link for a family that has so successfully moved in the post war years from coalowning into the finance capital professions. Another similar link via intermarriage can be seen in the case of J.E. Benson (FT4), whose wife is the cousin of Sir Kenneth Keith, chairman since 1972 of both the merchant bank Hill Samuel and Rolls Royce.